IMAGES
of America

PENNSYLVANIA AVENUE

ON THE COVER: This view from the south lawn of the Treasury Building looks down Pennsylvania Avenue toward the US Capitol building in August 1935. For nearly a century, this was a favorite site for photographers to capture America's most important street, the symbolic link between the Capitol and, behind the photographer, the White House. (Library of Congress.)

IMAGES
of America

Pennsylvania Avenue

Christopher P. Cavas

ARCADIA
PUBLISHING

ISBN 978-1-4671-0297-1

Published by Arcadia Publishing
Charleston, South Carolina

Printed in the United States of America

Library of Congress Control Number: 2018955605

For all general information, please contact Arcadia Publishing:
Telephone 843-853-2070
Fax 843-853-0044
E-mail sales@arcadiapublishing.com
For customer service and orders:
Toll-Free 1-888-313-2665

Visit us on the Internet at www.arcadiapublishing.com

For my grandmother Minnie Davis Kimel McMullen. She loved this city.

Contents

Acknowledgments

I am indebted to John DeFerrari, author of several fine books on Washington history and creator of the excellent website streetsofwashington.com. John graciously read through the manuscript, providing helpful suggestions and corrections, and allowed the use of several images. I am grateful to Alex Neil, my longtime colleague at the former Army Times Publishing Company, for reading through the manuscript and adding his editorial expertise. And my thanks go to author and editor Rick Burgess for putting me in contact with Arcadia Publishing.

Unless otherwise noted, all images in this book are from the collections of the Library of Congress. Images credited DDOT are courtesy the DC Department of Transportation.

Introduction

Pennsylvania Avenue is one of the world's best-known streets, an icon representing the US capital and the presidents who have lived there. Thousands routinely flock to the street's sidewalks every fourth January, when a newly inaugurated chief executive makes the triumphal journey from the Capitol building to the White House along a modest, 1.2-mile route heavy with symbolism, connecting the executive branch with the other two branches of the US democracy, the Congress and Supreme Court.

That symbolism is no accident. It was intended from the beginning, when Frenchman Pierre L'Enfant drew up his grand plan for the city in the early 1790s and conceived of the avenue as the most important street in the new capital. But the journey of "the Grand Avenue" over more than two centuries did not always live up to those early expectations. Like the city around it, Pennsylvania Avenue was a muddy mess well into the mid-19th century, prone to flooding, smelly from sewage and marsh, and not always a healthy place to live.

Yet the street was lively from the beginning. Hostels and rooming houses sprang up as soon as the federal government moved in during 1800. Eateries, places of entertainment, and merchants of all types rapidly followed. Some of the city's finest establishments opened for business along the avenue, and some of the most disreputable operations could be found just a few doors off the street. It was a rambunctious place, home to the city's largest market and the nexus of all its transportation lines.

Much of that life began to be sucked out of the street with the erection in the 1930s of the Federal Triangle, a huge construction project that demolished most of the structures on the avenue's south side and replaced them with huge, looming office buildings, full of federal workers by day but empty at night. The post–World War II decline of major urban cities struck Pennsylvania Avenue hard, to the point that Pres. John F. Kennedy, just after his inaugural parade in January 1961, termed the avenue's appearance a national disgrace. The years of decline continued into the 1980s, when new and often controversial schemes to revitalize the avenue began to bear fruit.

The focus of this book is on that core of the avenue—America's Main Street—where virtually every block is steeped in often colorful history. The entire roadway is much larger. To the northwest beyond the White House, the avenue continues another dozen blocks or so to cross Rock Creek and enter Georgetown. On the southeast side of the Capitol, the street runs more than three miles through Capitol Hill, across the Anacostia River, and to the Maryland line, where it continues more than 14 miles to finally end near the Patuxent River. But the stories about those portions of the avenue are beyond the scope of this work.

A note on location references: Washington is laid out in unequal quadrants centered on the US Capitol building—Northeast, Southeast, Southwest, and Northwest—and all addresses properly should indicate their quadrant (for example, "NW" or "SE"). Pennsylvania Avenue runs diagonally southeast to northwest, extending about two dozen blocks into Northwest and much further into Southeast. The core of the avenue that is the focus of this book is in Northwest, thus all addresses are in that quadrant unless otherwise noted.

One

L'Enfant's Grand Vision

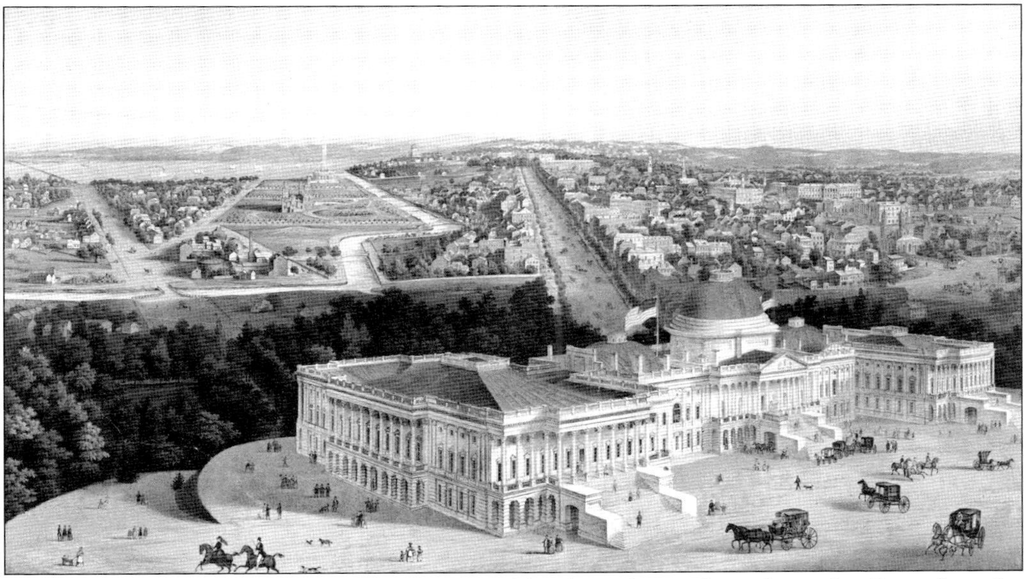

Pierre L'Enfant envisioned a grand ceremonial boulevard stretching from the Capitol to the executive mansion to symbolically link the branches of government. The city plan featured numbered north-south streets and lettered east-west streets overlaid with diagonal avenues, of which Pennsylvania Avenue became key. Although a federal city, the government owned only specific lots, with privately owned land and commercial and residential development filling in the spaces between. The city was slow to develop due to a lack of private investment and congressional disinterest, but it had become more defined by the time of this 1852 lithograph. The view looks down from Capitol Hill at Pennsylvania Avenue stretching northwest to the White House a mile away. The Washington Canal is at center, coming down from the Potomac River and taking a right turn across the Mall, which already features the Smithsonian Institution's castle. At the far end, the Washington Monument is still incomplete. Note how close the river is in this view from before the creation of the Tidal Basin. Note also the built-up nature of the city at right at the foot of Capitol Hill.

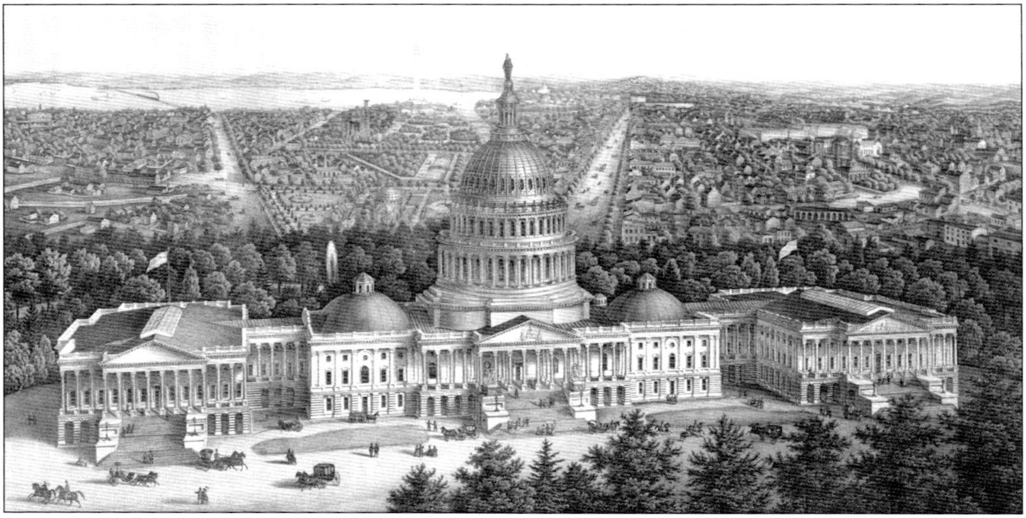

By 1871, the avenue had become more defined, even as the city grew around it. This lithograph—like the preceding illustration created by A. Sachse & Co. of Baltimore—depicts the Capitol with its new dome, while the unfinished Washington Monument would not be completed until the mid-1880s. The Mall has become much more cluttered, and the stretch of the Washington Canal crossing the Mall has been filled in.

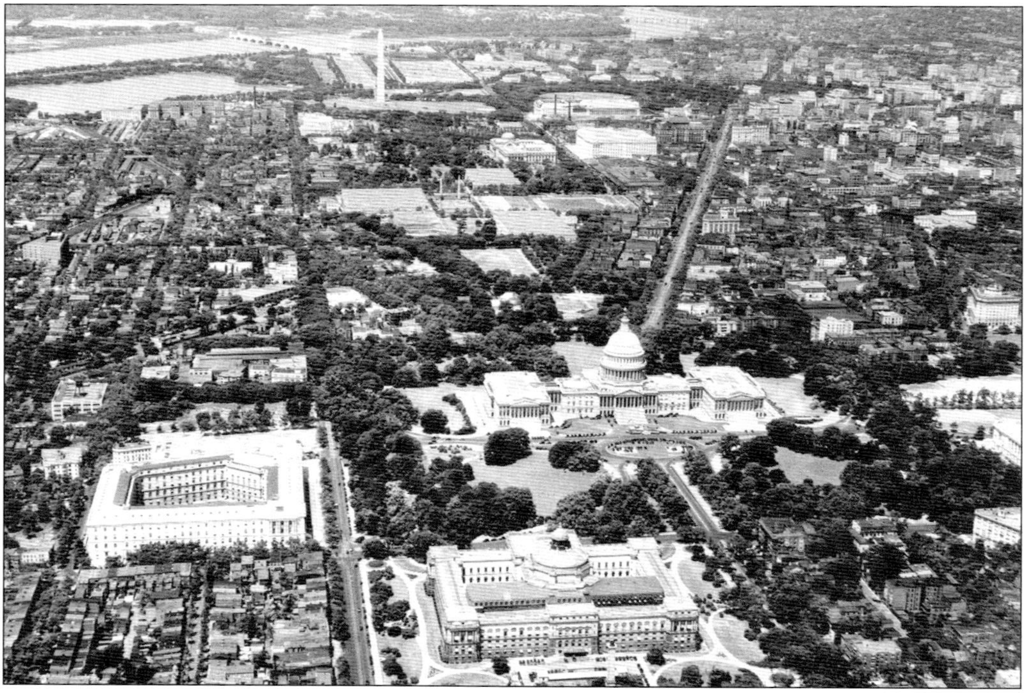

This 1931 aerial photograph shows that even after a century, L'Enfant's vision had yet to be fully realized. Buildings clutter the avenue at right, while the Mall has become a jumble of plantings, World War I temporary office buildings, and commercial structures. The Library of Congress main building is at lower center, with the House Office Building—later the Cannon building—at lower left.

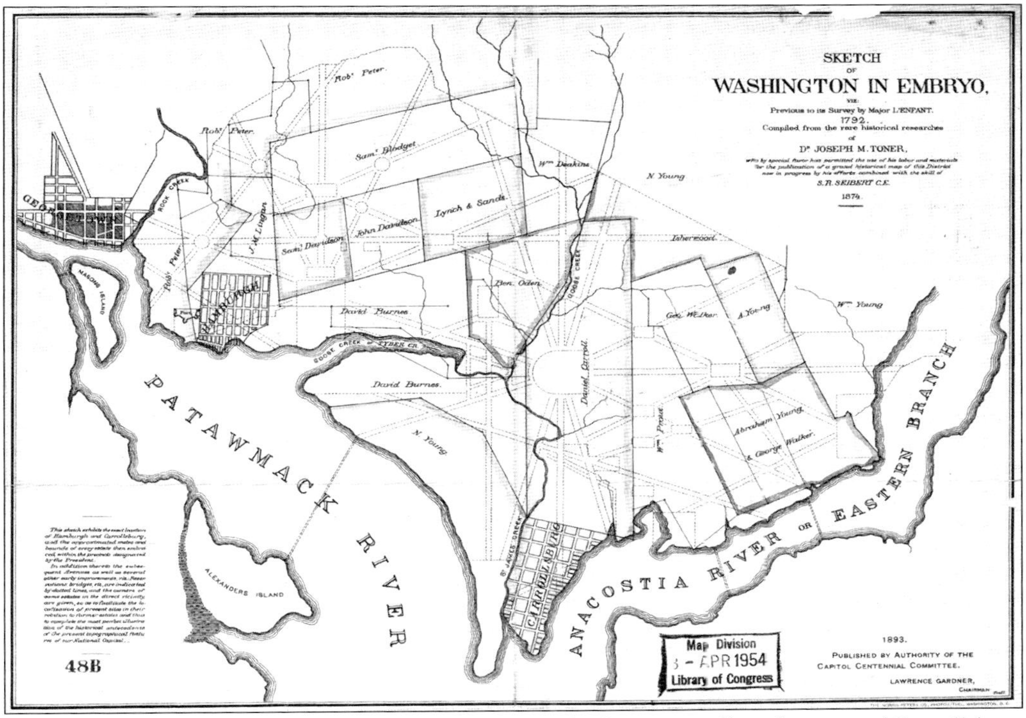

Washington was laid out over hilly farmland where only the two small settlements of Carrollsburg and Hamburgh existed before the site was chosen as the capital. This map from 1874 shows L'Enfant's street plan sketched over the pre-1792 lay of the land, with the Capitol's location prominent at center. Pennsylvania Avenue stretches to the northwest, skirting Tiber Creek, then a fairly sizeable waterway. Georgetown, at left, was its own city.

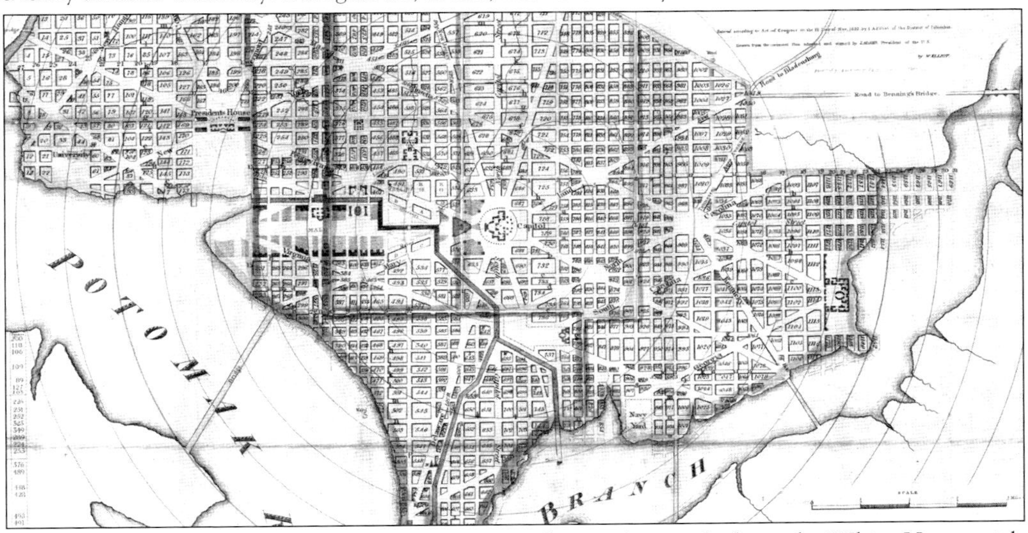

This map from 1822 illustrates the vision of Pennsylvania Avenue linking the White House with Congress. The avenue is bisected by Market Square, where a major city market was established on the street's south side by 1802. It would later be known as Center Market. The Washington Canal is shaded as it cuts into the city from Tiber Creek.

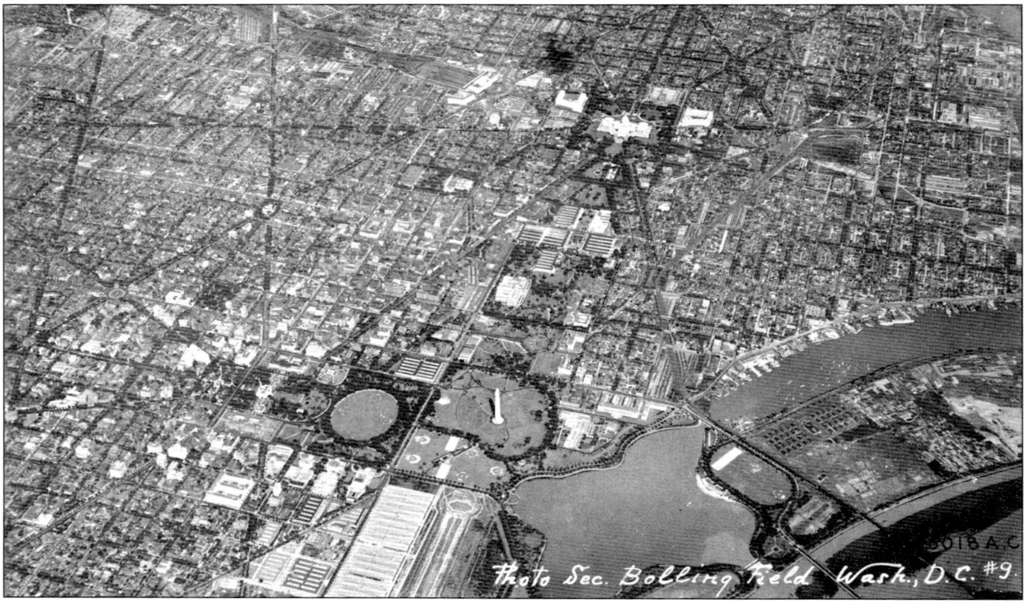

Washington's street plan is evident in this view from 1928. Pennsylvania Avenue is visible between the Capitol at top center and the White House at lower left, just to the left of the grass circle of the Ellipse. Note how Maryland Avenue at right center is a mirror to the southwest of Pennsylvania Avenue's northwest march. Although broken in line by the Capitol, the avenue continues to the southeast at upper right, crossing the Anacostia River toward Maryland. (National Archives.)

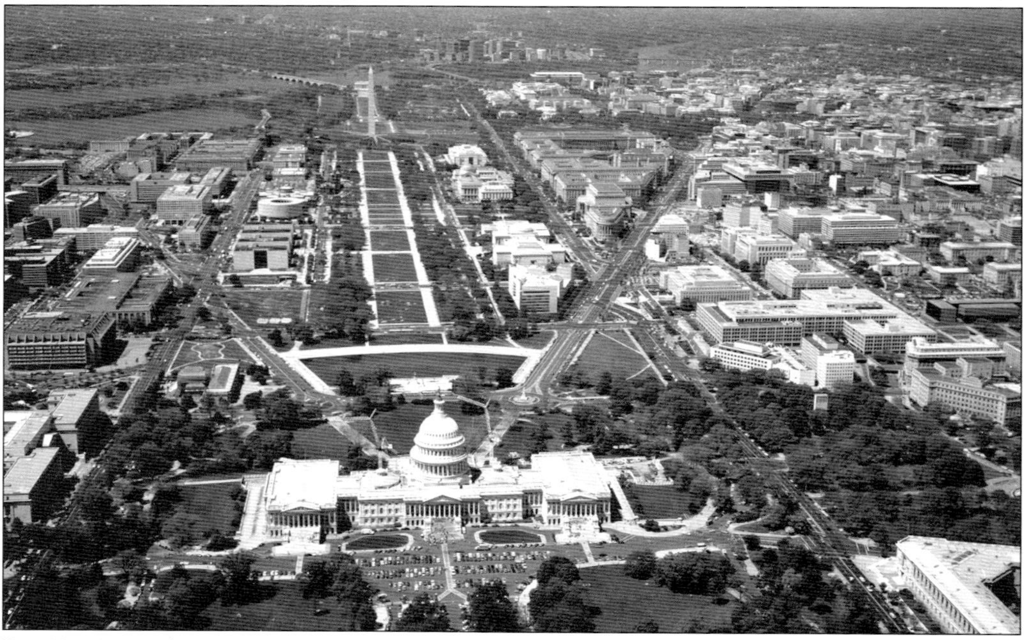

By 1990, Pennsylvania Avenue was finally surrounded by a sense of order. The Mall has been cleared and lined with museums. The clutter at the foot of Capitol Hill is long gone, swept away by landscaping and more ordered development. The Federal Triangle has replaced the chaotic neighborhood between the avenue and Constitution Avenue, which covers the former Washington Canal.

Two

City of Mud

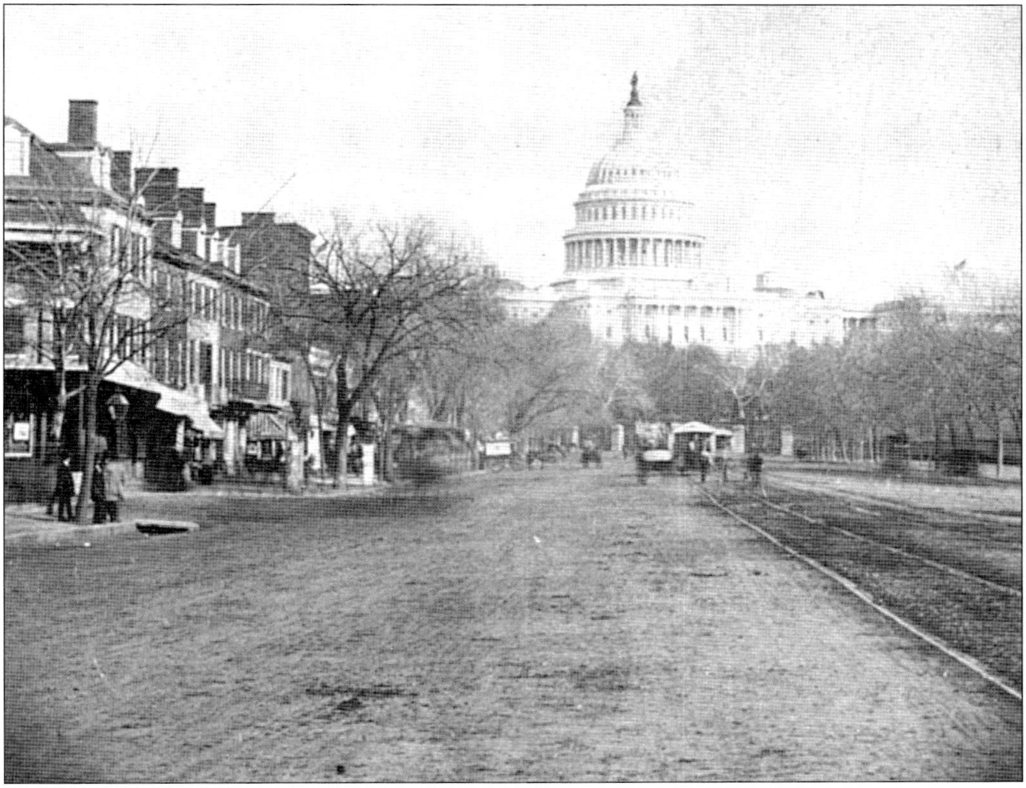

Early Washington was a paradox. Although laid out from scratch with a sophisticated urban road plan, the city lacked basic necessities, including a water supply and sewage system. Roads were unpaved and remained unimproved for decades. All the city's systems were challenged by an enormous influx of people during the Civil War, and the alleys behind many buildings were filled with malodorous filth. This 1870 view of Pennsylvania Avenue looks at the Capitol building from about Second Street. The road has been paved with wooden blocks, and cobblestones fill the spaces between the tram tracks at right. A rudimentary drainage system runs under the intersection at left. A street lantern sits on the corner—a rather luxurious feature of the avenue, where lighting was installed earlier than the rest of the city. As soon as Congress moved to Washington, there arose a need for housing for members, their employees, and those seeking to do business with the government, and lodging houses quickly sprang up virtually from the foot of Capitol Hill.

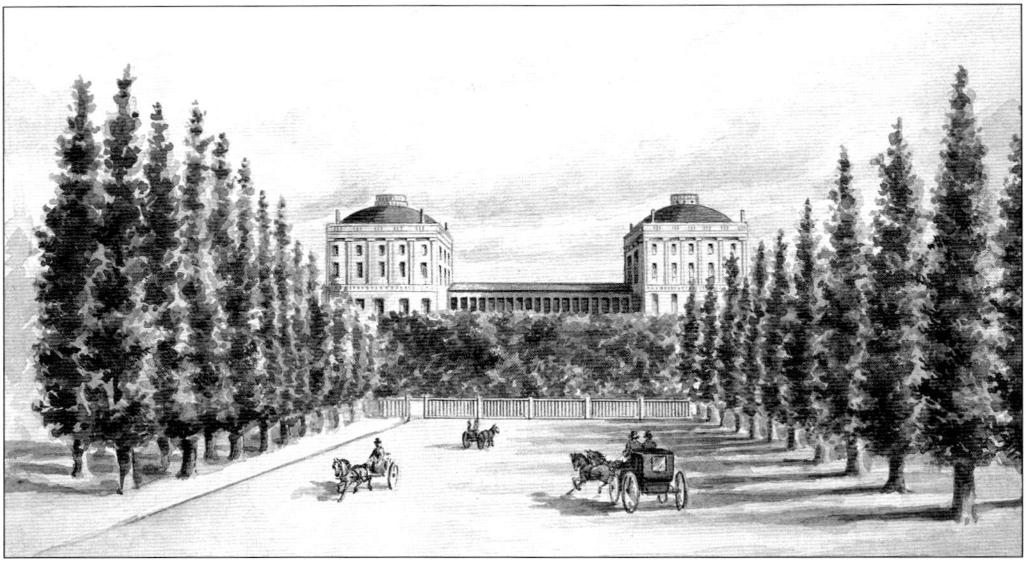

Thomas Jefferson was the first president to begin his term in Washington, and although he supported federal projects in the city, he opposed most civic improvement schemes and projects not on federal property. He did, however, direct that Lombardy poplar trees be planted at the foot of Capitol Hill, an idea he borrowed from the French. This idyllic depiction of Pennsylvania Avenue in 1812 was painted in 1819 from memory by Capitol architect Benjamin Latrobe and shows the building with a wooden structure linking the House and Senate Wings.

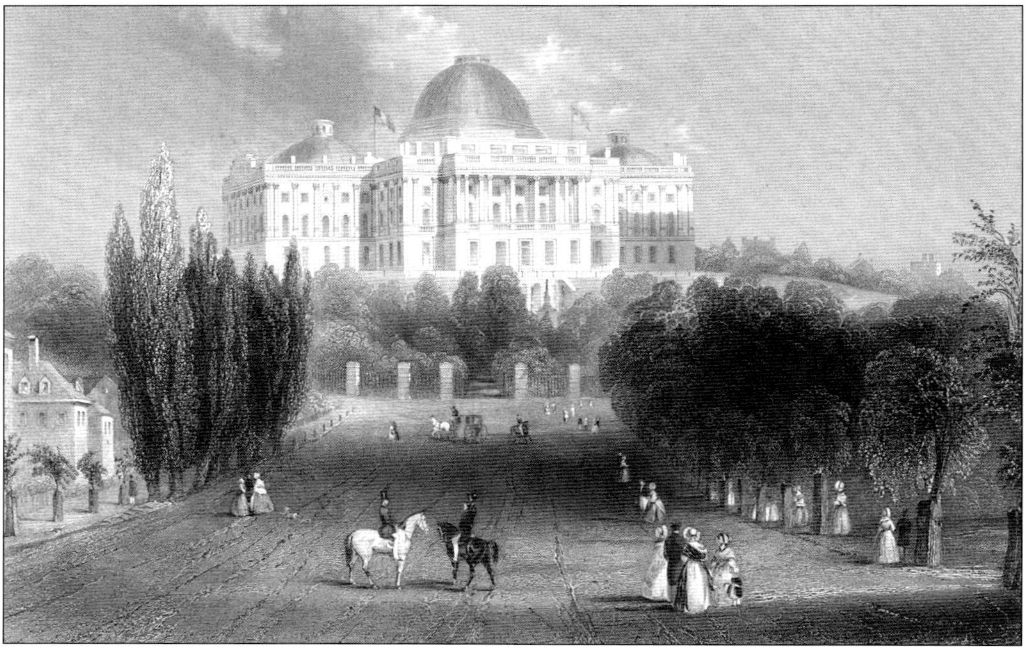

This 1848 engraving depicts virtually the same scene as the previous illustration but with the Capitol rebuilt, enlarged, and fitted with the green copper-covered dome designed by Charles Bulfinch and completed in 1823. This and similar prints gave an impression of gentility, but visitors to the capital found few of the refinements of most American metropolitan centers.

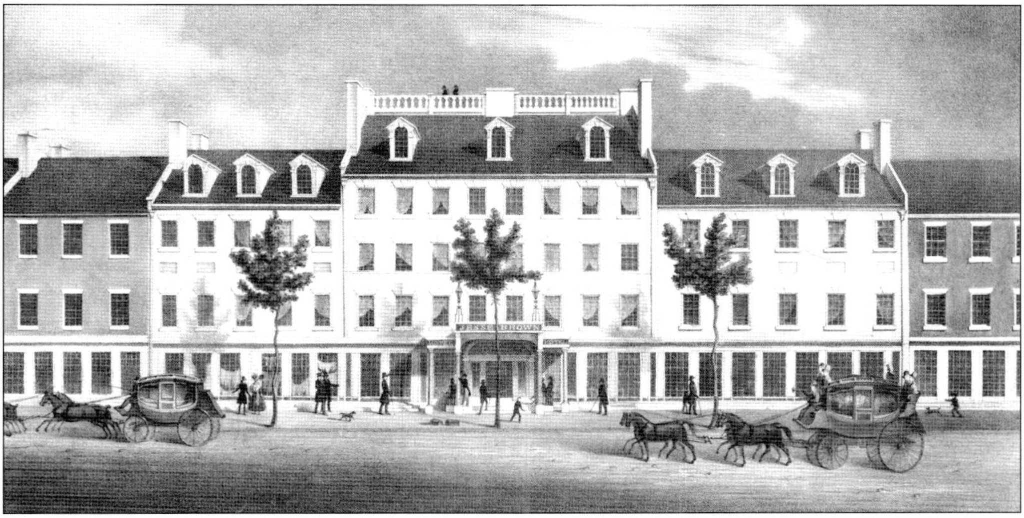

One of the city's earliest hotels, the Davis Hotel, began operating in 1802 on the northwest corner of Sixth Street and Pennsylvania Avenue. The establishment was purchased in 1820 by Jesse Brown, who greatly enlarged and modernized the building, reopening it in 1823 as the Indian Queen Hotel, also known as Brown's Hotel. It quickly gained a reputation as one of the finer hotels in the city and continued in operation until, as the Metropolitan Hotel, it was razed in 1935.

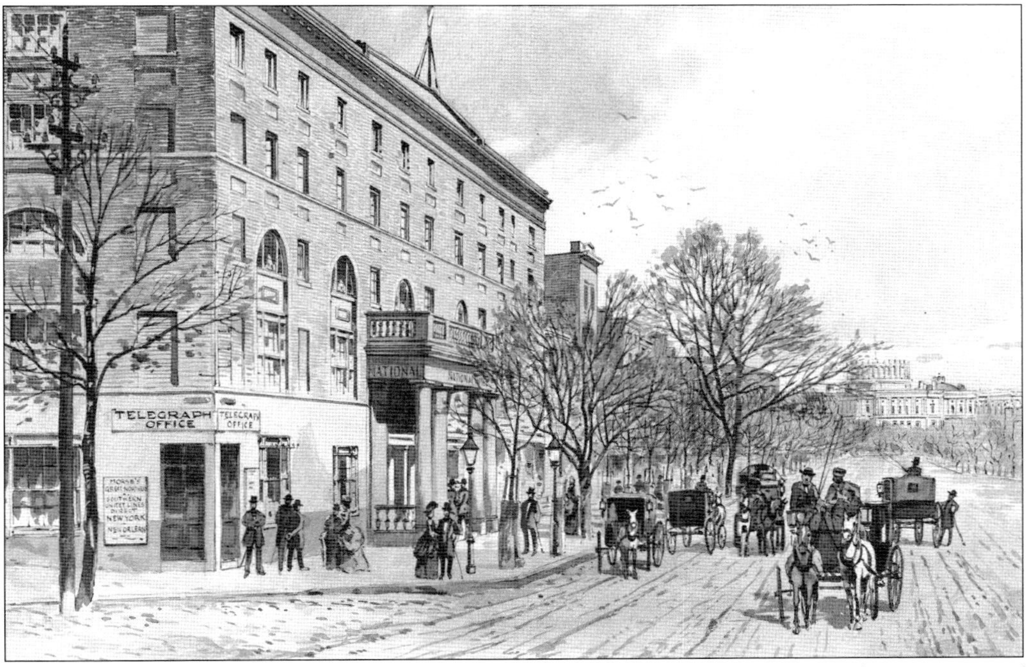

Across the street from the Indian Queen was the National Hotel, on the northeast corner of Pennsylvania Avenue at Sixth Street. A row of six houses built in 1816 was remodeled in 1826 to become the 200-room National, which soon outpaced Brown's to become Washington's leading hotel. English novelist Charles Dickens stayed there in 1841. The hotel was remodeled and enlarged in 1844 and 1857. This illustration shows it in 1860, with the unfinished Capitol dome in the distance.

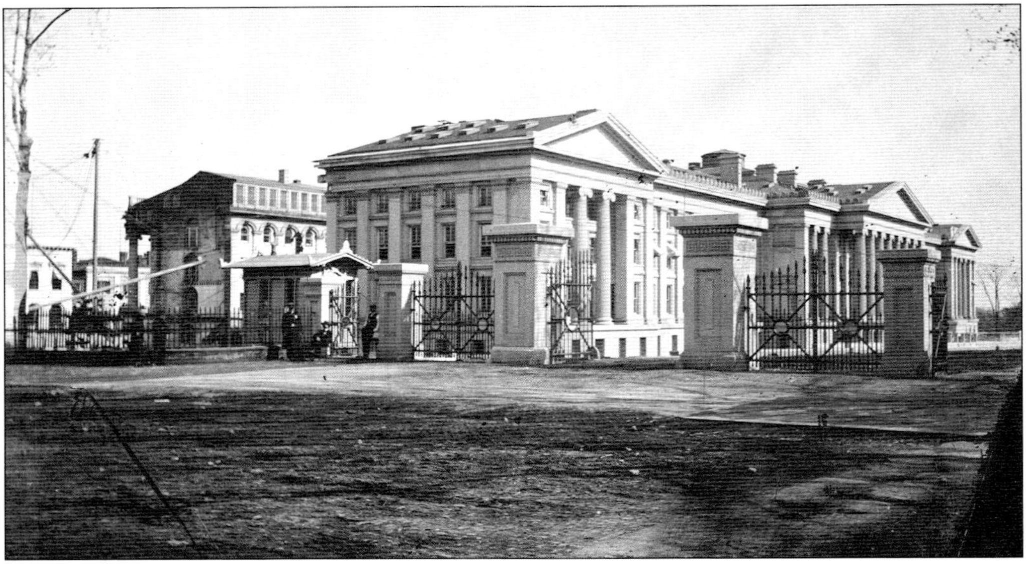

A new location for the US Treasury Department was sought after an 1833 fire destroyed the original building. After three years of indecision, a location was chosen on federal land adjacent to the White House on Fifteenth Street, linking Pennsylvania Avenue to the north of the mansion. Objections arose when it became apparent that the huge new building would obliterate the sweeping view between the Capitol and the president's house, but relocation would have been costly and time-consuming, and opposition eventually ceased. This view from about 1860 looks southeast from what is today Executive Drive in front of the White House, just out of view to the right.

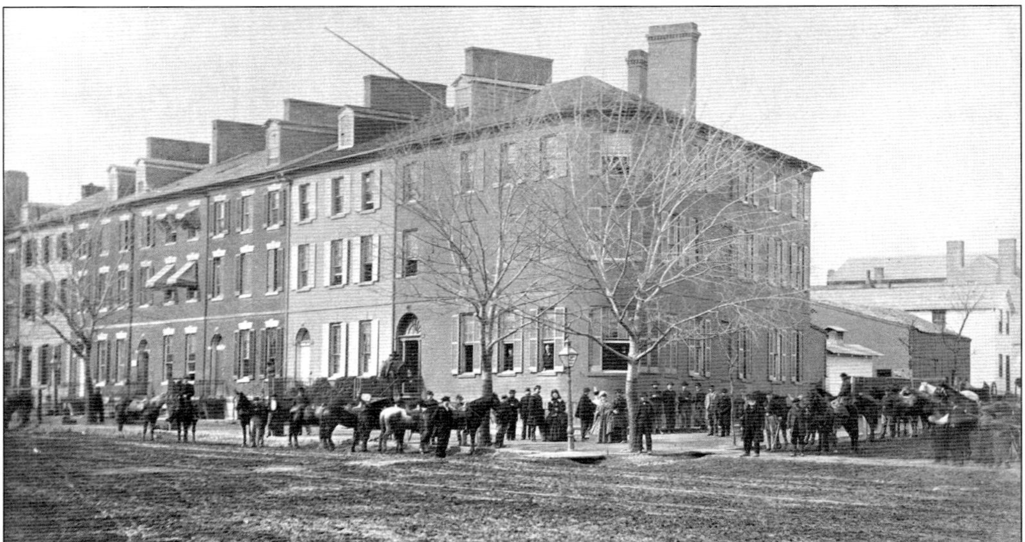

Another view of wartime Washington shows how the city's finest residents lived among mud and muck. This group of Federalist-style rowhouses on Pennsylvania Avenue at Nineteenth Street was known as the Seven Buildings, and during the Civil War, it provided headquarters and lodging for senior Union army officers. Pres. James and Dolley Madison lived in the corner house after the burning of the White House in 1814. Seen in April 1865, the facades of the last two houses on the left survive today incongruously incorporated into a modern office building.

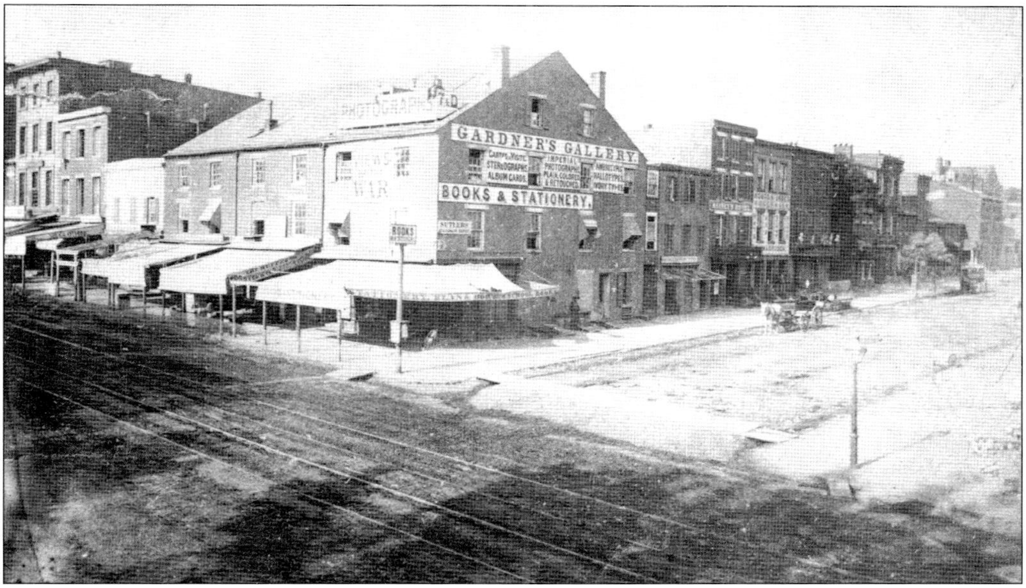

Two blocks up from Pennsylvania Avenue at the northeast corner of Seventh and D Streets stood the gallery of Alexander Gardner, a Scottish immigrant previously employed by Matthew Brady who became one of the best-known photographers of the Civil War. This 1863 view, at the height of the Civil War, shows his thriving establishment along the dusty streets of the capital. Note the raised wooden planks for crossing the street, with channels for rainwater.

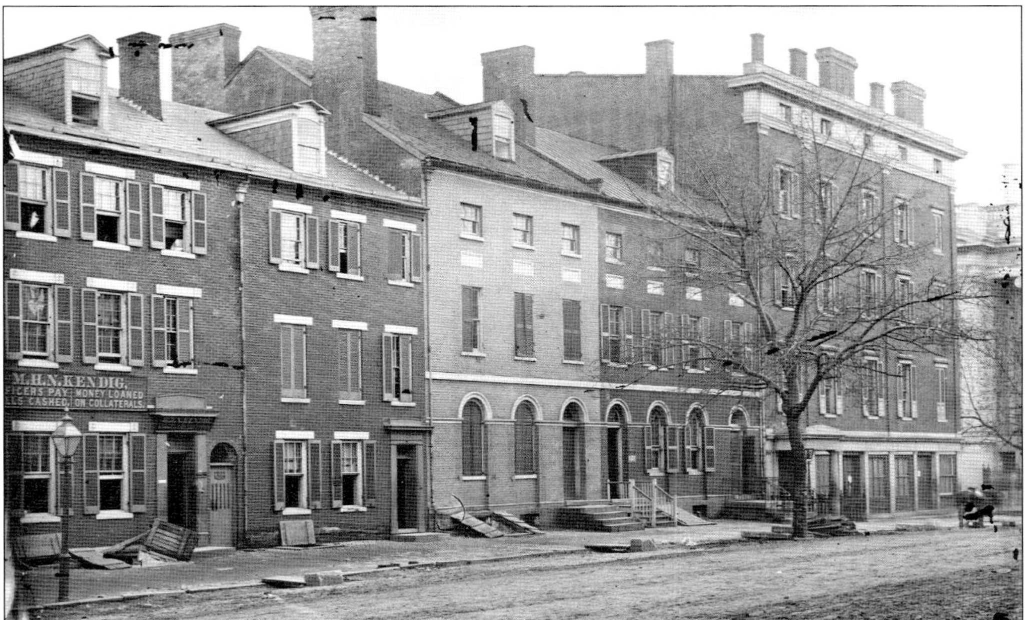

These F Street rowhouses seen in April 1865 display Greek Revival (left) and Federal architecture (center), along with the Greek Revival Corcoran Building at right. The Treasury Building is at far right across Fifteenth Street. Note the muddy street and bricked sidewalks, typical of the city at the time. This location today is the site of the north end of the Willard and Washington Hotels.

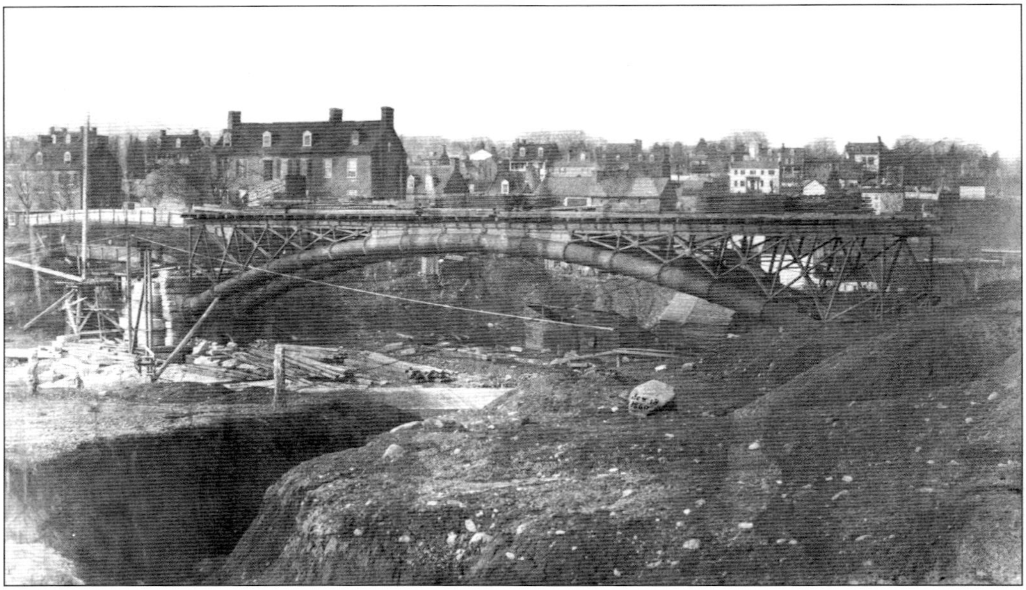

The burgeoning city outgrew the wells, springs, and cisterns of its early years, and a more reliable and plentiful water supply was sorely needed. In 1853, Congress voted $2 million to fund the huge project, designed and overseen by Army officer and engineer Montgomery Meigs. His innovative aqueduct brought water from Great Falls on the Potomac more than 18 miles to downtown Washington, all without pumps. One of the most impressive achievements was construction of an arch over Rock Creek, above which a roadway connected Pennsylvania Avenue's northwest leg to Georgetown. When the waterworks opened on January 3, 1859, Washington had a water supply with a capacity of 67 million gallons, twice what was required for New York City. The view above shows the roadway being built atop the aqueduct's massive 48-inch-diameter pipes, while the view below shows the Pennsylvania Avenue bridge in 1859, shortly after its completion. While the aqueduct solved the water supply problem, a municipal sewer system remained a pressing need.

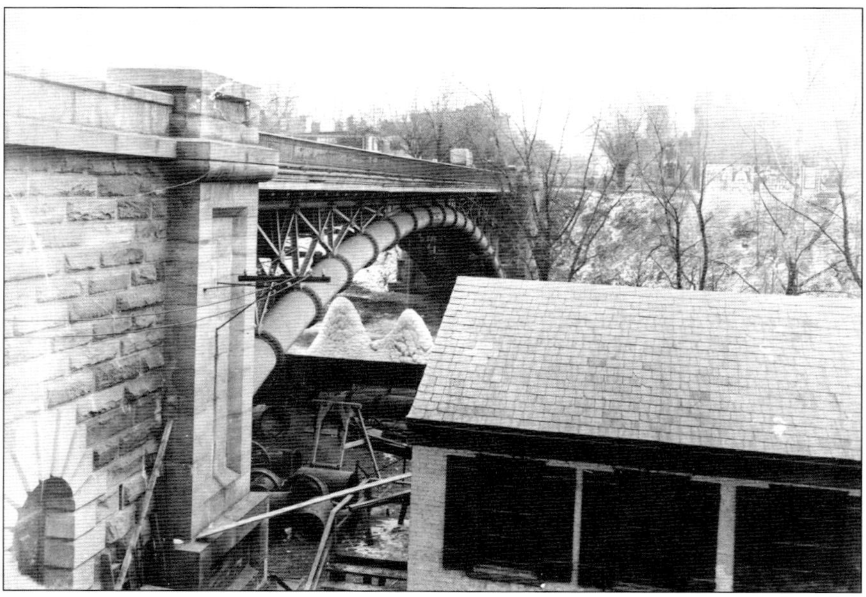

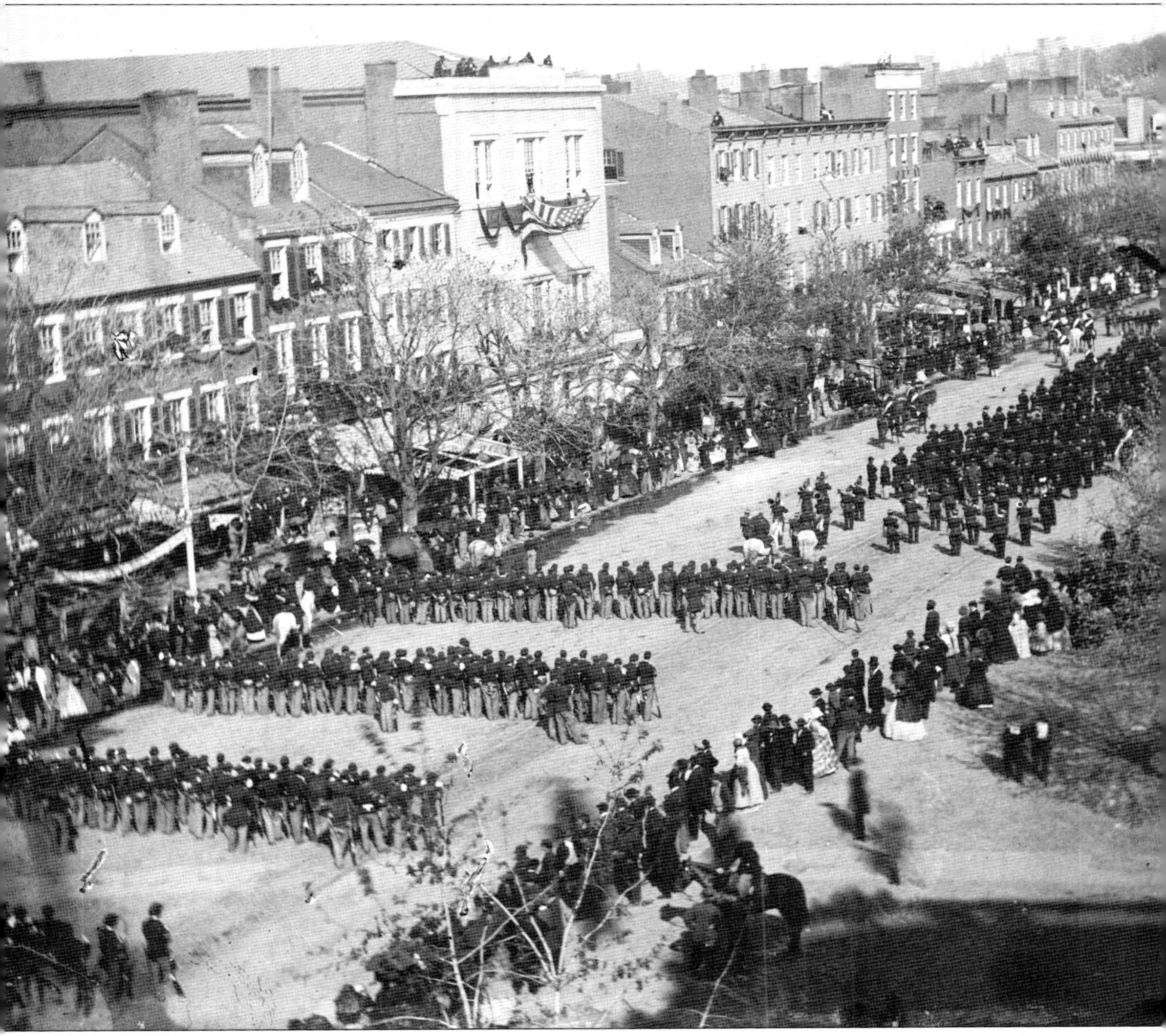

The Civil War had an enormous and transformative effect on the capital, causing an influx of thousands of people—soldiers, war wounded, civilian government employees, freed slaves, war profiteers, and many others. The city's population of 75,080 in 1860 more than doubled by 1863 and caused enormous strain on the infrastructure. The already inadequate sewer facilities were thoroughly overwhelmed, and crime and arrests rose dramatically. The end of the war in the spring of 1865 saw a relatively new phenomenon on the avenue with a number of military parades by the victorious Union army. A more somber occasion took place on April 19, 1865, when Abraham Lincoln's funeral procession made its sad way from the White House to the Capitol, where the slain president would lie in state. Here, dignitaries, a military band, and soldiers follow Lincoln's funeral car to the Capitol. Black bunting drapes an American flag and several buildings.

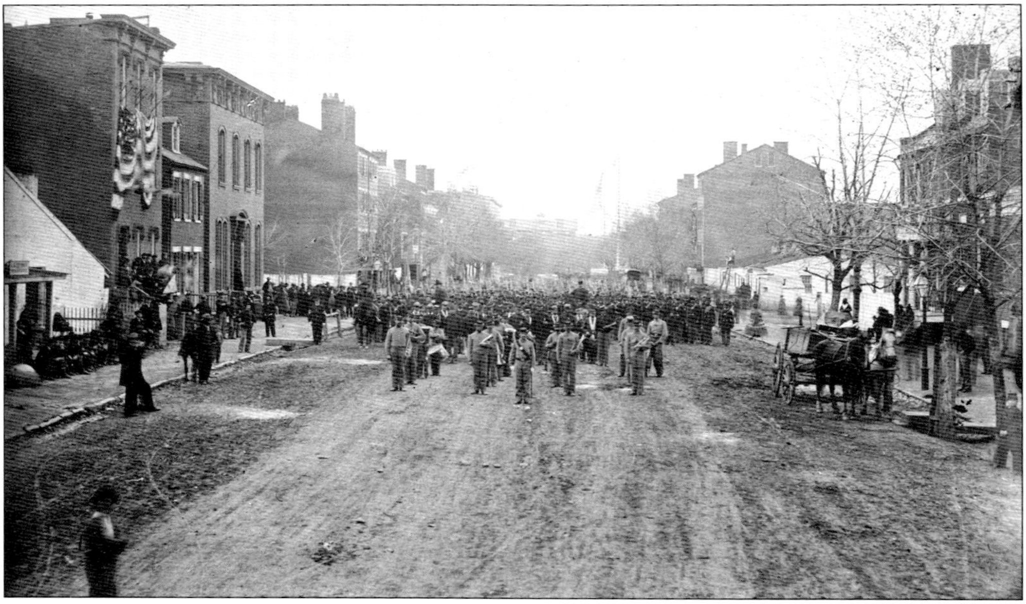

This scene along F Street in Washington shows a group of Union troops carrying out a victory parade in March 1865. F Street and Pennsylvania Avenue were two of Washington's prime shopping streets, linked to each other by Seventh Street. Despite the street's importance, it is just a dirt road, although lined by brick sidewalks. The soldiers are Gen. Winfield Scott Hancock's Veteran Corps of the 1st US Volunteer Infantry, made up of men who had been wounded and were unable to serve on the front lines.

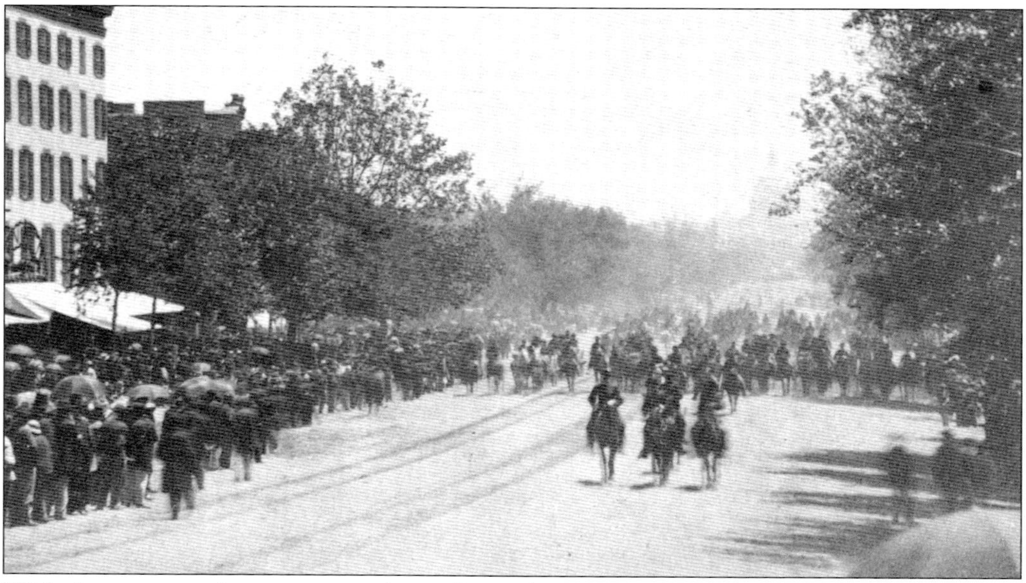

With the war won, the victory parades on Pennsylvania Avenue reached a crescendo on May 23 and 24, 1865, with the Grand Review of the Armies. About 80,000 soldiers of the Army of the Potomac paraded on May 23, while the following day saw about 65,000 troops of the Army of the Tennessee and the Army of Georgia. The festive mood was in direct contrast to the gloom a month earlier of Lincoln's funeral processions.

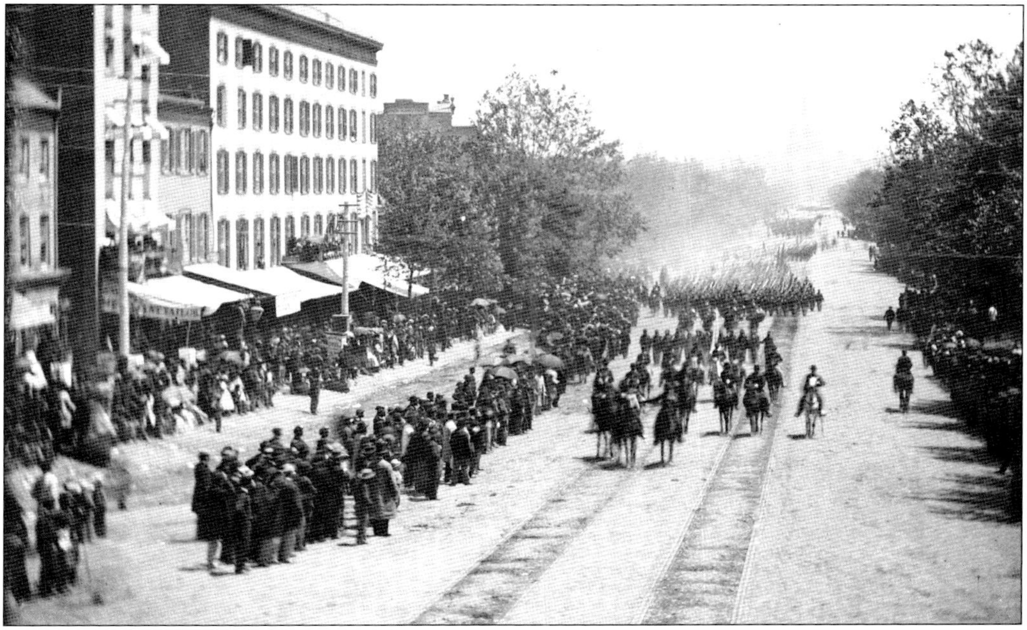

The Grand Review of the Armies continues in these views from the same vantage point on May 23 and 24, 1865, photographed by the studio of Matthew Brady. The troops are about to turn right up Fifteenth Street to head to the White House, having passed the Willard Hotel at left center on the corner of Fourteenth Street. A hotel first existed on this site in the early 1820s and emerged in 1850, after a major enlargement and remodeling, as the Willard, run by the four Willard brothers. Another enlargement in 1858 transformed the Willard into perhaps Washington's leading hotel. Before the outbreak of war in 1861, historian James Goode wrote, Southern sympathizers used the Fourteenth Street entrance to stay on one floor, while Unionists used the Pennsylvania Avenue door. The hotel was routinely filled to overflowing during the war and become a leading meeting place for members of the military and government. Julia Ward Howe composed "The Battle Hymn of the Republic" while staying at the Willard.

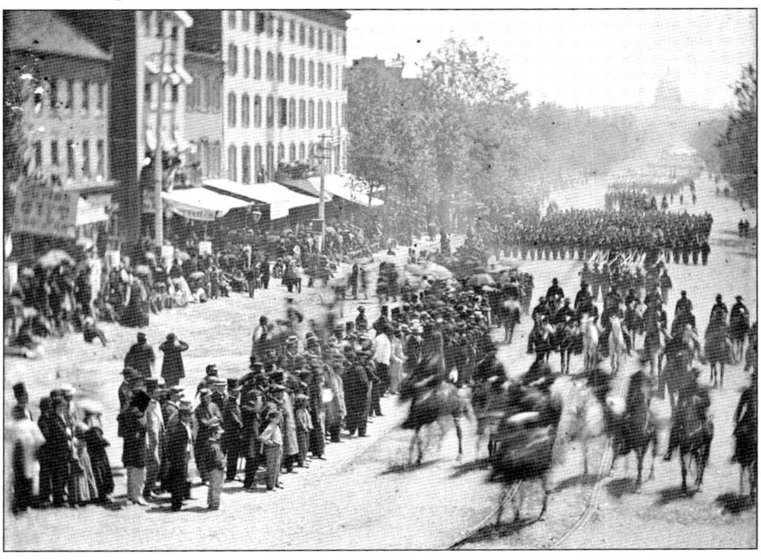

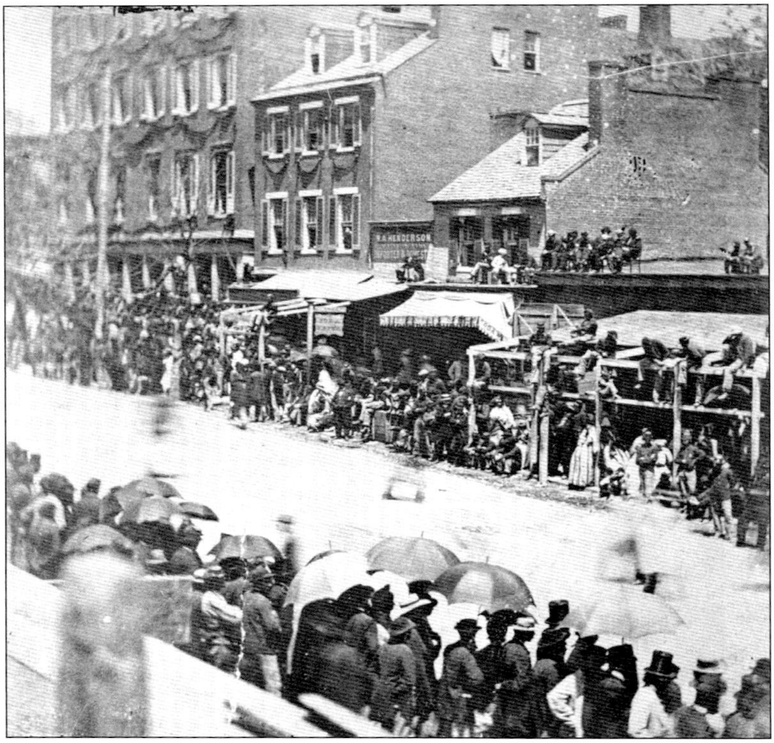

Crowds line Fifteenth Street between Pennsylvania Avenue and the White House as they await the passing of the Grand Review of the Armies. Note the men sitting in chairs on the roof at right, some of whom seem to be in uniform. The photograph was taken from the Treasury Building. Some maps of the period show this section of Fifteenth Street as Pennsylvania Avenue, a confusion that still exists today.

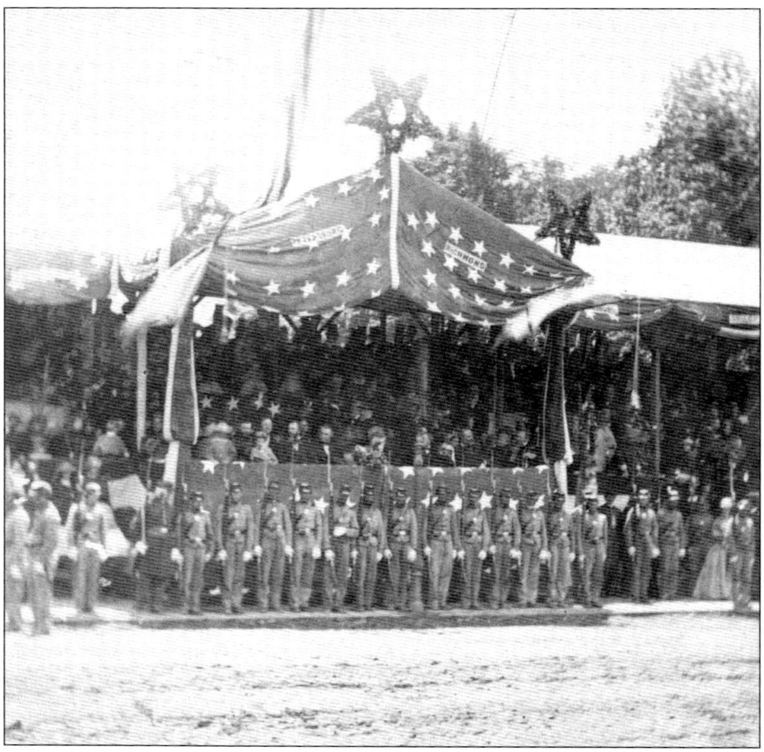

The presidential reviewing stand for the Grand Review of the Armies was set up for the occasion to the north of the White House along Pennsylvania Avenue. Pres. Andrew Johnson is at left center of the main stand, looking to his right; on the left appears to be Secretary of War Edwin Stanton. At far right by the front of the stand are Gen. Ulysses S. Grant and Gen. William T. Sherman (next to flag), who seem to be looking at each other.

Washington's roads remained in a sorry state after the war, although the avenue was probably the city's best street. Twin streetcar tracks ran down the center, with cobblestones between the rails, while the street itself was decked over with wood paving. Here, carriages for hire await fares at the foot of Fifteenth Street in 1870. The single horse is probably a hill horse, hitched on for extra power to get the streetcars up hills. (John DeFerrari.)

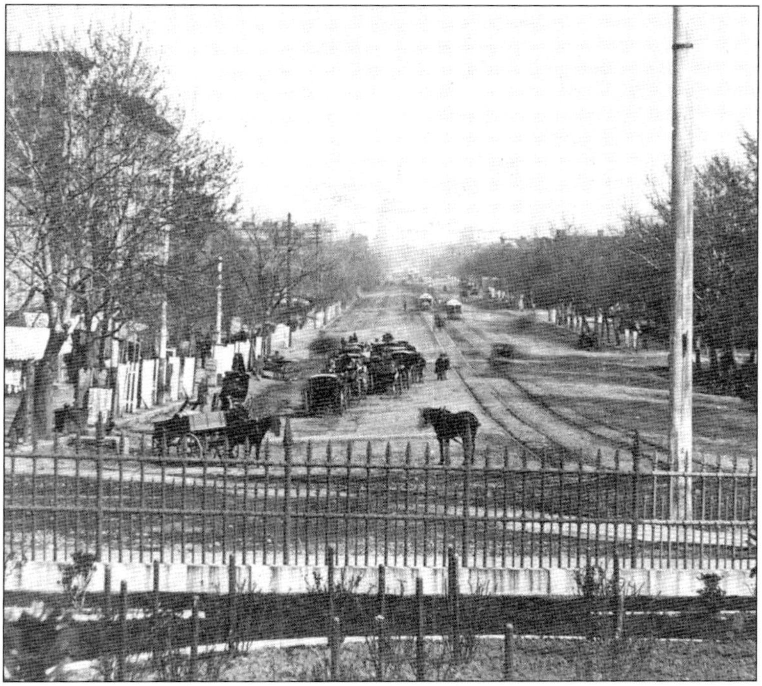

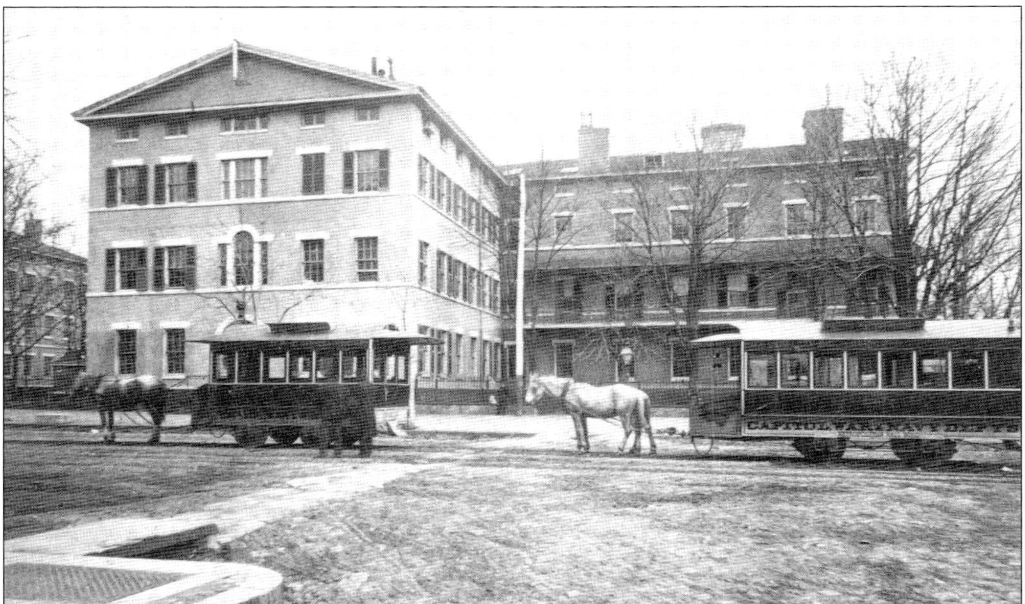

Two Metropolitan Rail Road horse-drawn streetcars await passengers by the Navy Department building on Seventeenth Street just below Pennsylvania Avenue around 1867. In 1864, the Metropolitan became the second street railway company chartered in Washington, following the 1862 opening of the Washington & Georgetown line. The smaller bobtail car at left ran between the Navy Department, the US Post Office, and Treasury, while the full-sized car at right ran between the Capitol and the War and Navy Departments.

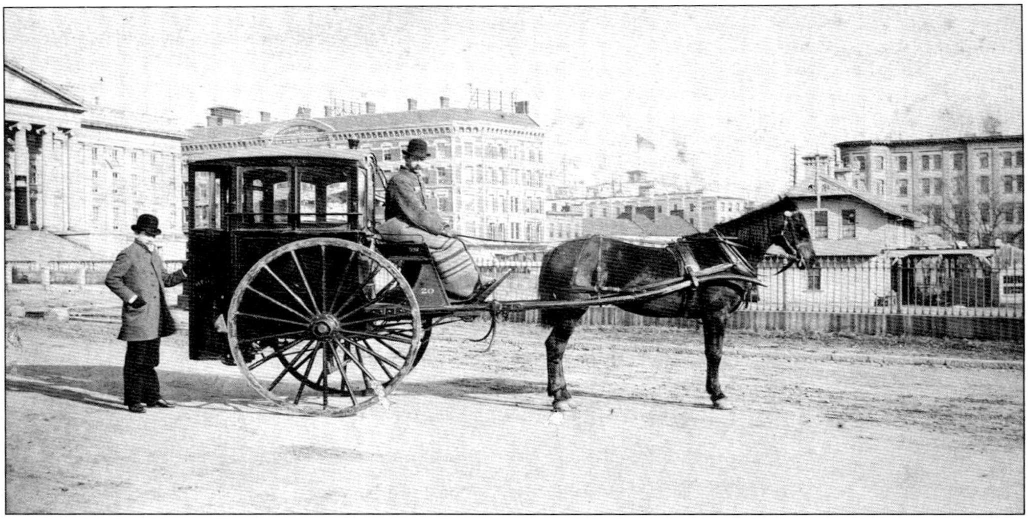

Two chilly men pose around the mid-1880s with a two-wheel horse-drawn carriage of the Herdic Phaeton Company. For nearly 30 years, Herdics were a popular form of urban transportation, not dying out until the mid-1910s. At left is the Treasury Building, while directly behind the carriage is the Corcoran Building on Fifteenth Street below F Street. Built in 1848, the Greek Revival Corcoran was one of the city's finest commercial buildings. Today it is the site of the Washington Hotel. Note that the street has yet to be paved.

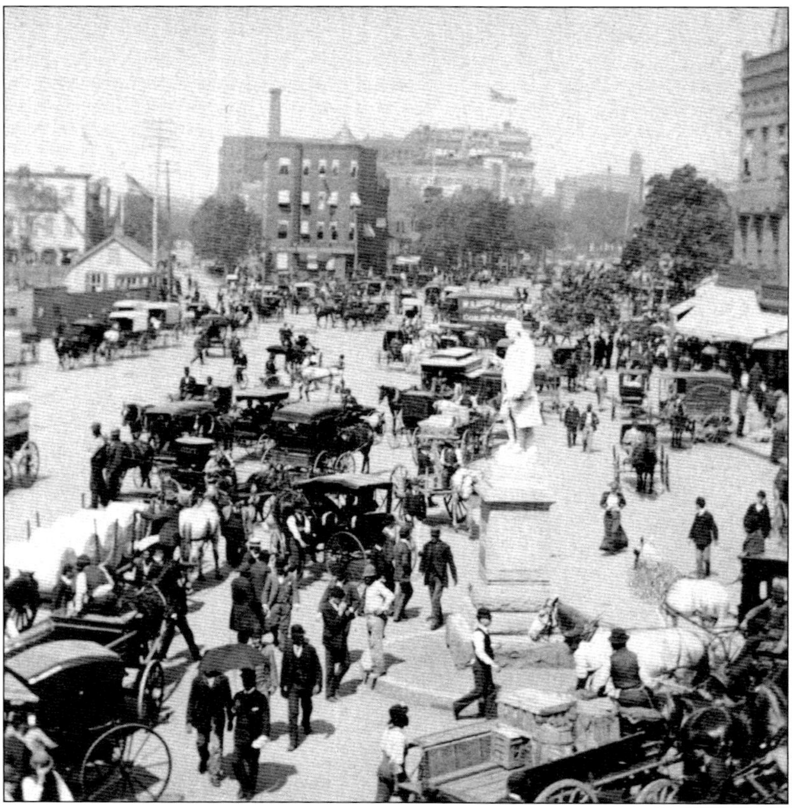

Few 19th-century photographs convey the hustle and bustle of the avenue like this view from about 1889 at the intersection with Tenth and D Streets. A statue of Ben Franklin looks down upon all manner of horse-drawn vehicles, including carts, carriages, and at least one omnibus. Note that even in this pre-automobile era, traffic kept generally to the right side of the roadway. Most of these conveyances had bells to warn pedestrians of their approach.

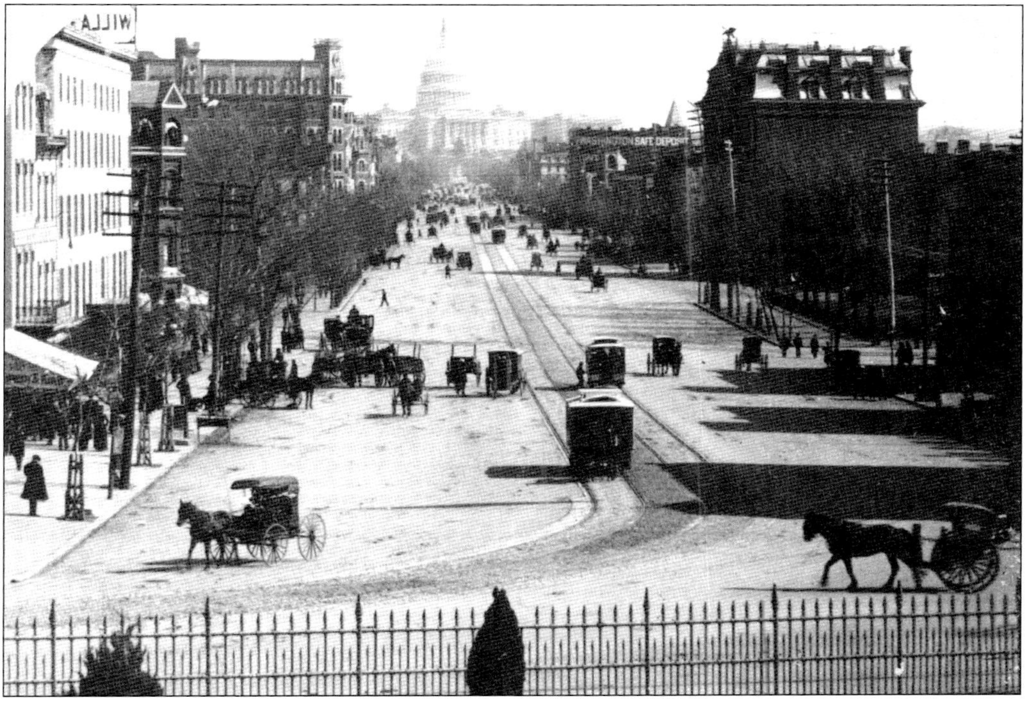

A major modernization effort spearheaded in 1870 by Alexander Shepherd, the director of public works, drastically changed Washington in only a few years at the cost of nearly bankrupting the city, and Shepherd falling from power. Among the improvements, thousands of trees were planted and streets were paved. The large building at left center is Shepherd's Centennial Building, completed in 1876 after he returned to private life. To settle debts, he soon sold the building, which in 1893 became the Raleigh Hotel.

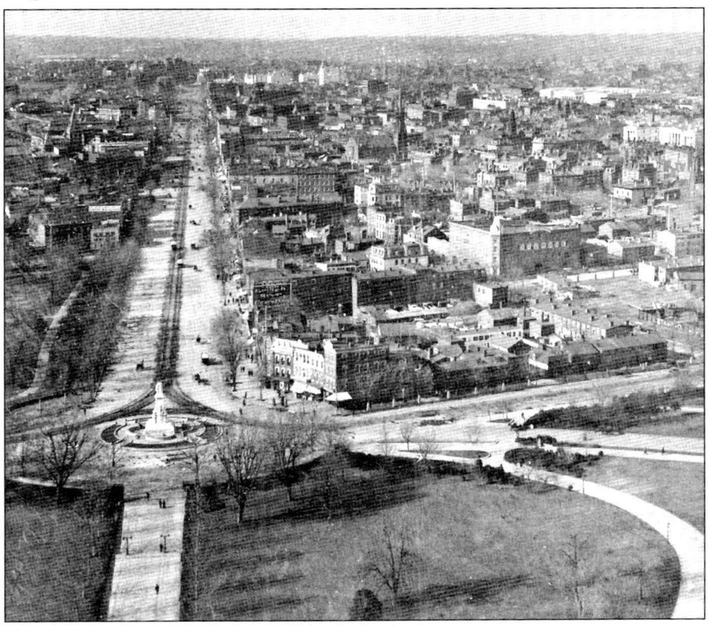

This 1883 view from the Capitol shows how city congestion came right to the foot of Capitol Hill at First Street in the right foreground. The city's Chinatown was centered in the first group of buildings on the avenue's southern side at left center, between Third and Fourth Streets. The large spire at upper left marks the Baltimore & Potomac Rail Road station, whose tracks lead across the Mall to the left. (John DeFerrari.)

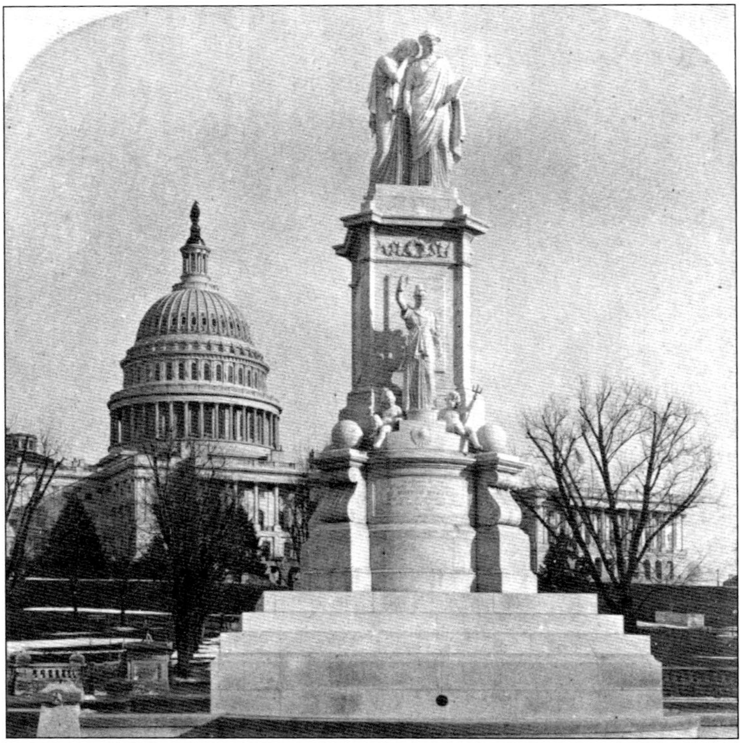

The Peace Monument was placed at the center of Peace Circle at Pennsylvania Avenue and First Street. Completed in 1878 and seen in 1880, it honored American naval deaths from the Civil War. While the circle has since been enlarged and the cityscape down the avenue completely changed, the monument remains in this location to this day and marks the starting point for many processions and parades.

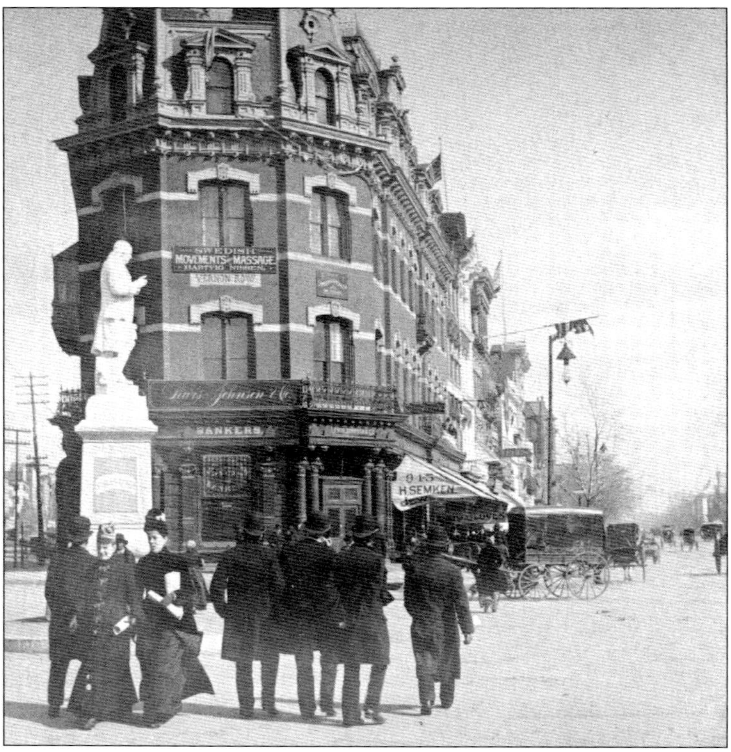

Ben Franklin's statue presides over a more orderly scene in this March 1889 view of Vernon Row, a group of commercial buildings at Tenth and D Streets and the avenue. The view looks east, with the avenue at right. Lewis Johnson & Company bankers occupy the ground floor, while Norwegian immigrant Hartvig Nissen's Swedish Movements and Massage take up the three floors above. The shop of noted silversmith H. Semken is at right on the building's Pennsylvania Avenue side.

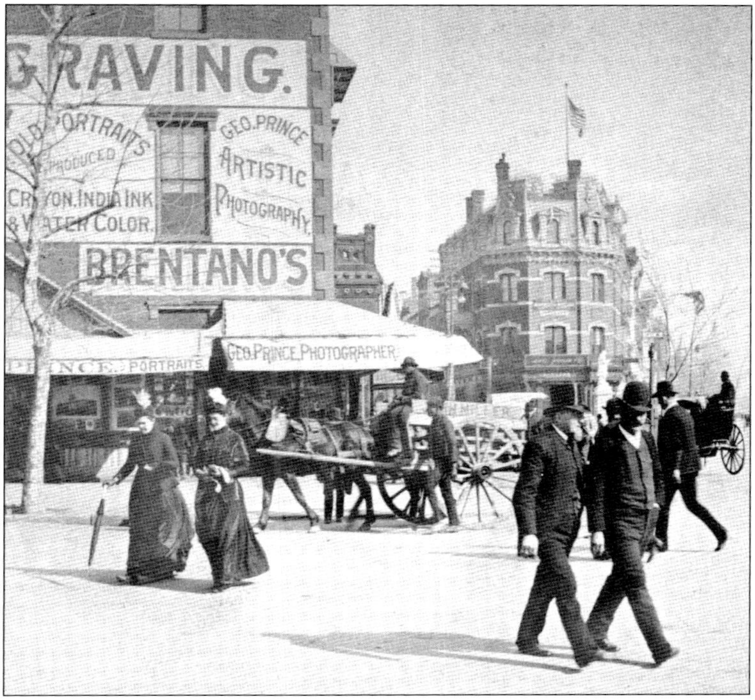

Well-dressed pedestrians stroll in May 1889 at Eleventh and D Streets and Pennsylvania Avenue. Founded in New York City, Brentano's books opened its first branch in 1883 in Washington, and within a few years, it became the country's largest bookseller. The company remained in business until 1984. George Prince was a noted photographer of the day who offered a variety of services, including drawings and watercolor portraits. Vernon Row is at right in the background.

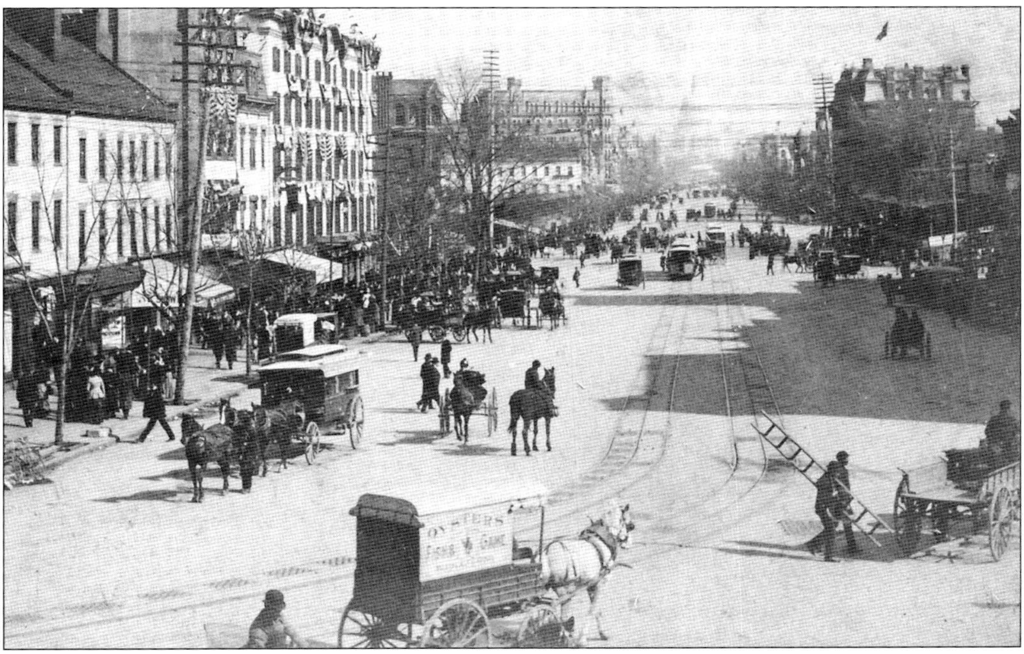

The avenue is seen in 1892 from the Treasury Building. The Willard Hotel at left is decorated with patriotic bunting, possibly for the Grand Army of the Republic encampment that September. Note the proliferation of telephone and electric wires overhead. Fears of increasing power line congestion drove a persistent opposition to overhead cable trolleys, and Congress mandated that, unlike in many cities, overhead wires would be prohibited in Washington. (John DeFerrari.)

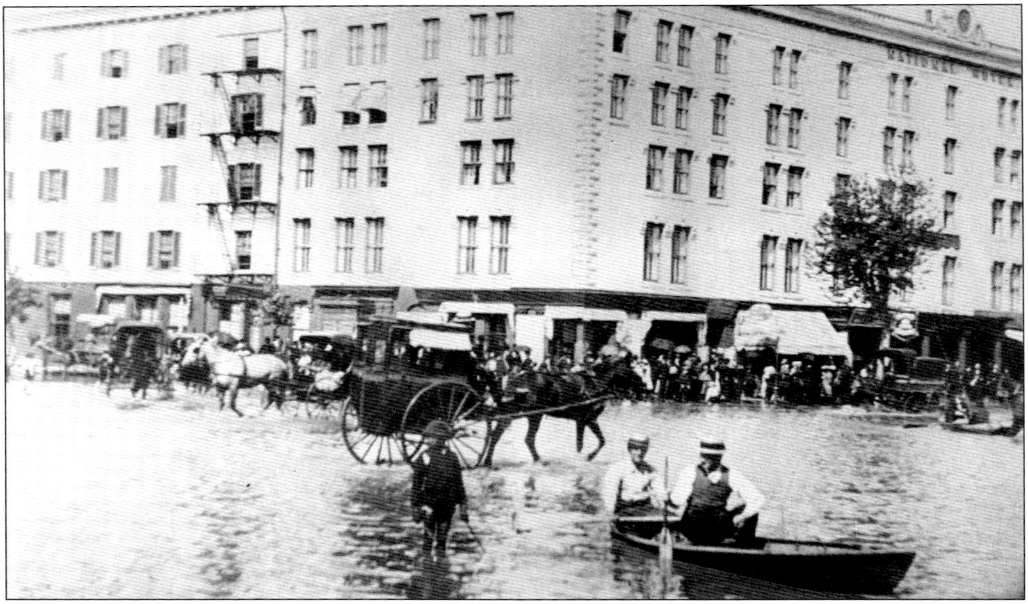

Flooding was a persistent problem along the low-lying portions of the avenue. On June 2, 1889, floodwaters lap at the National Hotel at Pennsylvania Avenue and Fourth Street. The waters rose from Tiber Creek, buried below the avenue when the streets were laid out in 1790, and from an inadequate sewer and drainage system. This flooding resulted from the same storm system that caused the Great Johnstown Flood in Pennsylvania, the most devastating US flood of the 1800s.

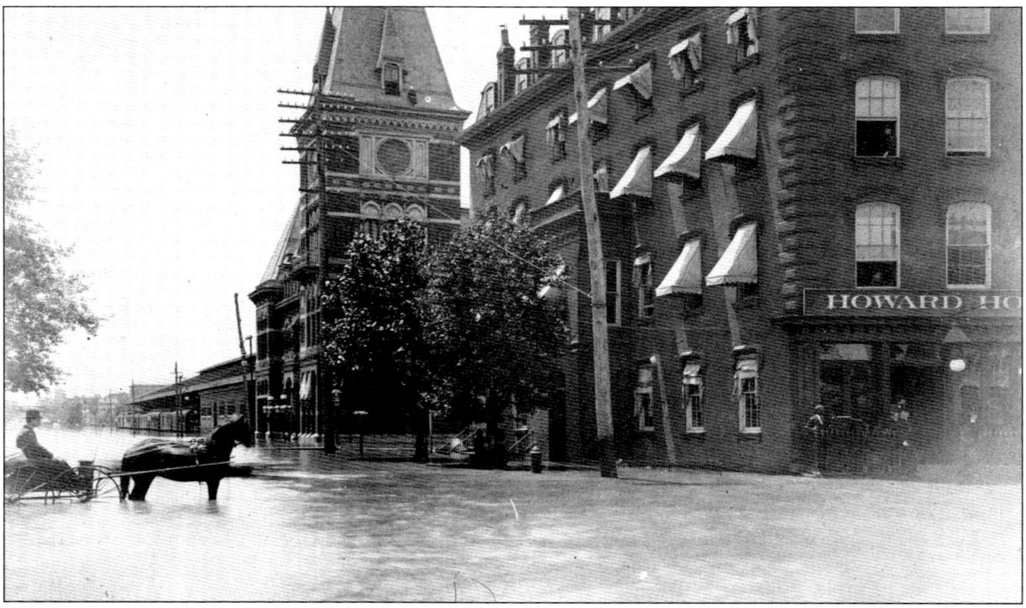

A view from the avenue looking south down Sixth Street on June 2, 1889, shows floodwaters surrounding the Howard Hotel at right and the Baltimore & Potomac (B&P) train station. Note the railroad cars on the tracks stretching across the Mall, just over the horse at left. Sixth Street ran straight down to the Washington Channel along the Potomac. The B&P station was controversial even before it was completed in 1878; it was demolished in 1908 with the opening of Union Station.

Three

The Modern City Emerges

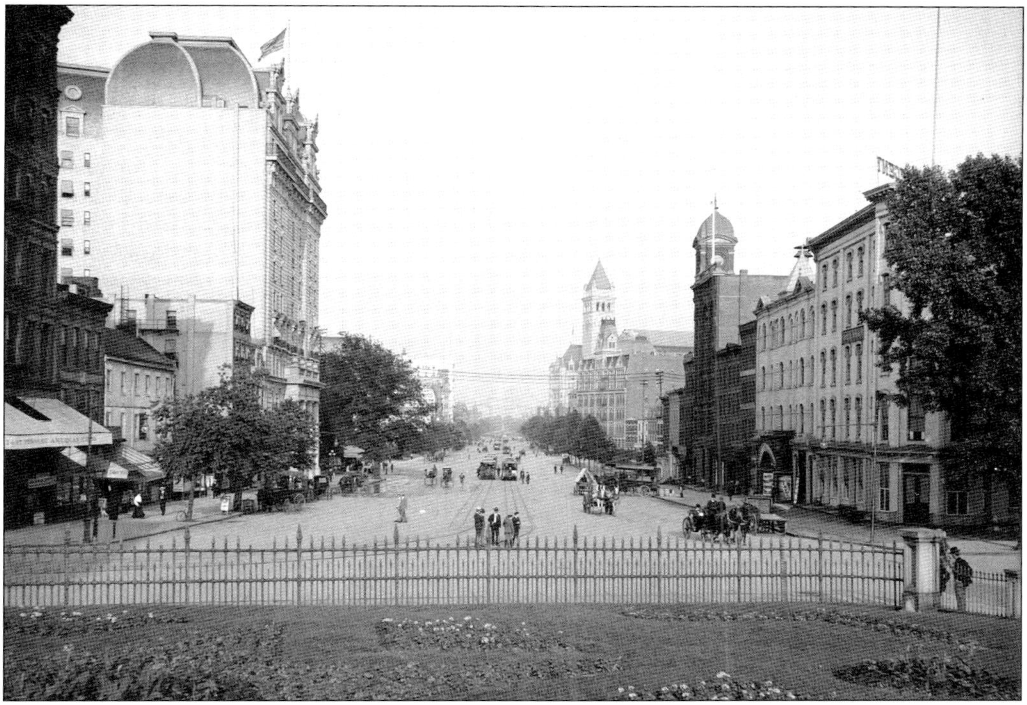

The end of the economically depressed 1890s saw a new burst of building development that gradually changed much of the avenue's character. In 1899, the new Post Office Building was completed at Twelfth Street, its Romanesque Revival clock tower rising to 315 feet and dominating the avenue. Two years later, a new, much larger Willard Hotel rose along Fourteenth Street, its Beaux-Arts bulk dominating the upper avenue. A few years later, the new District Building rose diagonally opposite the Willard on Fourteenth Street, its more subdued, classical American Beaux-Arts style presenting a sense of stability and permanence. Seen here in June 1903, the view from Treasury has been altered by the huge Willard, at left, and the Post Office's clock tower at right center. The scene, probably photographed on a Sunday, lacks the bustle of a weekday, with a group of men conversing in the center of the lightly populated street. Within a few years, the advent of the automobile would sweep away this tranquility.

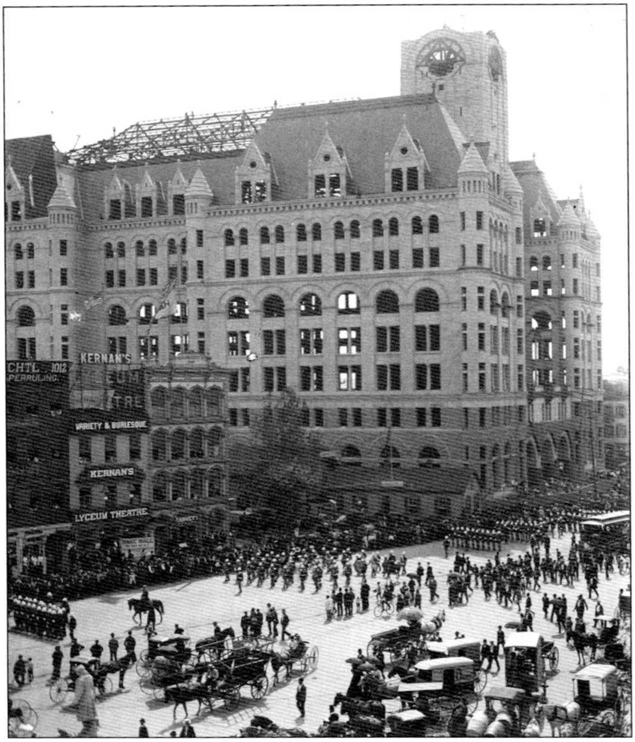

Construction of the new Post Office Building began in 1892 and took seven years to complete. The building was needed to replace an 1839 facility up on F Street that was no longer sufficient for the needs of the rapidly growing city. On September 3, 1894, a parade marking the first federal observance of Labor Day passes by the building, which fills the block between Eleventh Street, at center, and Twelfth Street, to the right.

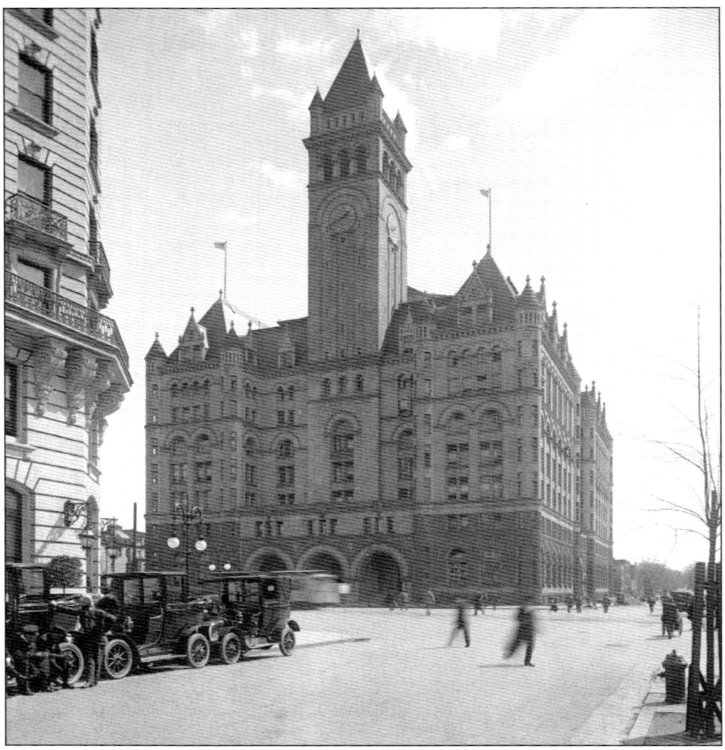

The Post Office Building is seen from Twelfth Street, with a line of taxicabs along the corner of the Raleigh Hotel in the left foreground. Despite appearances, the facility turned out to be drastically inadequate, and plans to turn over one floor to the Treasury Department were shelved for lack of space. The clock tower only just preceded Congressional height restrictions enacted in 1899, just as the building was being completed.

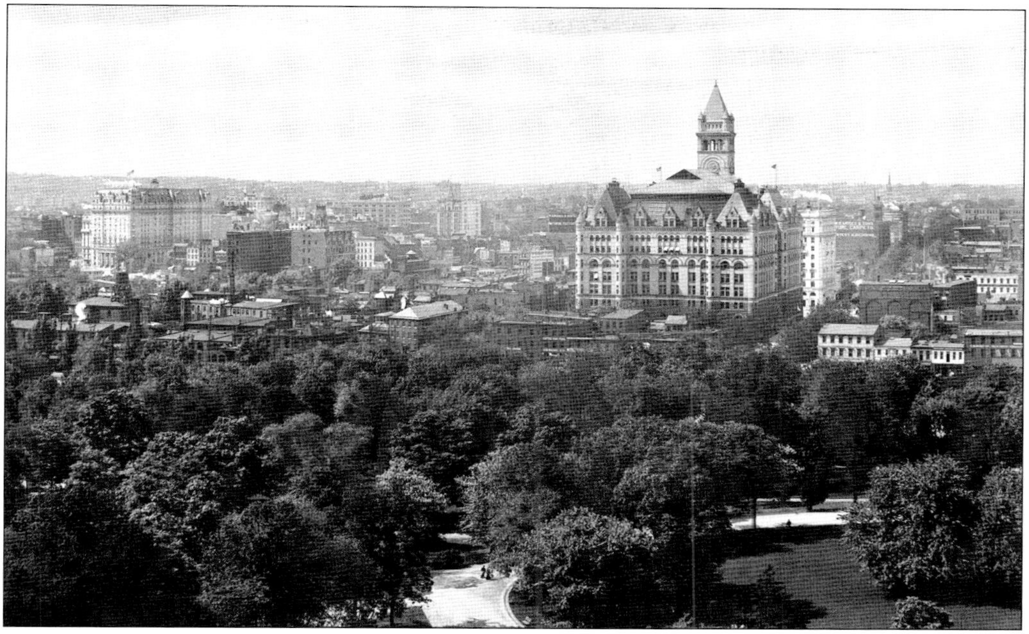

These views from the south side of the National Mall, before the buildup of the city, display the vast bulk of the Post Office Building in ways no longer possible. The view above, from 1904, looks out from the tower of the Smithsonian Institution's castle across a heavily wooded Mall. The low-lying buildings just beyond the trees mark the neighborhood once known as Murder Bay, one of the most disreputable parts of town during the mid-1800s. At far left is the Willard Hotel, while the white building just peeking from behind the Post Office at right is the Evening Star Building. The view below dates from the late 1910s. The Post Office Building featured an A-framed glass roof over its large atrium.

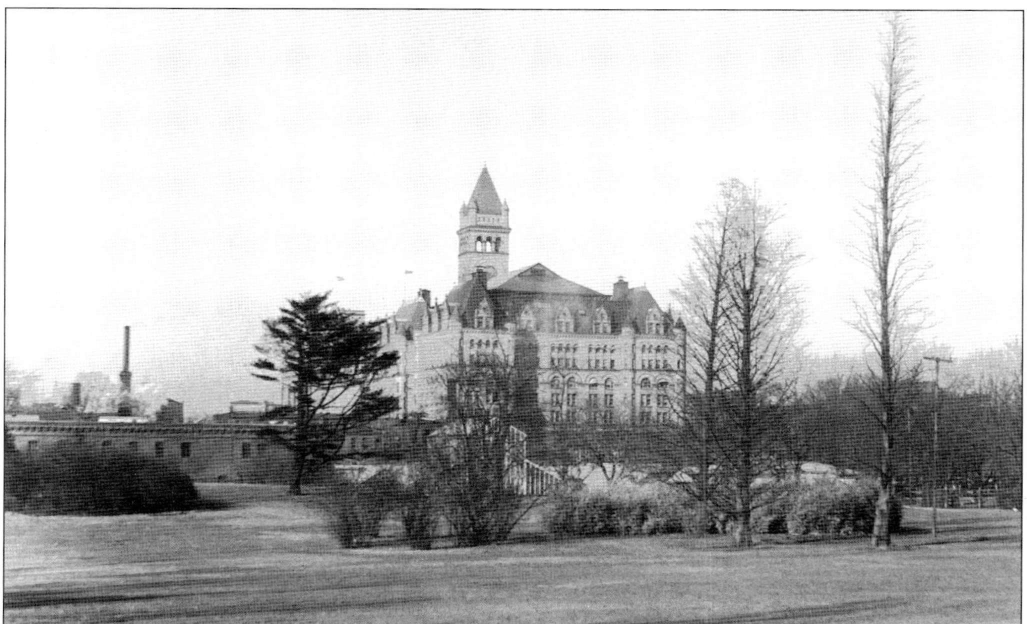

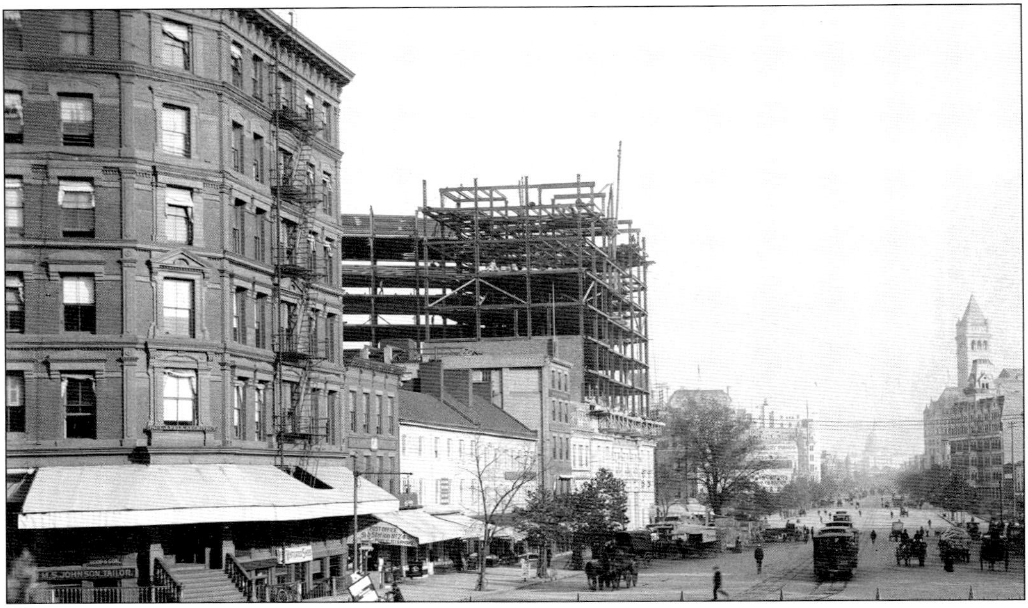

The steel girders of the new Willard Hotel rise in November 1900 above the location occupied by the establishment since the 1820s. The middle group of buildings at center date from about that time. At left on Fifteenth Street is a corner of the Corcoran Building, one of the city's finest office buildings. The second floor displays a sign for Paul J. Pelz, a German-born immigrant who became the primary architect for the exterior of the Library of Congress.

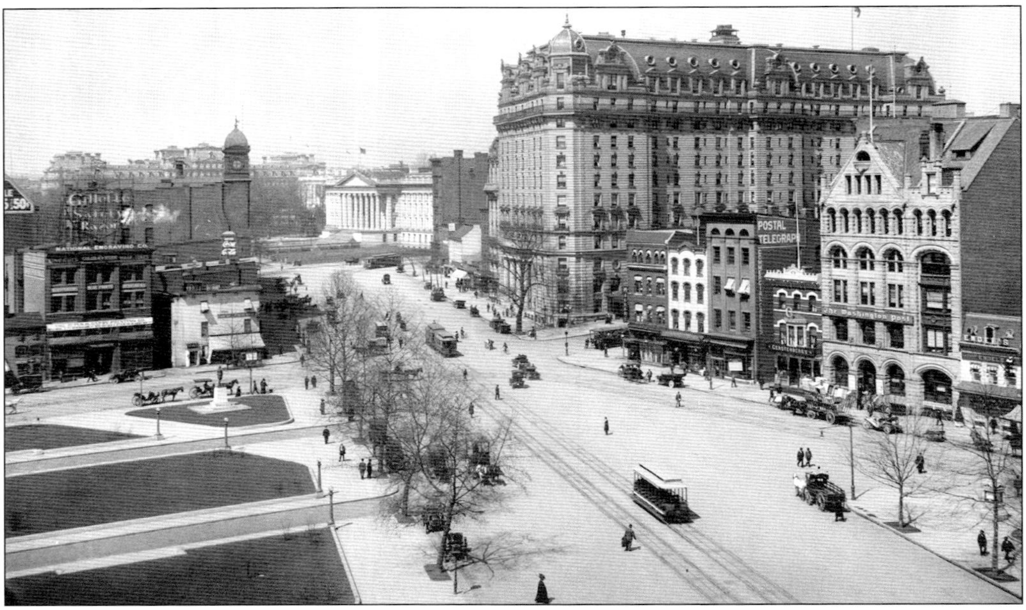

The new Willard dominates this view from about 1907 of the intersection of Pennsylvania Avenue with E Street, at right, and Fourteenth Street, next to the hotel. In the middle distance, a streetcar is turning up Fifteenth Street in front of the Treasury Building. The Romanesque Revival building at far right is the home of the *Washington Post*, one of several newspaper and telegraph offices giving the strip the moniker "Newspaper Row."

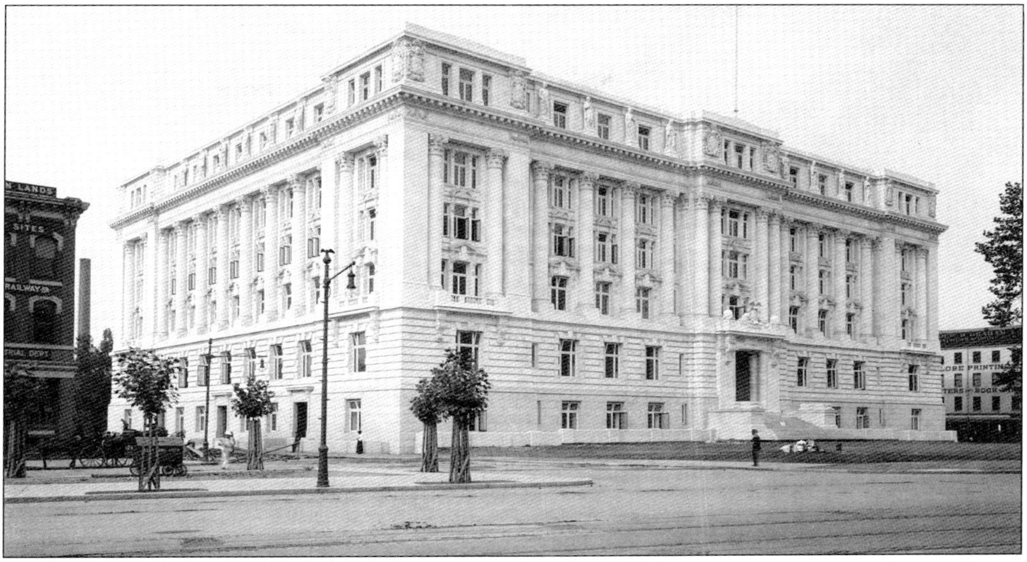

The District Building is seen soon after its 1908 completion. The prominent site on the southeast corner of Fourteenth Street and Pennsylvania Avenue became available after the Capitol Traction Company's power plant burned in 1897. Congress purchased the land in 1902 for a sorely needed District municipal building. The American Beaux-Arts structure with a granite and marble exterior took four years to build and continues in use as the city's town hall. In 1994, it was renamed the John A. Wilson District Building.

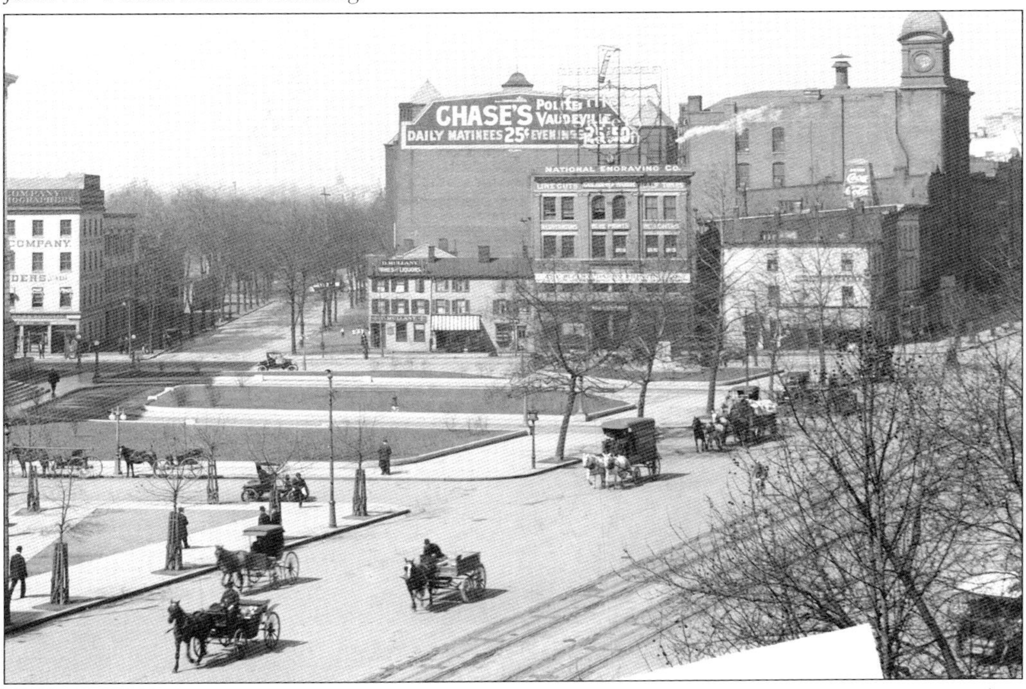

The pace of life seems pretty sedate in this view along Fourteenth Street at the avenue and in front of the District Building, just out of view to the left. Chase's Polite Vaudeville theater, along E Street at center, was one of a number of theaters in the neighborhood.

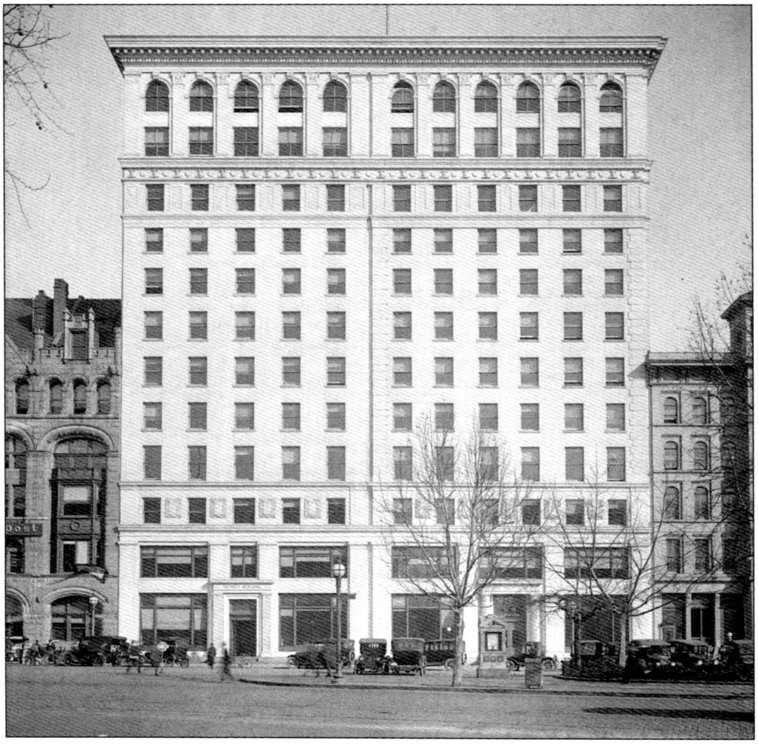

The Munsey Building is pictured in 1919, shortly after a major remodeling effort virtually doubled the structure's size, filling the space between the Washington Post Building at left and the National Theater. Frank Munsey claimed he spent nearly double the price per foot on the building's construction to install items such as marble floors and expensive wood and brass finishings. A vigorous preservation effort in the late 1970s failed to save the structure, which was demolished in 1980.

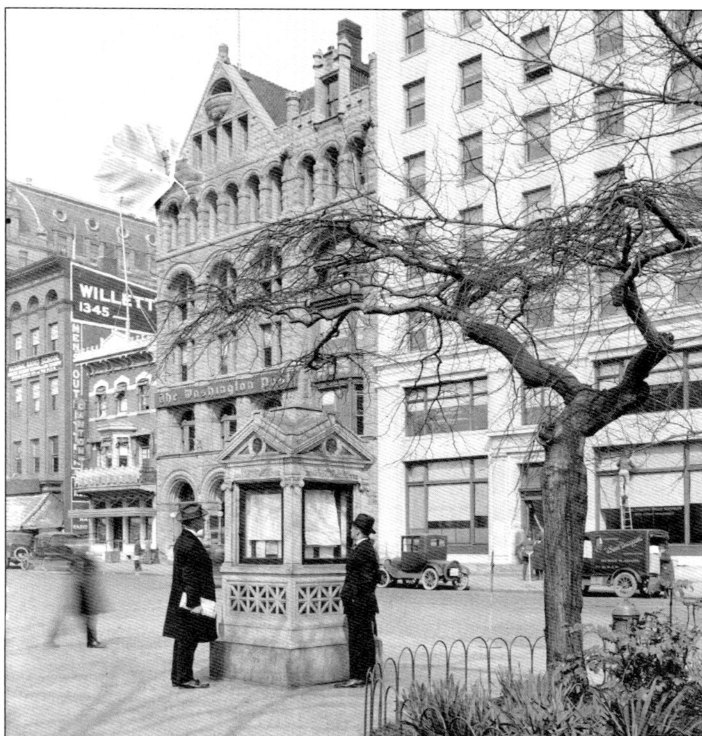

Two men peruse the latest weather reports around 1920 posted in a special US Weather Bureau kiosk in front of the Munsey Building. The kiosk was actually an elaborate weather station, housing thermometers, rain gauges, thermographs, and other instruments, all displayed in one of the structure's windows. The installation was completed in 1908 and was initially popular, but it soon gained a reputation for exaggerating temperatures, particularly in hot weather, a function of its location surrounded by pavement. It was dismantled in early 1933.

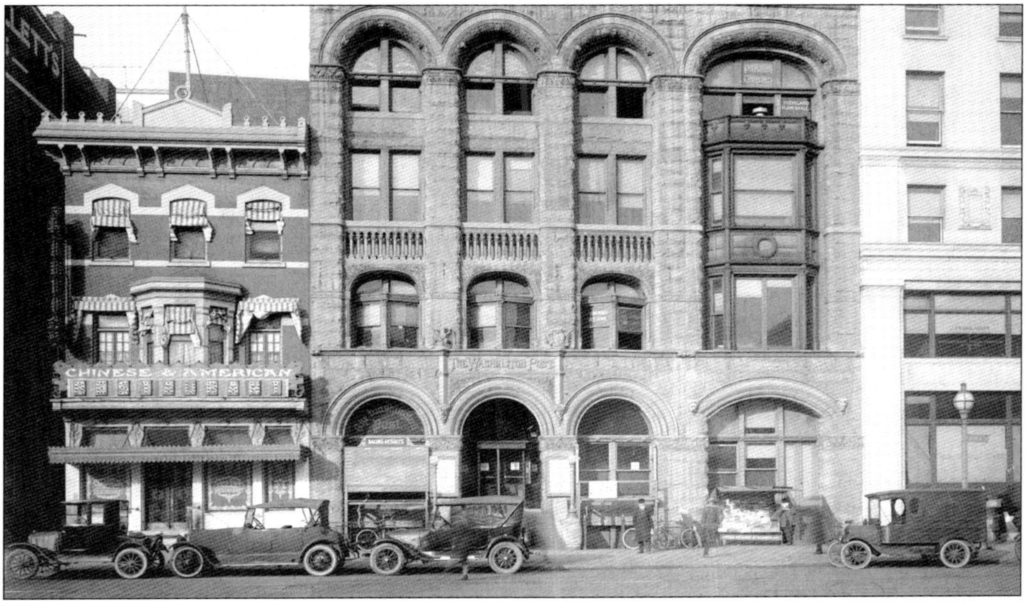

The *Washington Post* newspaper began publishing in 1877 but did not find a permanent home until the 1893 completion of this building at 1337 E Street in the heart of Newspaper Row. The Romanesque Revival structure was enlarged in 1905 with an east bay, seen to the right up against the Munsey Building. Another bay was added on the west side in 1934. The *Post* later constructed a new building on L Street, and the E Street structure was demolished in 1954.

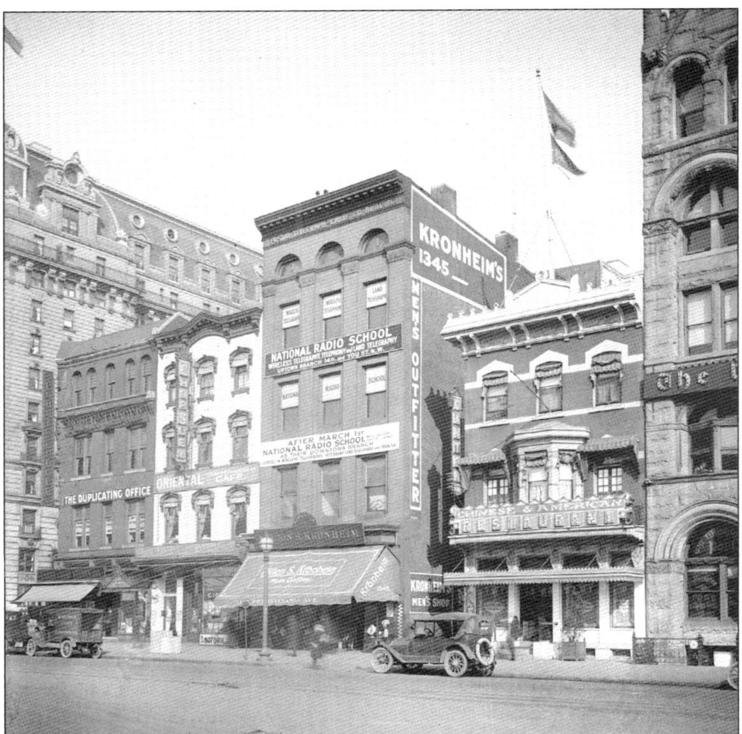

Another view shows Newspaper Row around 1920. The National Radio School (NRS) opened in 1914 with classroom instruction on how to become a "radio expert," according to its ads. It soon expanded into the National Radio Institute, offering correspondence courses in radio technology and operation. The NRS building is flanked by the Oriental Café and the Canton Pagoda, two popular Chinese restaurants. The building at left prominently advertises the Washington bureau of the *Public Ledger*, a major Philadelphia newspaper.

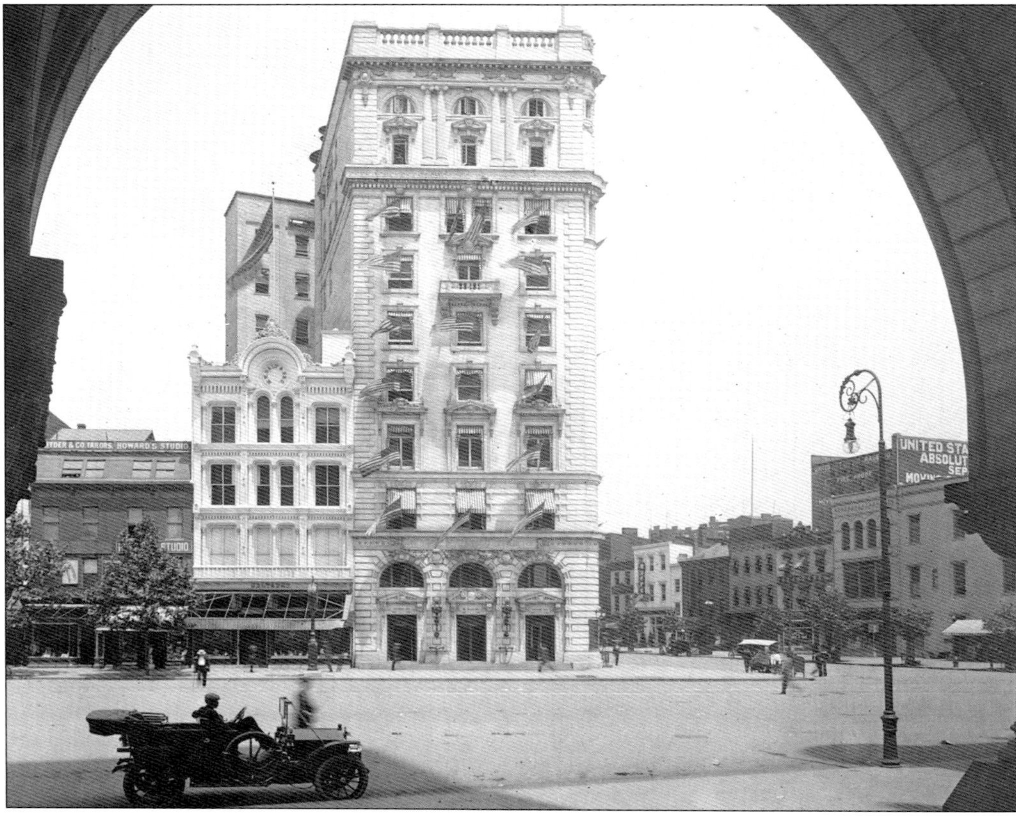

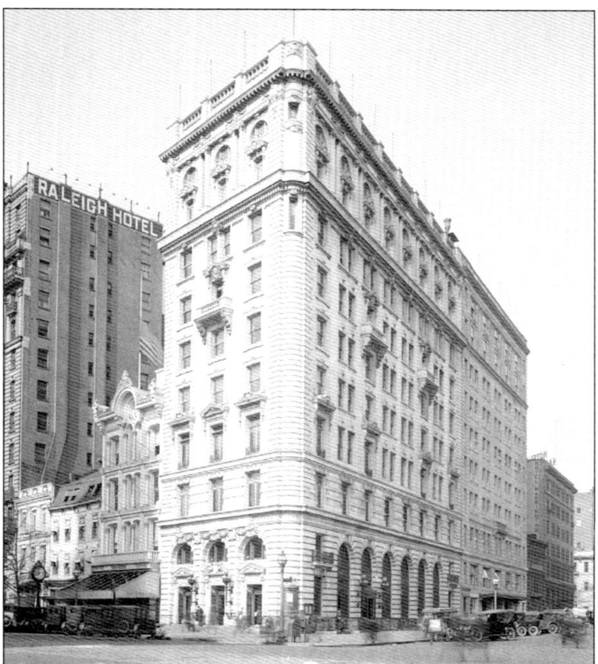

Washington's leading newspaper for many decades was the *Evening Star,* which was published in this building from 1899 to 1955. The elegant marble structure was completed in 1900 on the northwest corner of Pennsylvania Avenue and Eleventh Street, greatly enlarging a previous structure from 1881. The Beaux-Arts edifice made a powerful statement as to the paper's importance with its white marble gleaming in the sunshine. An annex, pictured at left on the right along Eleventh Street, was added in 1919. The four-story building immediately to the left housed Galt & Bro., for two centuries one of the city's premier jewelers. The family-owned company operated in various locations from 1802 to 2001. Edith Galt, the last owner with the family name, became the second Mrs. Woodrow Wilson. The view above is from 1907; the one at left, about 1920.

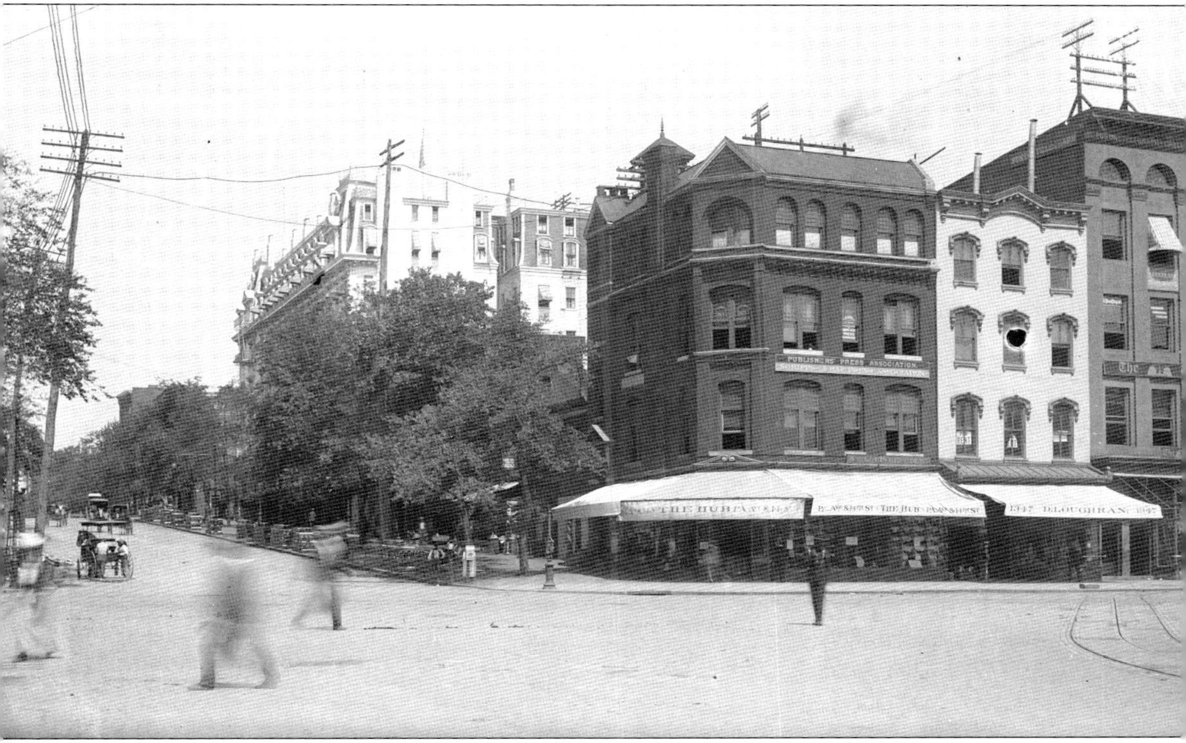

The northeast corner of Fourteenth Street and Pennsylvania Avenue was one end of Newspaper Row, where a number of newspaper and telegraph companies kept offices. In this 1901 view, the Publisher's Press Association, Scripps-McRae Press Association, and *St. Louis Republic* newspaper all have offices in the corner building above the Hub store, with the *Wcrld* newspaper and Postal Telegraph Cable Company at far right. Up the hill is the Ebbitt House hotel, demolished in the 1920s for the National Press Club building.

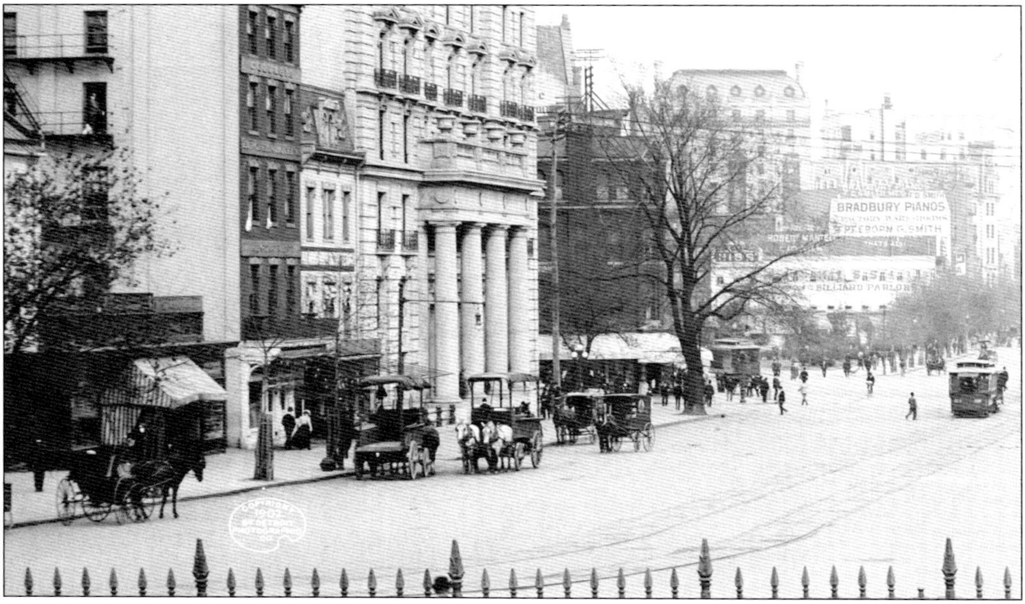

Even after the city's streetcars were electrified in the 1890s, horses remained the region's prime movers. This 1902 view of Pennsylvania Avenue shows horse-drawn carts and carriages parked in front of the Willard Hotel and several restaurants. Pedestrians cross the street unconcerned by fast-moving vehicles, a situation that would change very soon.

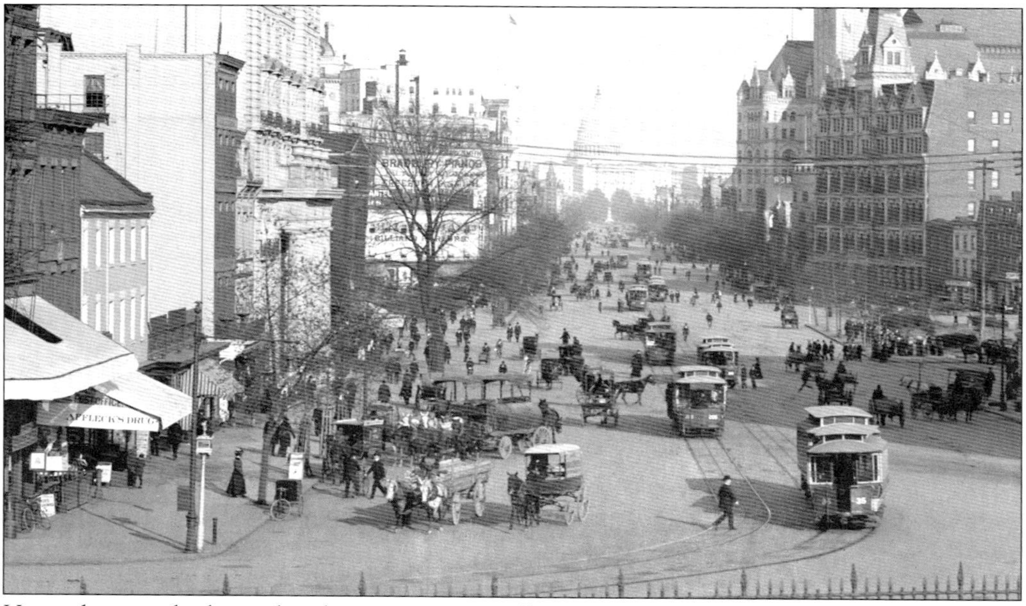

Horse-drawn vehicles and pedestrians cross at all points along a busy Pennsylvania Avenue in 1902 between the steady progression of dozens of streetcars. Some of the streetcars, including the No. 35 in the right foreground, are two-car trains, with a powerless second car being towed to increase the number of passengers. Each streetcar, however, had only one motorman and one conductor, and the two-car arrangement increased their workload and was dangerous. The two-car trains were dropped after 1910.

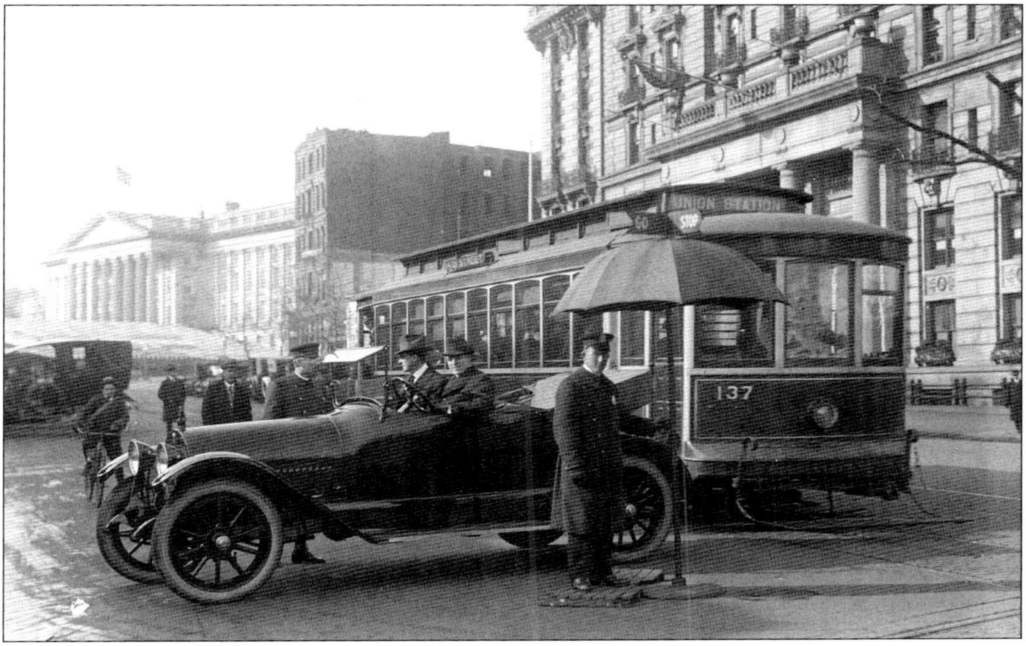

The explosion of automobiles in the 1900s quickly revealed flaws in the city's traffic systems, and clearly more was needed. Among the new innovations were rotating stop and go signs placed in the middle of intersections, controlled by a traffic policeman. These two photographs are part of a series taken in 1913 showing two men in a Haynes Model 22 Roadster stopped in the center of Fourteenth Street and Pennsylvania Avenue, with E Street in the background below. The traffic cop is operating a stop and go sign outfitted for his comfort with an umbrella. Inside the streetcar, the motorman can be seen at the head, just inside the glass, while the conductor looks out from the car's rear door. A wire cowcatcher is fitted on the streetcar's front end to prevent debris, animals, and people from being run over. The small, hand-operated stop and go signs quickly proved inadequate and were soon replaced.

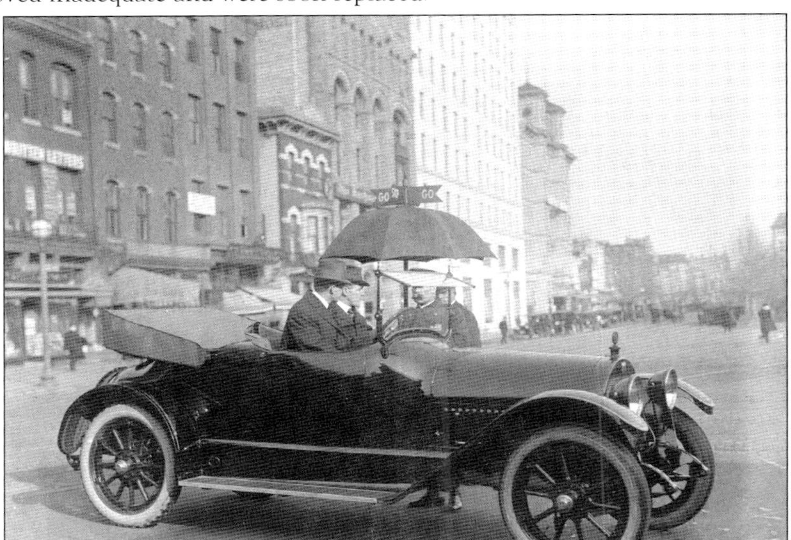

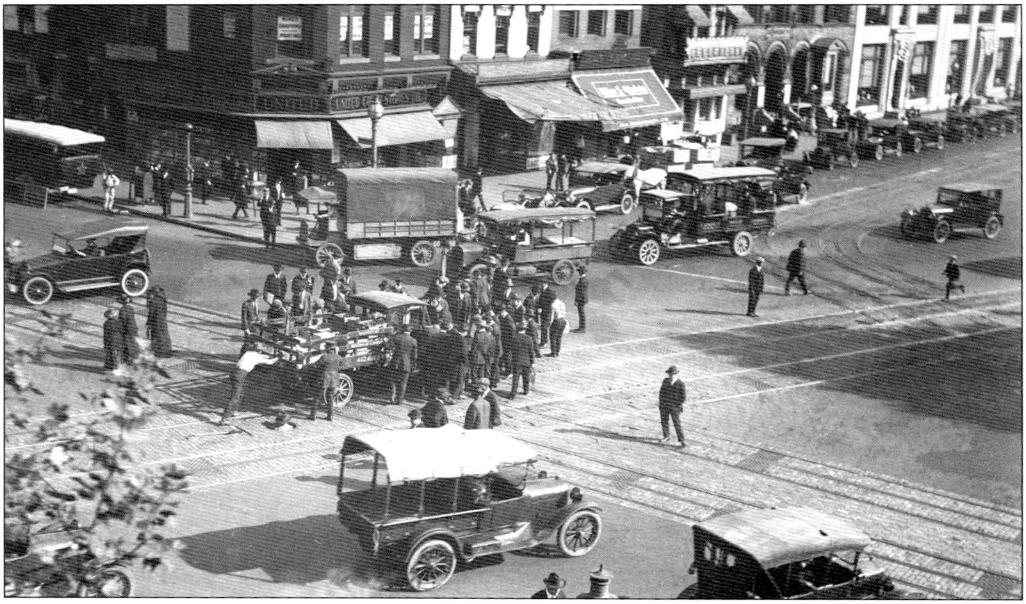

The same intersection is seen around 1920 with some sort of traffic altercation going on. A Washington Beverage Company truck seems to have broken down in the middle of Fourteenth Street and Pennsylvania Avenue. One man appears ready to push at the vehicle's rear, directed by a policeman, while a group of men is clustered around the engine. Note the man popping out of the manhole by the truck's rear, in between two streetcar tracks. Not a single horse is in view.

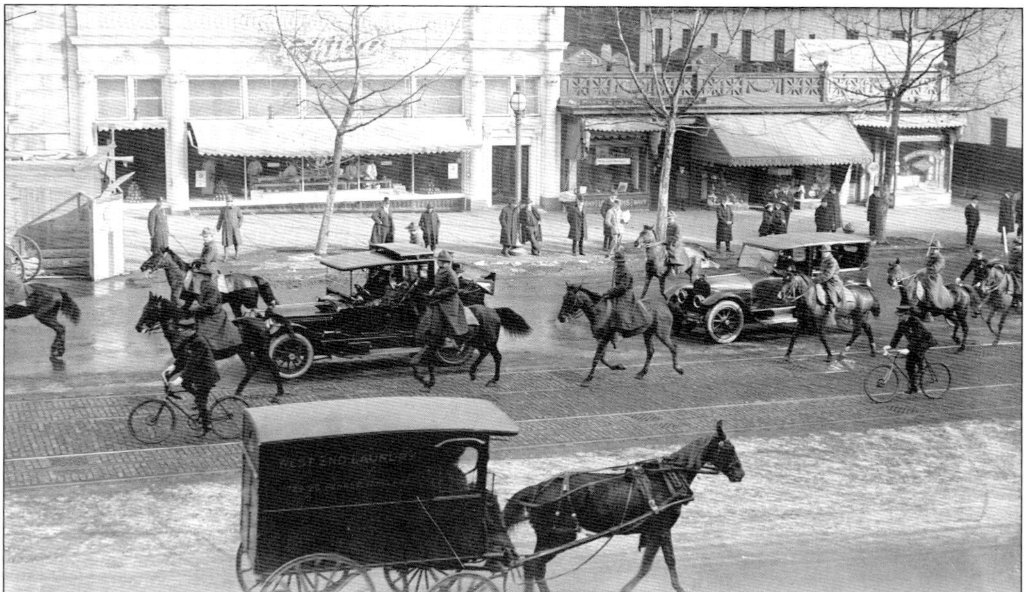

Passersby stop to watch mounted US Army cavalry escorting two limousines passing Childs Restaurant at 1423 Pennsylvania Avenue. The autos might be carrying a diplomatic mission from Serbia that visited Washington from December 1917 to January 1918. Childs was a national dining chain that began in New York City, and this, the first location in Washington, opened in 1913. The Childs building was torn down in the early 1950s and replaced by a parking garage.

Pennsylvania Avenue is seen from Thirteenth Street on a cold winter's night in 1924, the camera's time-exposure creating the illusion of the street being deserted. The Raleigh Hotel rises in the distance. Despite the banning of alcohol sales during the 1920s, supper and dance clubs thrived in hotels like the Raleigh.

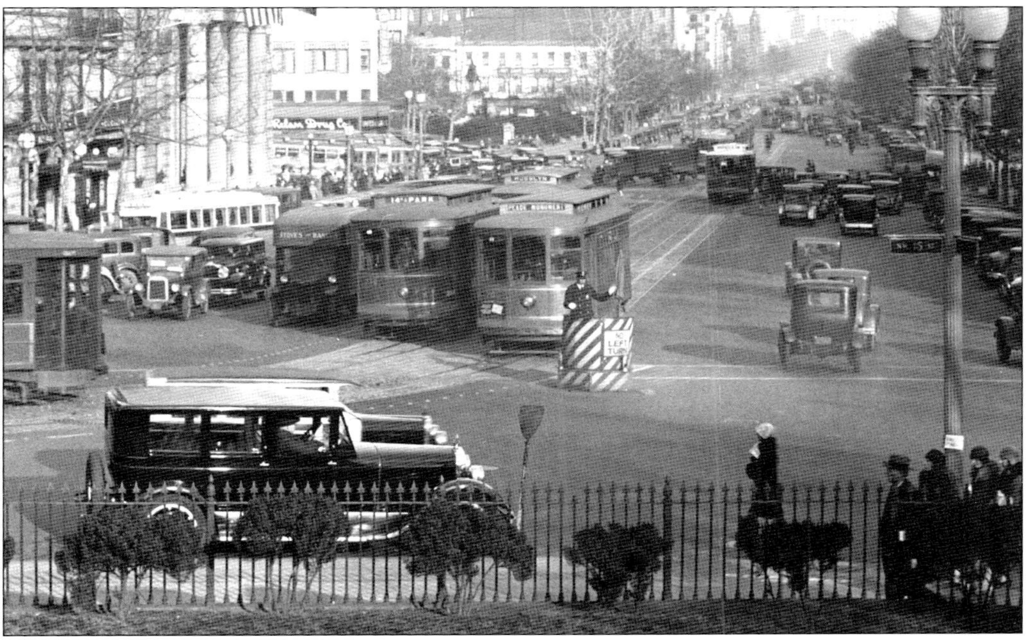

Afternoon rush hour is pictured at Fifteenth Street and Pennsylvania Avenue in March 1930. Despite the development of electric traffic lights in the 1910s, it remained easier to manually control many intersections where a live traffic officer could direct streetcars, trucks, cars, and pedestrians. This officer has been given a more substantial concrete stand, which still appears to offer little protection.

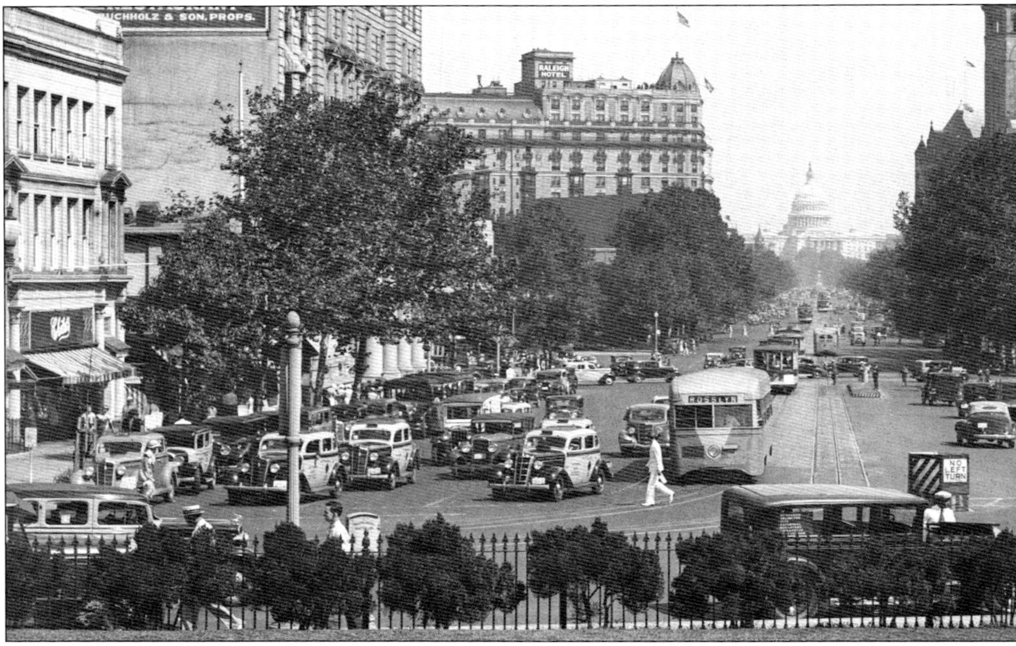

A summertime view down the avenue in August 1935 shows quite a few Diamond Cabs. A tourist car for hire is in the right foreground looking for a fare. The Capital Transit streetcar at center is headed for Rosslyn, in Virginia opposite Georgetown. The route would run up Pennsylvania Avenue around the White House and on to M Street in Georgetown, then cross Key Bridge into Virginia.

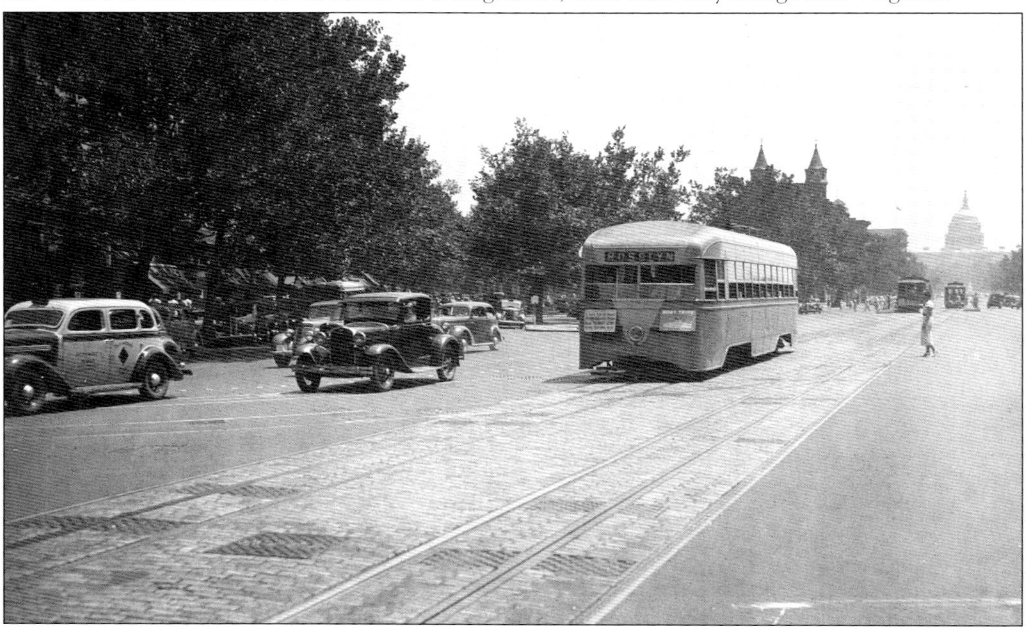

A Capital Transit Company streamliner streetcar bound for Rosslyn comes up Pennsylvania Avenue around Ninth Street in July 1936. Signs on the front of the car advertise the company's *Transit News* publication, along with boat trips to Mount Vernon on the Wilson Line, which ran excursion vessels from Washington's southwest waterfront.

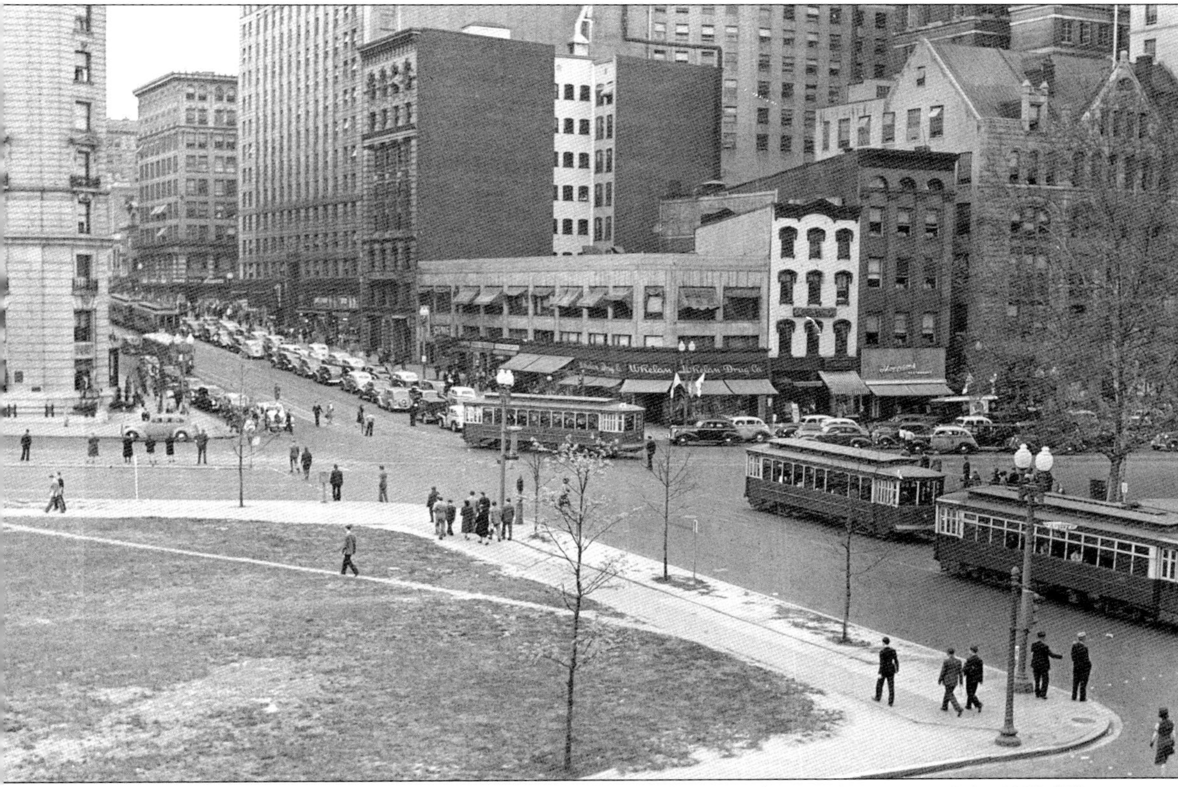

This view looks up Fourteenth Street from E Street and Pennsylvania Avenue in July 1939. The United Cigar store that had occupied the corner on Fourteenth Street now houses a Whelan Drug store. Brothers Charles and George Whelan founded the United Cigar chain in 1901, and two of Charles's sons began the affiliated Whelan Drug chain. The Washington Post Building, at far right, displays a western addition made in 1934.

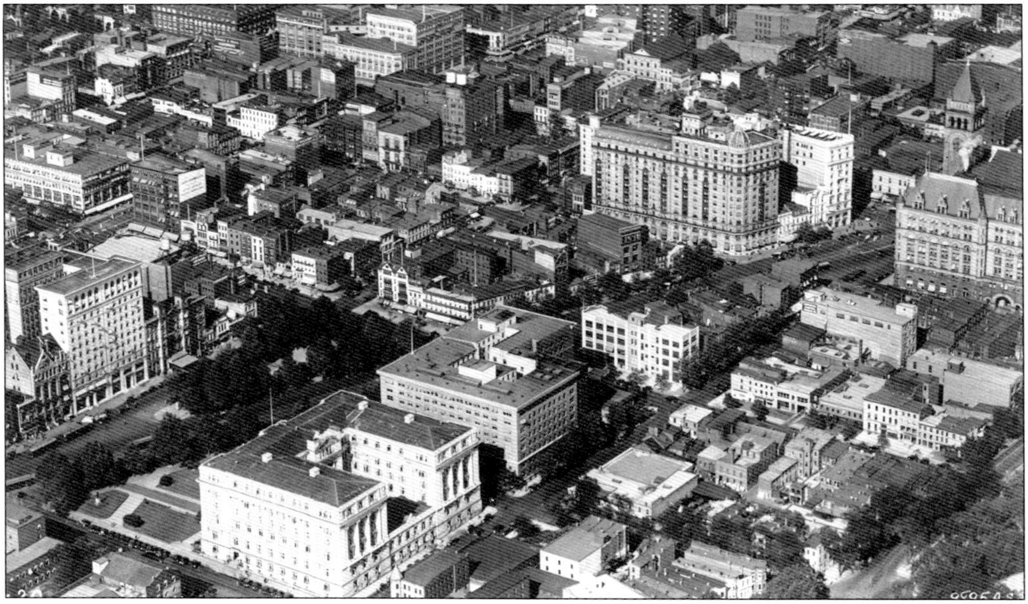

This aerial view from August 1921 looks down at the avenue around Thirteenth Street. The District Building is at lower center, and across Pennsylvania Avenue to the left are the Munsey and Washington Post Buildings. Marked with its distinctive cupola, the Raleigh Hotel on Twelfth Street is at right center, with the gleaming white Evening Star Building to its right. The Post Office is at center far right. (National Archives.)

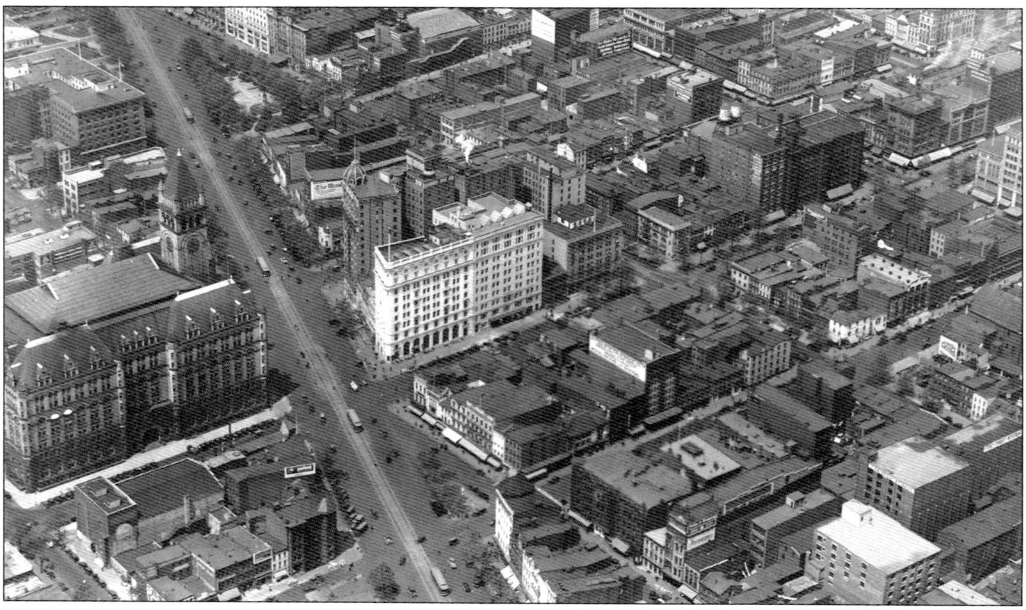

Pennsylvania Avenue runs top to bottom at left in this aerial view from May 2, 1922, looking at Eleventh Street. The Post Office Building is at left, with the Evening Star Building directly across the street in the center of the photograph. Note how D Street cutting in from the lower right forms one of Washington's characteristic triangular blocks when it hits the diagonal of the avenue. (National Archives.)

Four

A SHOPPING AND ENTERTAINMENT CENTER

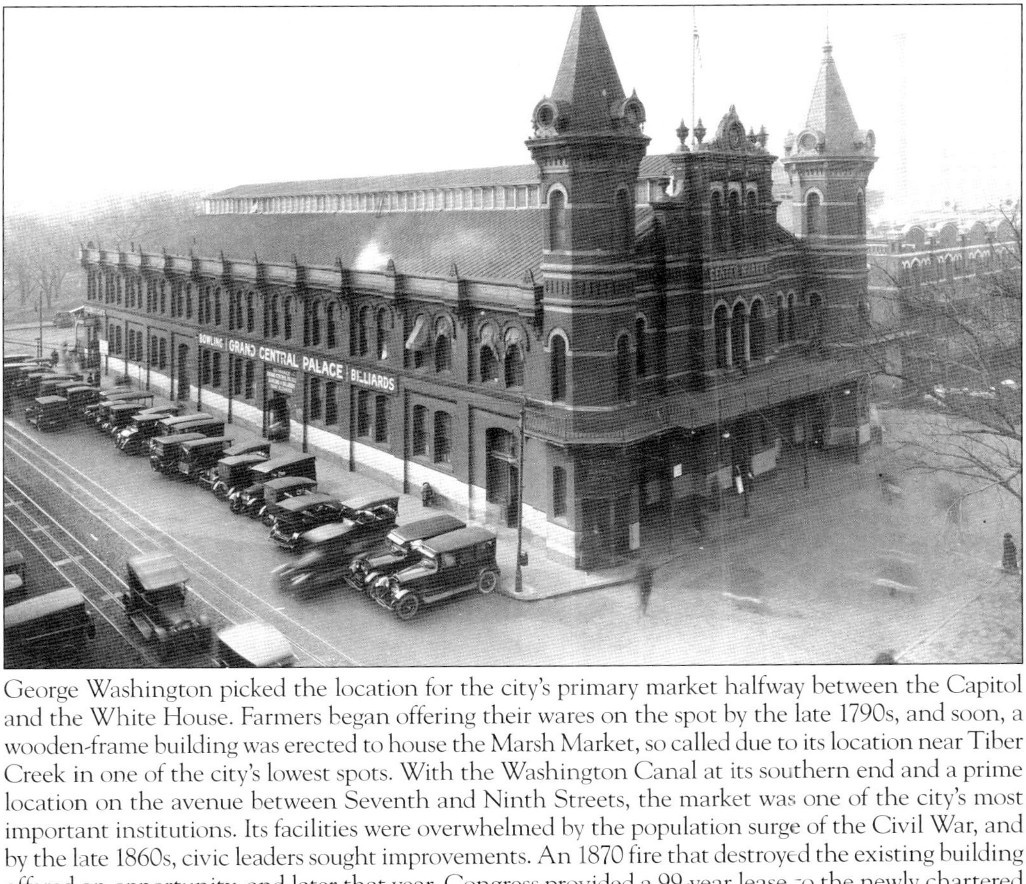

George Washington picked the location for the city's primary market halfway between the Capitol and the White House. Farmers began offering their wares on the spot by the late 1790s, and soon, a wooden-frame building was erected to house the Marsh Market, so called due to its location near Tiber Creek in one of the city's lowest spots. With the Washington Canal at its southern end and a prime location on the avenue between Seventh and Ninth Streets, the market was one of the city's most important institutions. Its facilities were overwhelmed by the population surge of the Civil War, and by the late 1860s, civic leaders sought improvements. An 1870 fire that destroyed the existing building offered an opportunity, and later that year, Congress provided a 99-year lease to the newly chartered Washington Market Company to operate a new facility. Adolf Cluss, the leading architect in the city, was engaged to design the new market, which, when it opened in 1871, was widely hailed as the most modern and sanitary facility in the country. It incorporated not just food stalls but also entertainment facilities, including billiard parlors, as advertised in this early 1920s view of the Grand Palace.

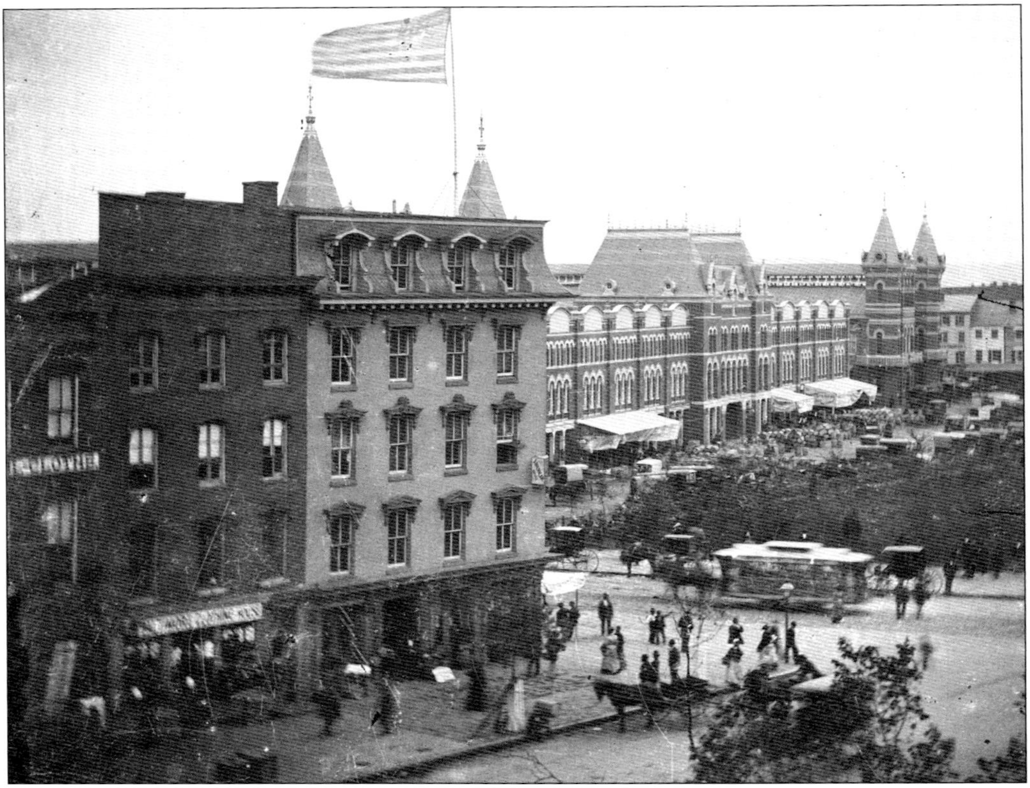

The long north facade of Center Market is seen beyond the building flying the large flag in this view from about 1881 from photographer Matthew Brady's studio on Pennsylvania Avenue. The horse-drawn streetcar is on Seventh Street. The sprawling market complex stretched two blocks from Seventh to Ninth Streets. Note the numerous outdoor stalls, some under awnings, which were cheaper to rent than those indoors.

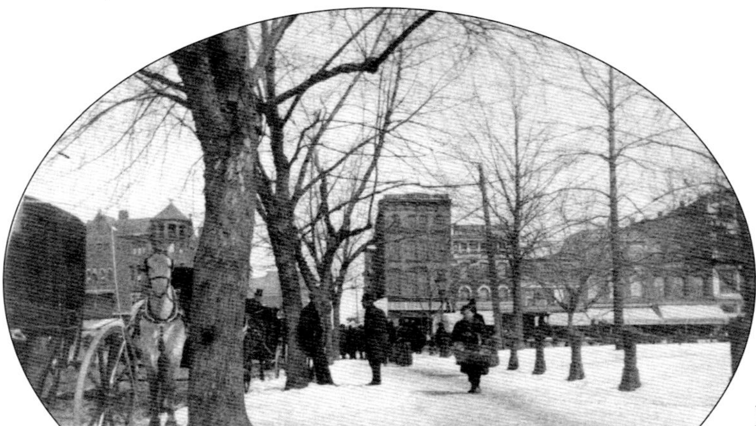

A snowy scene is pictured near Center Market in 1889. Carriages similar to those parked at left normally were used by wealthier people or those able to afford herdics, privately owned carriages similar to taxis. Most of the market's patrons walked to market or traveled by streetcar.

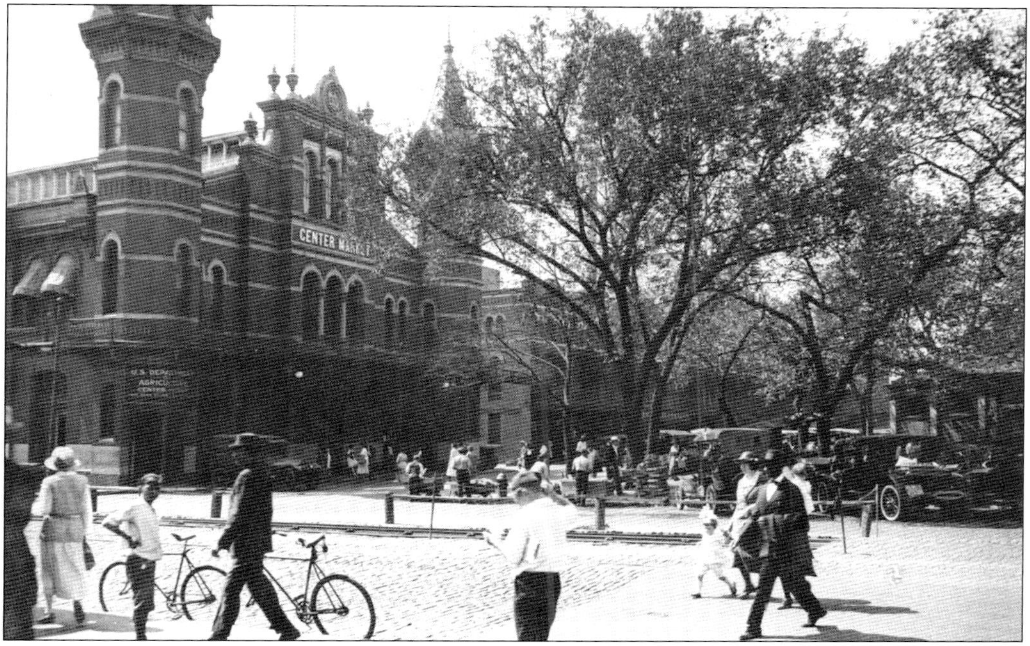

Passersby outside the Seventh Street entrance to Center Market enjcy a fine autumn day in October 1922. Note the Department of Agriculture sign just above the corner entrance, a sign of new ownership. In 1922, Congress abolished the Washington Market Company over concerns of monopoly, and management of the facility was turned over to the Agriculture Department, which ran the market until it closed in 1931. (National Archives.)

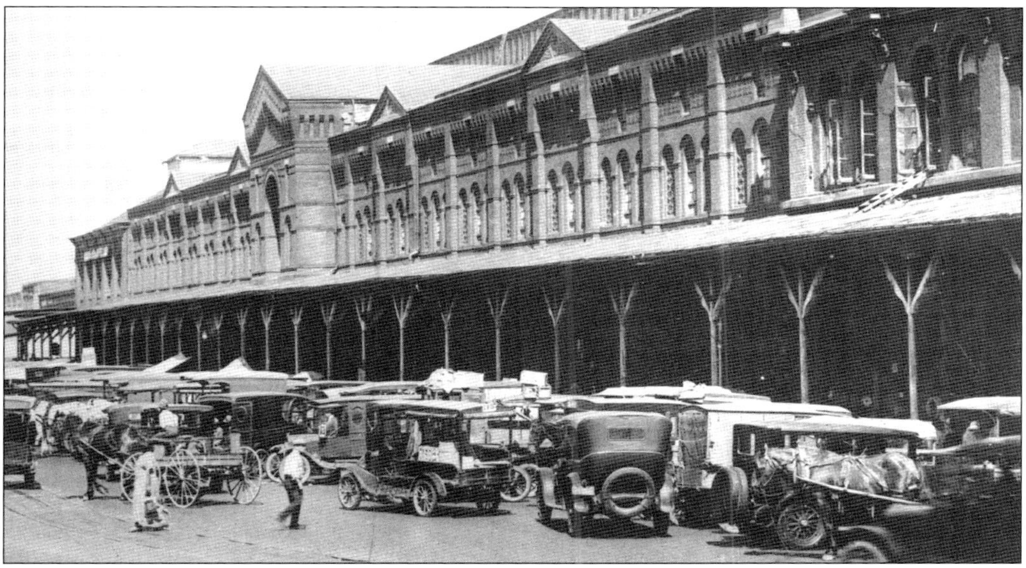

Trucks, cars, and horse-drawn carriages crowd the scene outside Center Market in this view from about 1920. As with all markets of the day, farmers brought their products in daily, some to sell to vendors inside and some to hawk outside on the street, where the market charged for the space. Competition was often fierce for these spots, and instances of corruption and violence were not unknown. (National Archives.)

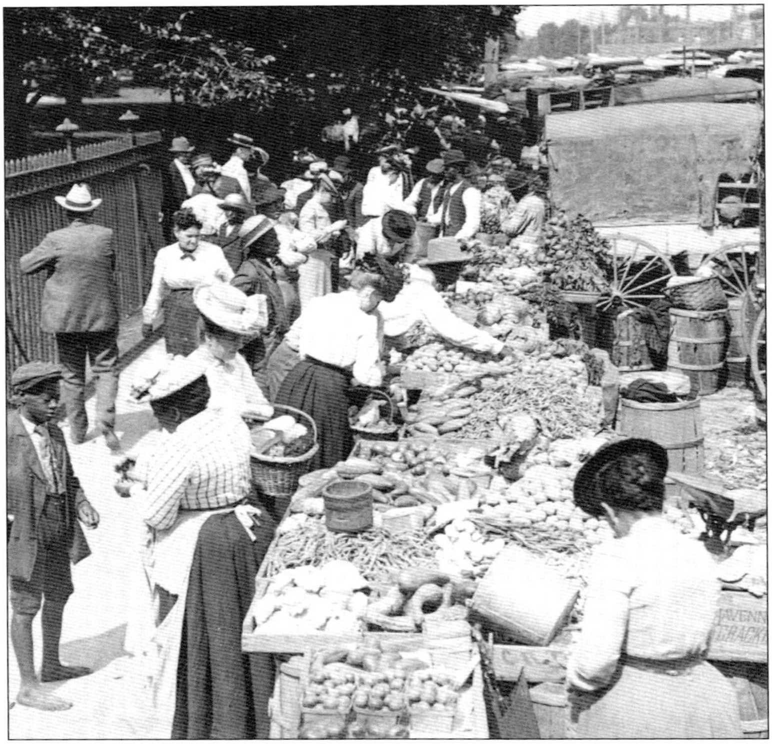

Customers pick over fruits and vegetables outside Center Market around 1904. The great bulk of food-buying in these times was carried out by women, while most of the vendors were male. The market was a great meeting place, as society matrons, working-class mothers, and servants all rubbed shoulders to purchase the best products. With refrigeration still a thing of the future, a run to the market was a daily task for many.

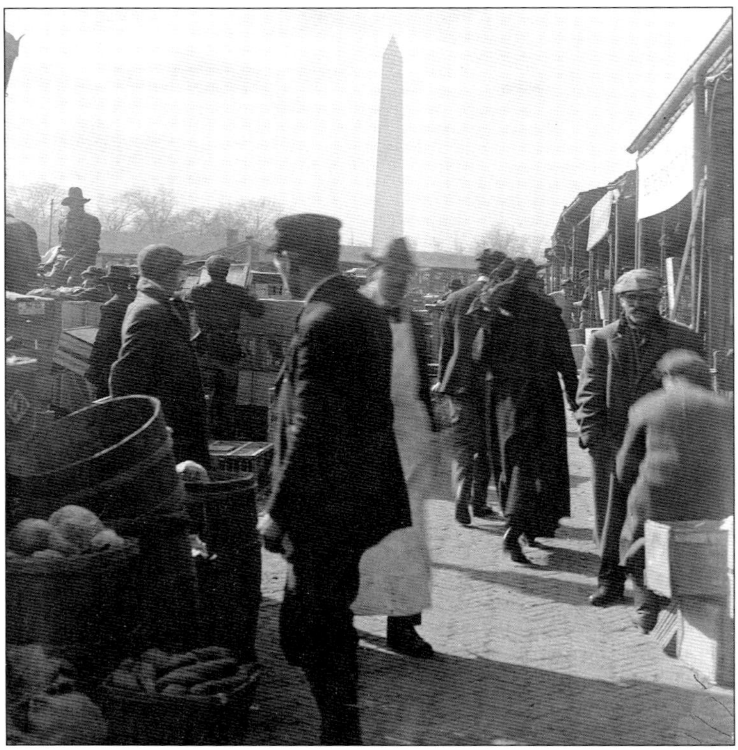

Vendors and customers mingle in a busy scene around 1917 outside the market's southern expanse near B Street, later to become Constitution Avenue. The Washington Monument rises to the west above trees on the National Mall.

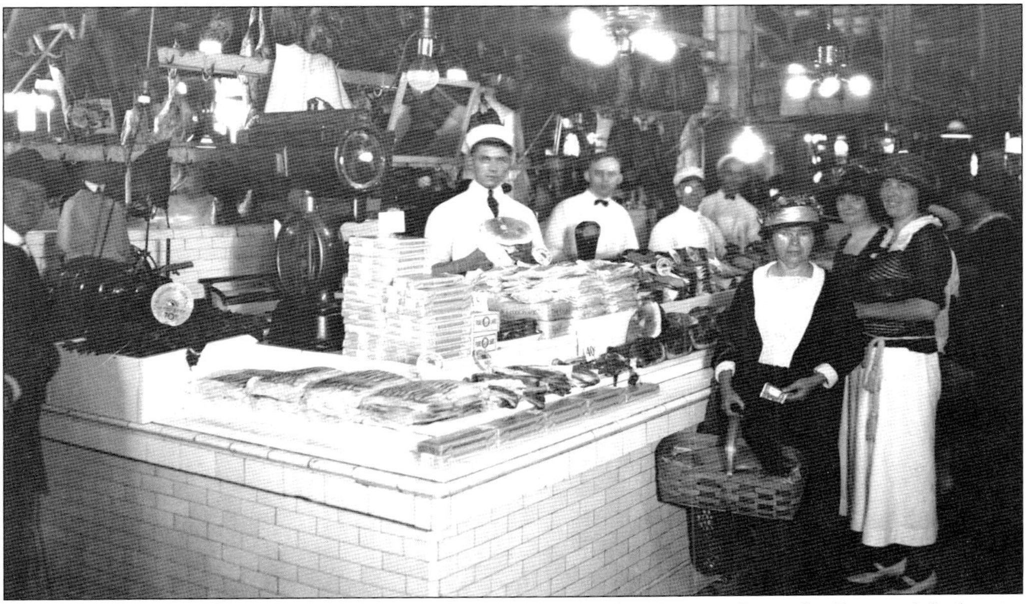

Customers and butchers smile for the camera at a cured meat stand inside Center Market in October 1922. Note the meats hung up at left behind the butchers. Then as now, quality assurance for meat products was always a concern, but the takeover in 1922 of the market's management by the Department of Agriculture helped to ensure better standards. The woman in the foreground seems to already have her cash in hand.

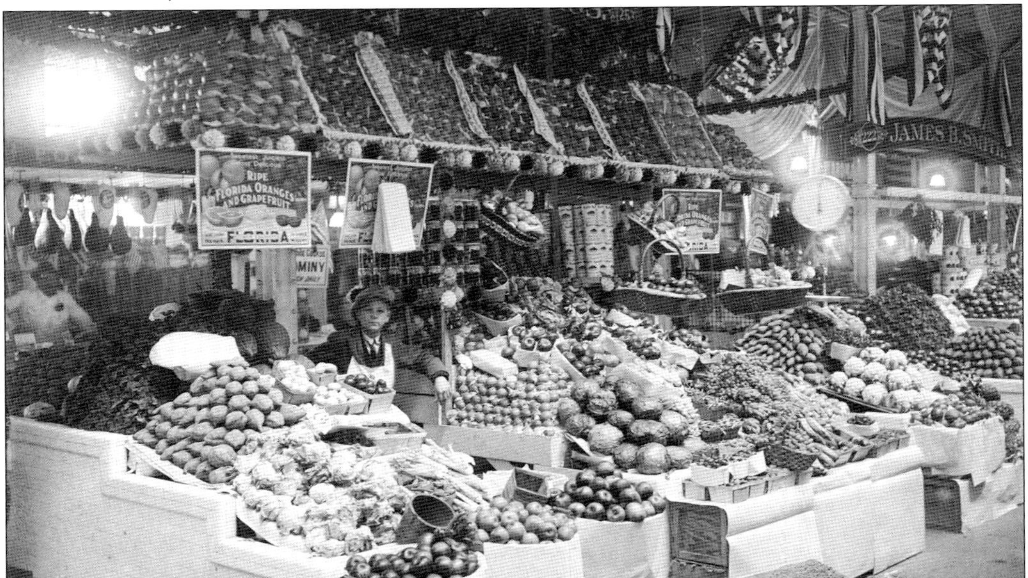

A young vendor stands proudly amongst his wares at a fruit stand inside Center Market in this photograph dated February 18, 1915. When it opened in 1871, the market was noted for its airiness and natural light, and the facility still seems bright 44 years later, aided by electric lighting. The market is decorated with patriotic bunting, perhaps for the birthdays of Presidents Washington and Lincoln, then celebrated separately on February 12 and 22. (National Archives.)

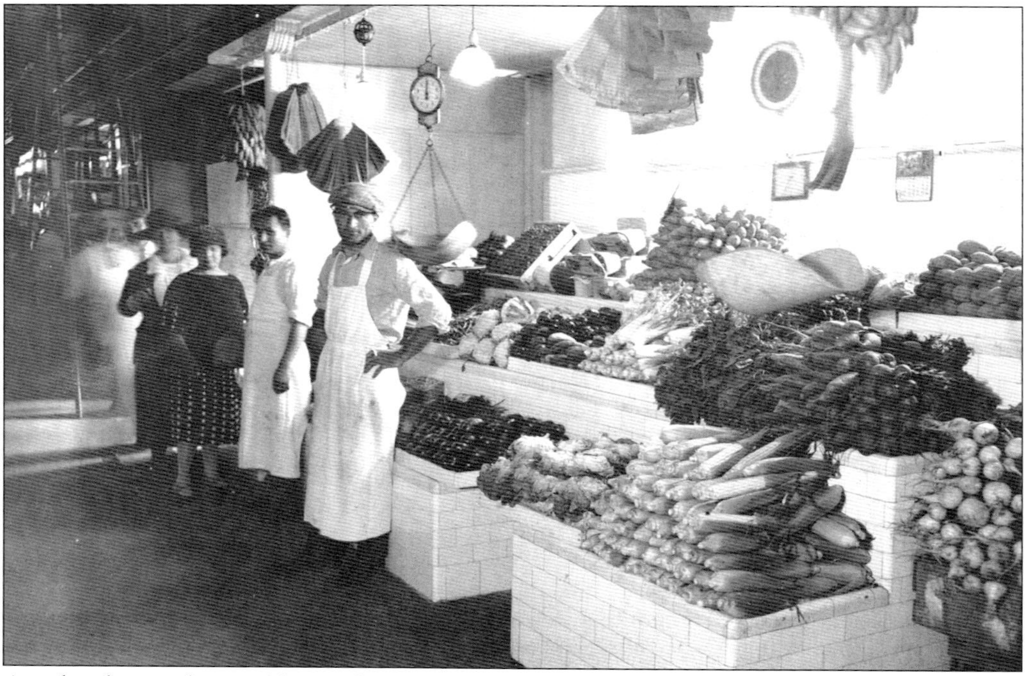

Another fruit and vegetable stand inside Center Market in October 1922 shows changes made by the Agriculture Department. Compared with the previous photograph from 1915, the stand is a bit more orderly, and produce is more accessible to customers. Although the stands were rented, vendors could operate from the same spot for many years. (National Archives.)

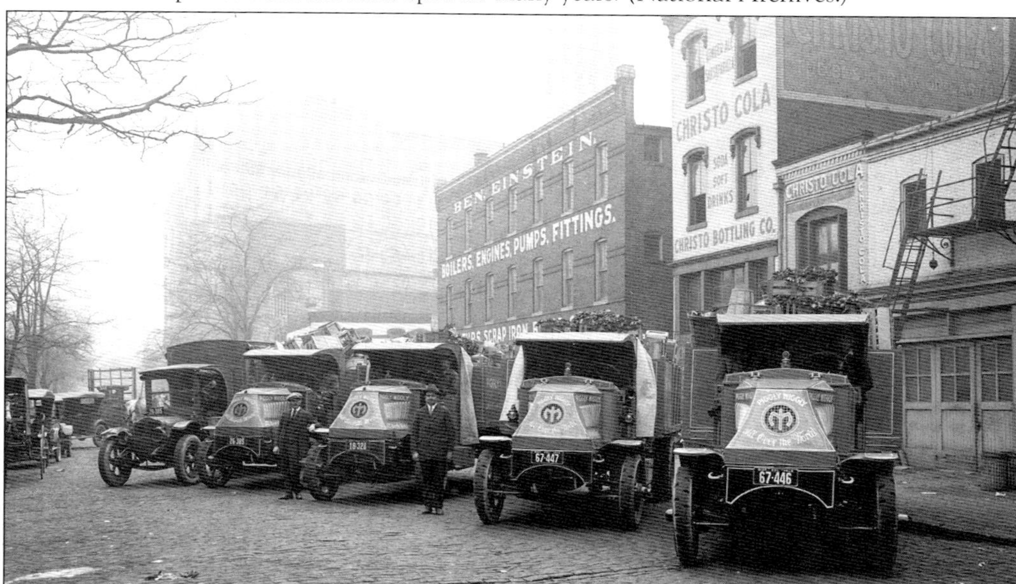

Piled high with fresh produce, loaded Piggly Wiggly trucks are ready to roll to outlying stores in this view along B Street outside Center Market in 1924. Each of the four Mack AC Bulldog trucks has a driver and loader sitting in the cab, while two men who might be managers stand almost at attention. The huge bulk of the Post Office Building rises in the background.

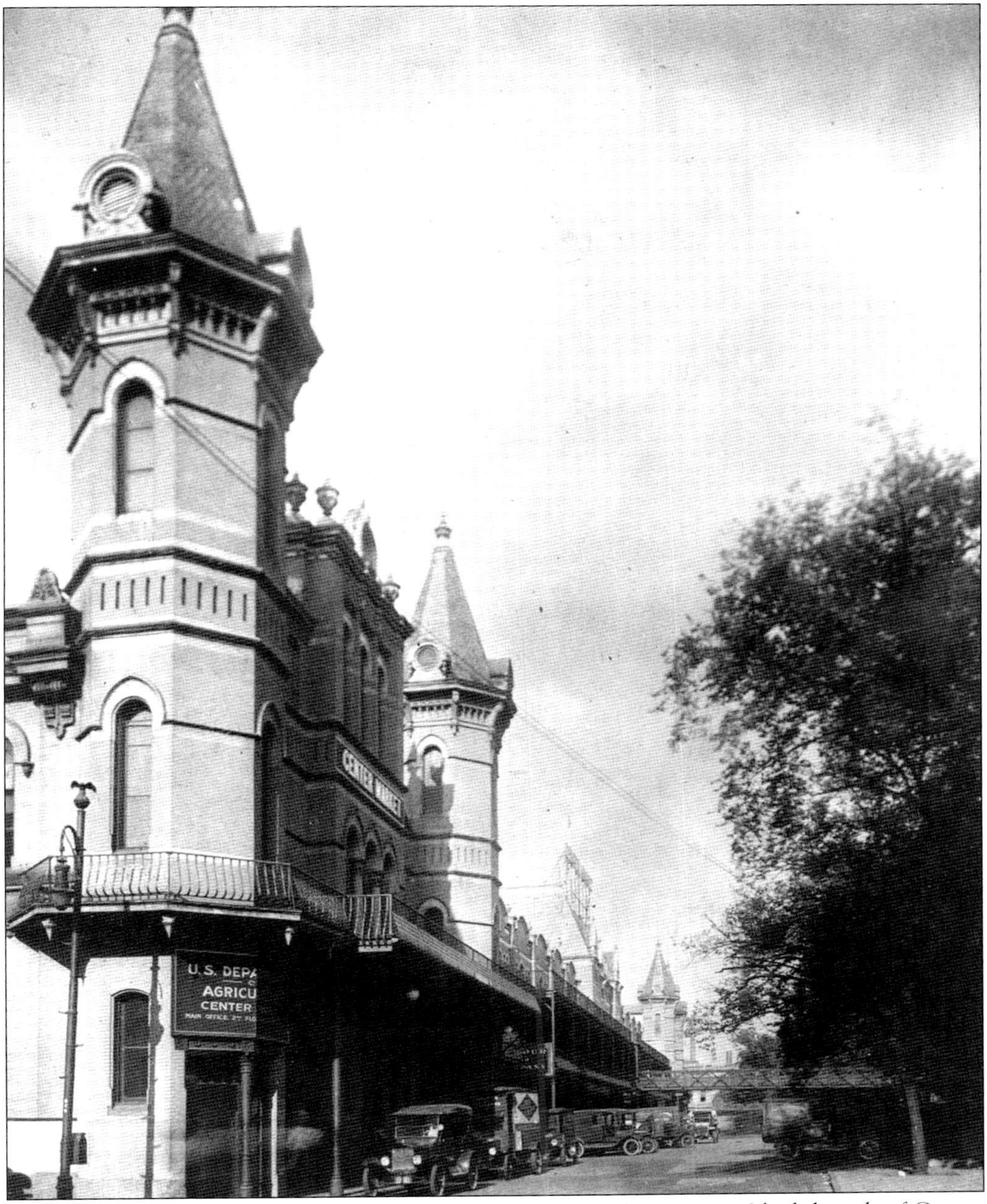

This view looking up from Seventh Street gives a sense of the vast two-block length of Center Market. The raised walkway gave direct access to the building's second floor, where eating establishments and lounges were located above the market's main floor. The similarity between the market and the Smithsonian's Arts and Industries Building on the National Mall's south side is no coincidence—both were designed by architect Adolph Cluss, who produced about a dozen public buildings in Washington. (National Archives.)

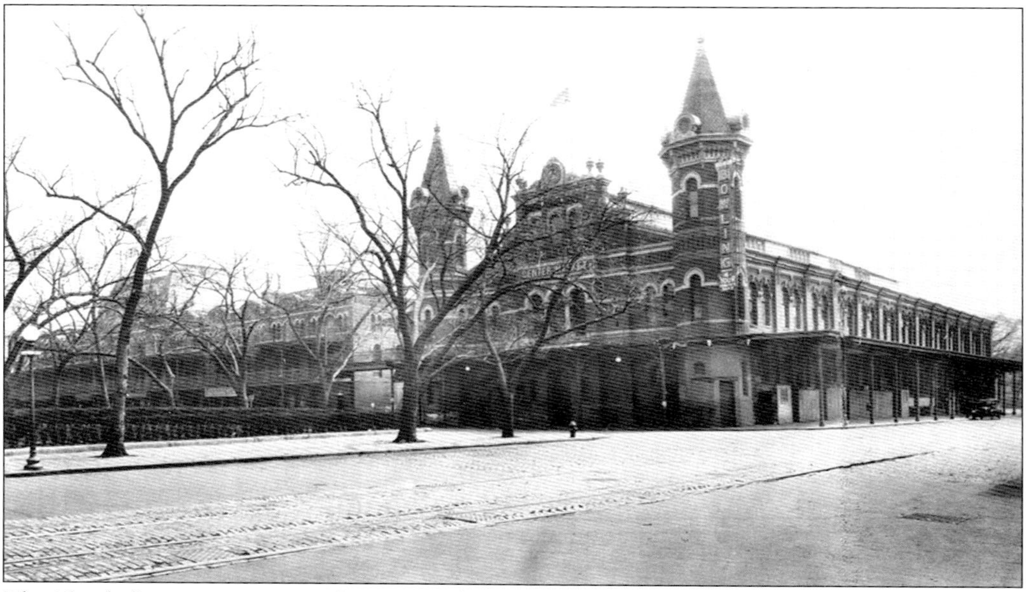

The Ninth Street entrance to Center Market in 1928 shows the entrance to the bowling alley, probably on a Sunday, when stores in Washington were closed. By the time of this view, the market's days were already numbered. The facility was becoming dirty and somewhat tawdry, and Congress had plans to demolish the market and most of the buildings around it for the Federal Triangle project of government office buildings. (National Archives.)

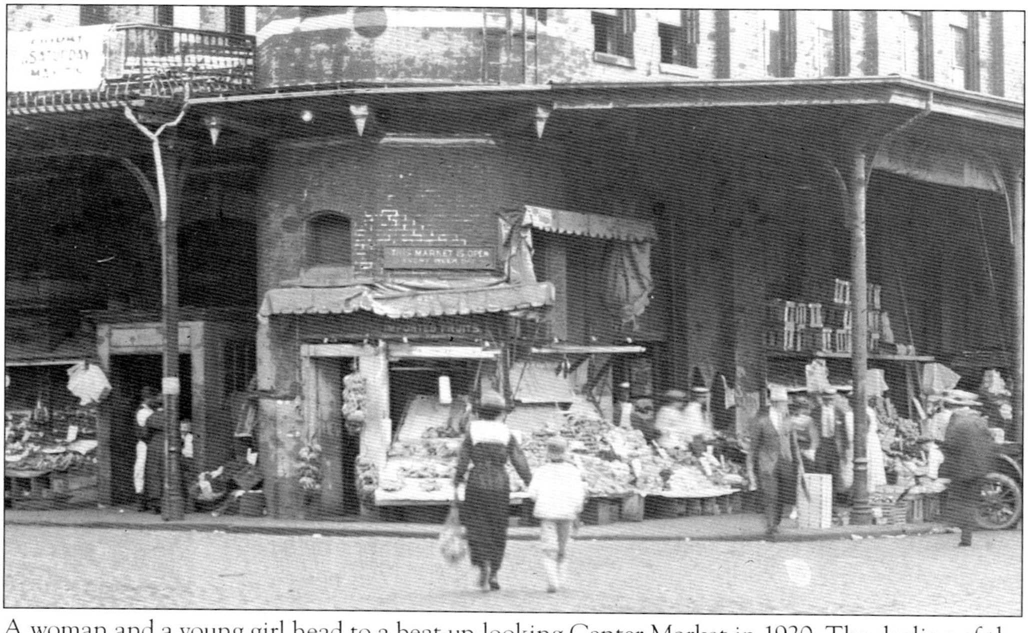

A woman and a young girl head to a beat-up-looking Center Market in 1920. The decline of the facility led Congress to transfer operation to the Agriculture Department in 1922, and although improvements were made, the heyday of large, centrally located markets was past. With the building's demolition, Center Market moved in 1931 to the former Northern Liberty Market at K and Fifth Streets NW, where it operated another three decades before closing in 1963.

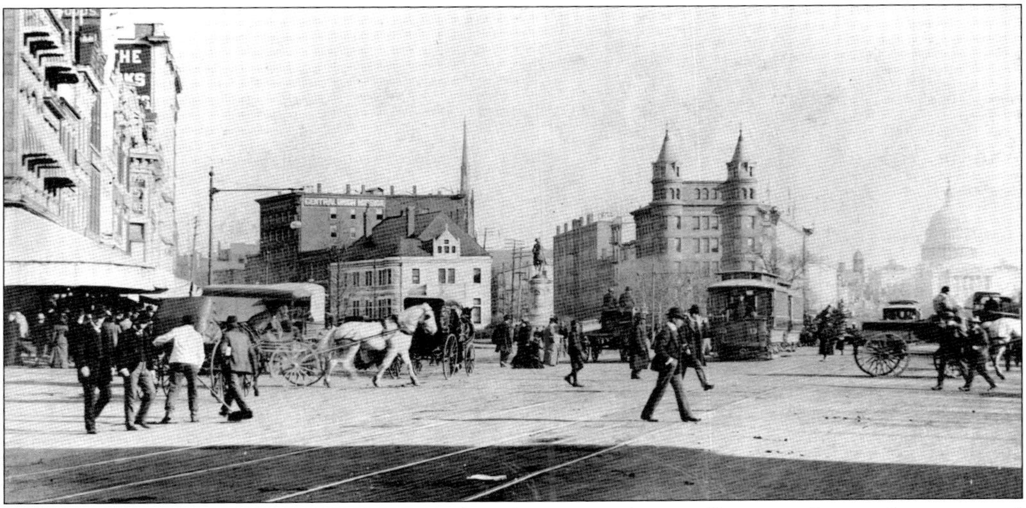

Directly north of Center Market was Market Square, at the confluence of several streets and avenues. This February 1901 view from Eighth Street and Pennsylvania Avenue looks east over an unhurried scene of pedestrians, street sweepers, horse-drawn carts, and electric streetcars. Louisiana Avenue (today's Indiana Avenue) is at left, C Street is at center, and the avenue is at right. The buildings on the left housed a number of specialty shops and Kann's department store.

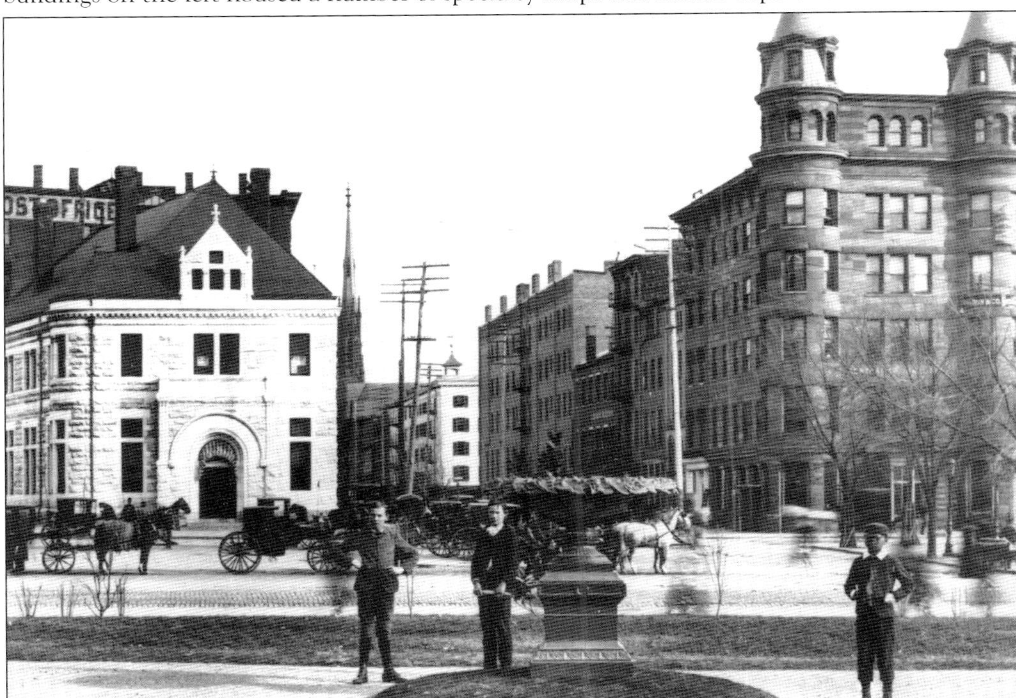

Three boys along Seventh Street in Market Square stare back at the photographer around 1890. The Romanesque building at left was completed in 1888 to house a branch of the Bank of Washington. The building at right was completed in 1860 as the St. Marc Hotel. Originally having a flat roof, it was converted to become a branch of the Central National Bank and in 1887 renovated with the distinctive twin towers on top.

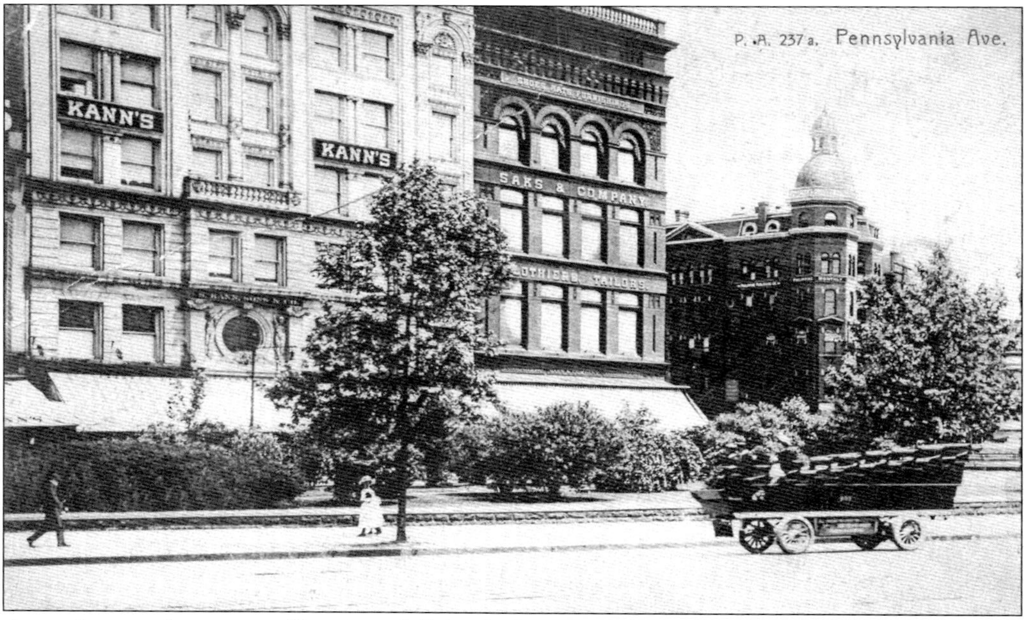

A tourist omnibus passes Kann's and Saks & Company department stores on Market Square around 1905. The three Kann brothers founded the store here in 1893 as one of several businesses on the block, including Saks & Company, which later became Saks Fifth Avenue. The Kanns gradually bought up the other businesses until they owned all the buildings on the south and east sides of the block. The domed structure at right is the Fireman's Insurance Company building, completed in 1882. (John DeFerrari.)

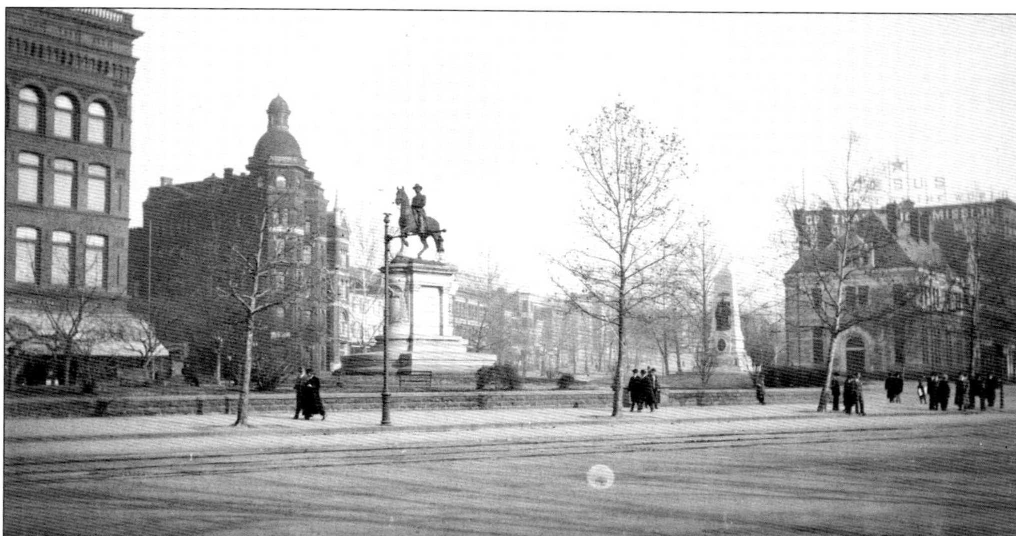

Market Square is pictured in 1914 on a quiet Sunday, judging by the empty streets. The equestrian statue at center was erected in 1896 to honor Civil War general Winfield Scott Hancock, a hero of the 1863 Battle of Gettysburg. The short obelisk-like monument at right is the Stephenson Grand Army of the Republic Memorial, dedicated in 1909 and named for the founder of the Grand Army of the Republic veterans' association. (Naval History and Heritage Command.)

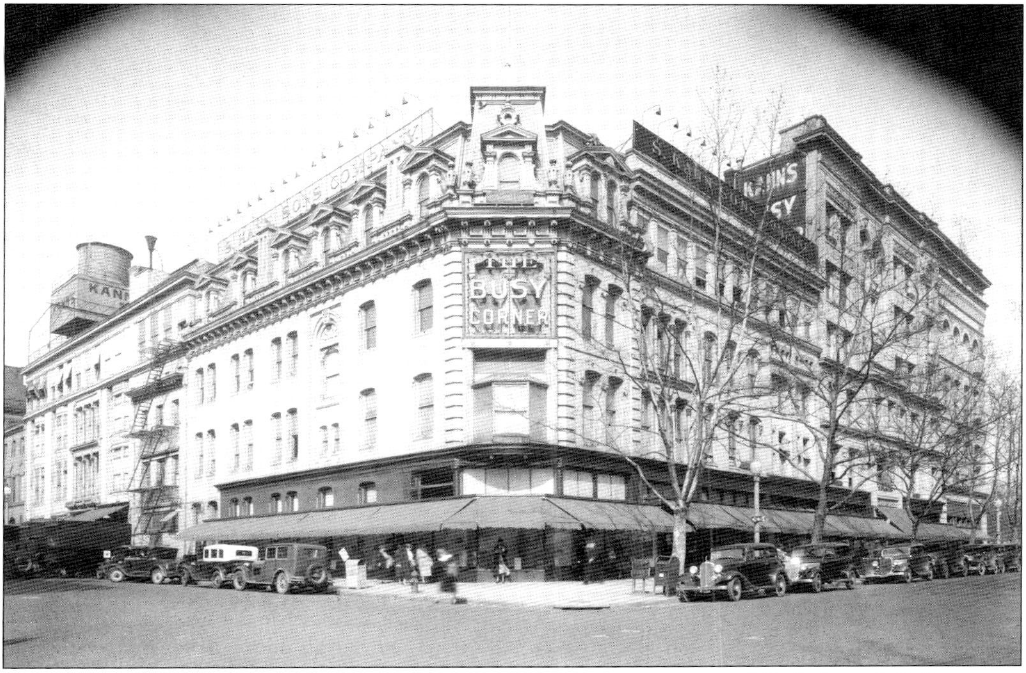

Kann's department store advertised its location at the intersection of Eighth and C Streets at Pennsylvania Avenue as "the Busy Corner," proclaimed by a large electric sign. Kann's was the second largest department store in Washington after Woodward & Lothrop and specialized in low costs along with a thriving mail-order business. Having gradually bought most of the buildings on its block, Kann's knocked out interior walls to create large floor spaces, a process that was largely complete by the time of this photograph from around 1935.

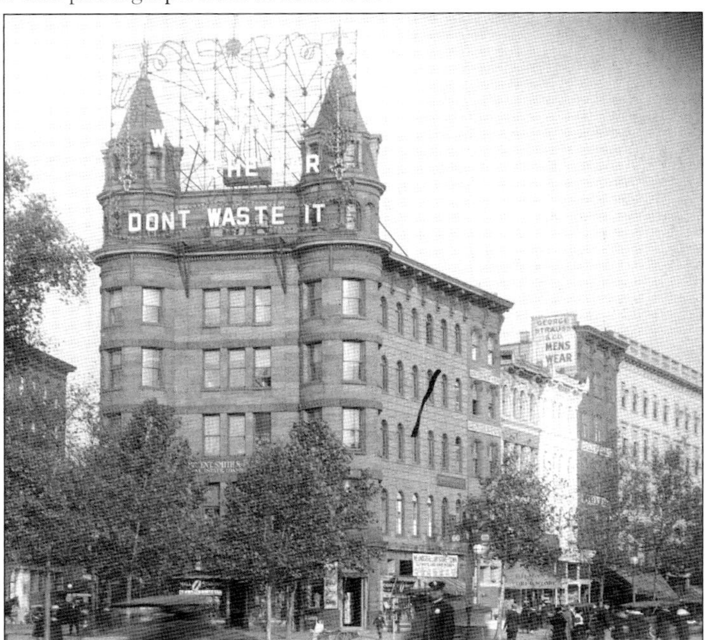

Sitting on the triangular intersection of Pennsylvania Avenue, C Street, and Seventh Street, the Central National Bank building was marked by its distinctive twin towers, which made excellent supports for ever-changing large electric signs. This view from December 1917, during World War I, shows a sign reading "Food Will Win the War Don't Waste It." In the 1860s, photographer Matthew Brady had his studio in an upper floor of 625 Pennsylvania Avenue, the four-story white building to the right.

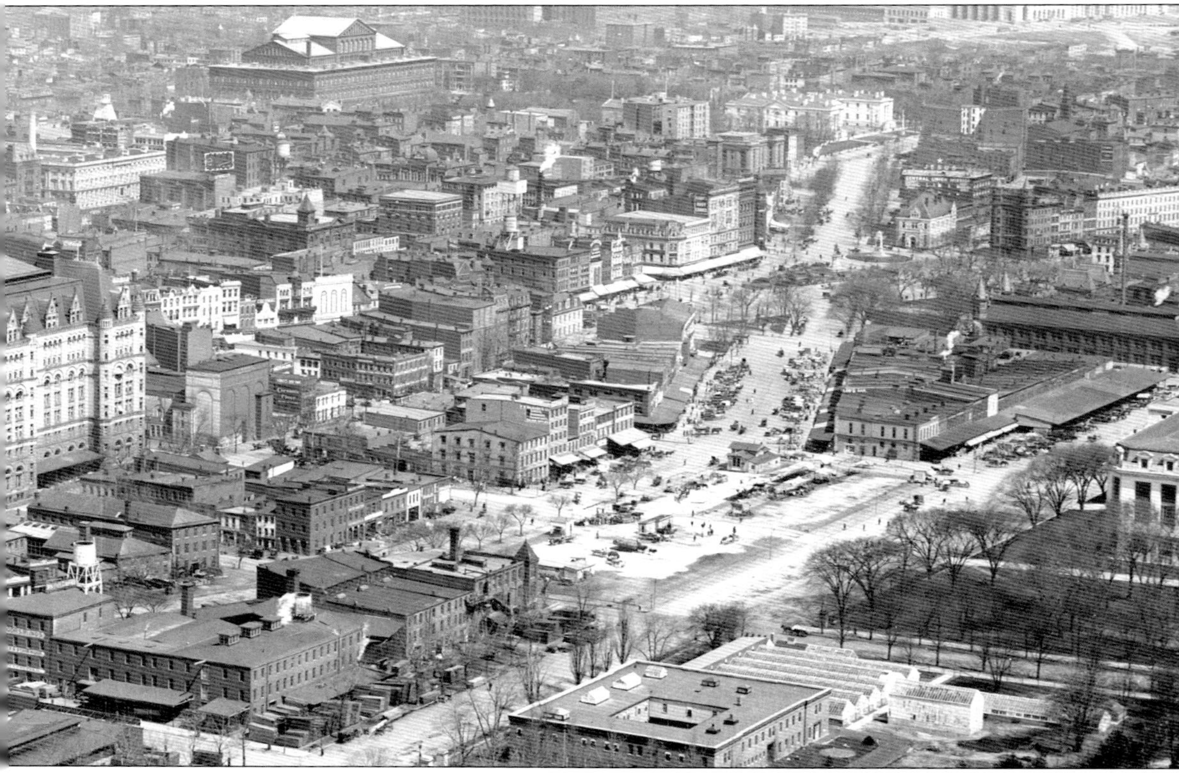

Louisiana Avenue is at center right in this 1910 view from the Washington Monument. Center Market is at far right, with B Street—today's Constitution Avenue—at lower right. In the middle of Louisiana Avenue is Market Square with General Hancock's statue, while at the head of the street is Washington's old city hall, by then in use as a federal court building. The very large building at upper left is the Pension Building.

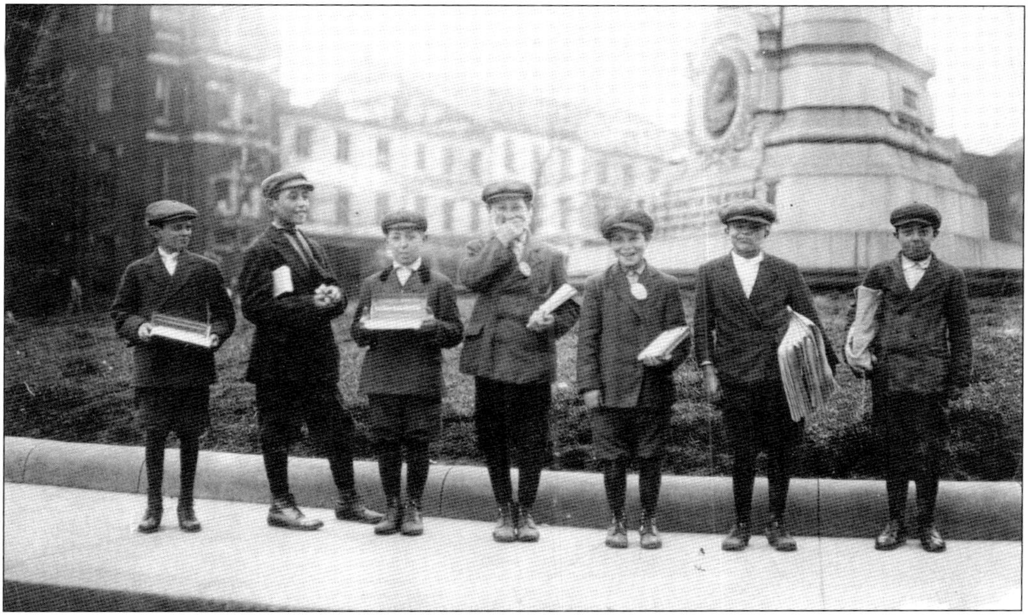

Amidst the stores and traffic and pedestrians were dozens of young boys selling newspapers, cigars, gum, and other items. The boys were often very young—11 or even younger—and rarely had any schooling. These photographs were taken around Market Square in April 1912 by Lewis Wickes Hine, a photographer and activist with the National Child Labor Committee, which sought rules and regulations to keep children from being exploited as workers. The boys above are standing next to the Grand Army of the Republic Memorial. Hine noted in the original caption that one of the youngest boys here, age 11, "is a truant on probation. Very defiant." The photograph below shows 11-year-old Solomon Sickle, whom Hine noted "says he sells until 8 p.m. Very illiterate, been in this country only six months."

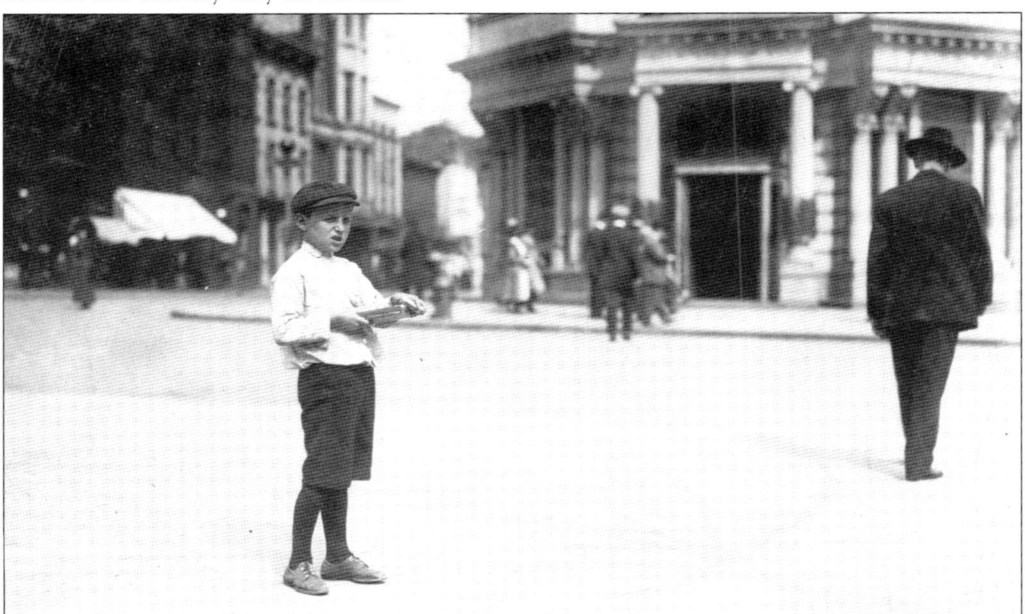

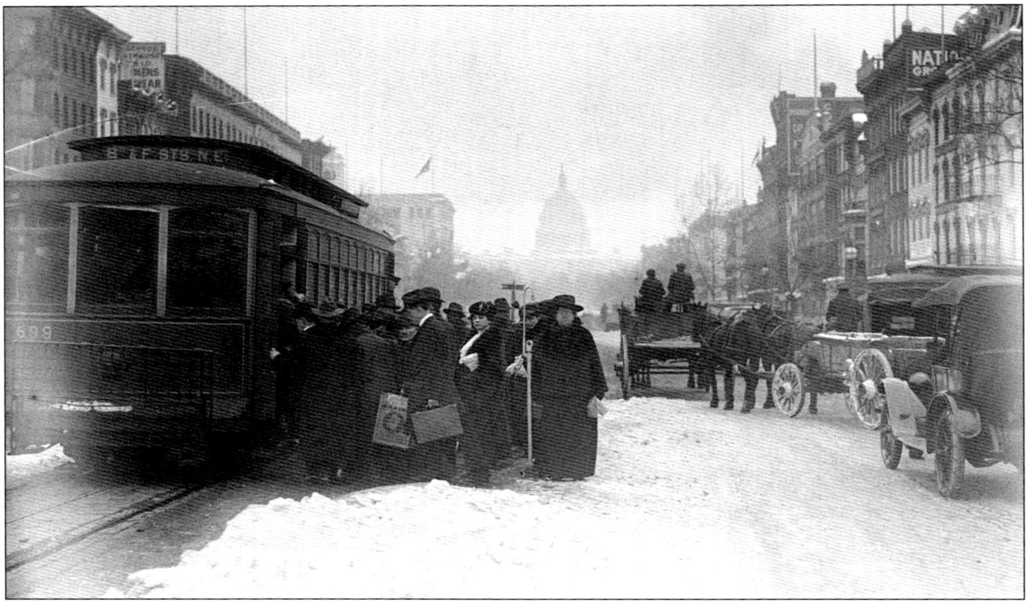

Passengers board a streetcar stopped at Seventh Street along a snowy Pennsylvania Avenue around early 1918. Many of them are shoppers carrying bags bought at the nearby Center Market or at a store. Many passengers had difficulty stepping up into the cars, a situation remedied a few years later when streetcar stands began to be built all over the city. Horse-drawn carts were especially valuable in bad weather, since horses were better able than automobiles to handle harsh conditions.

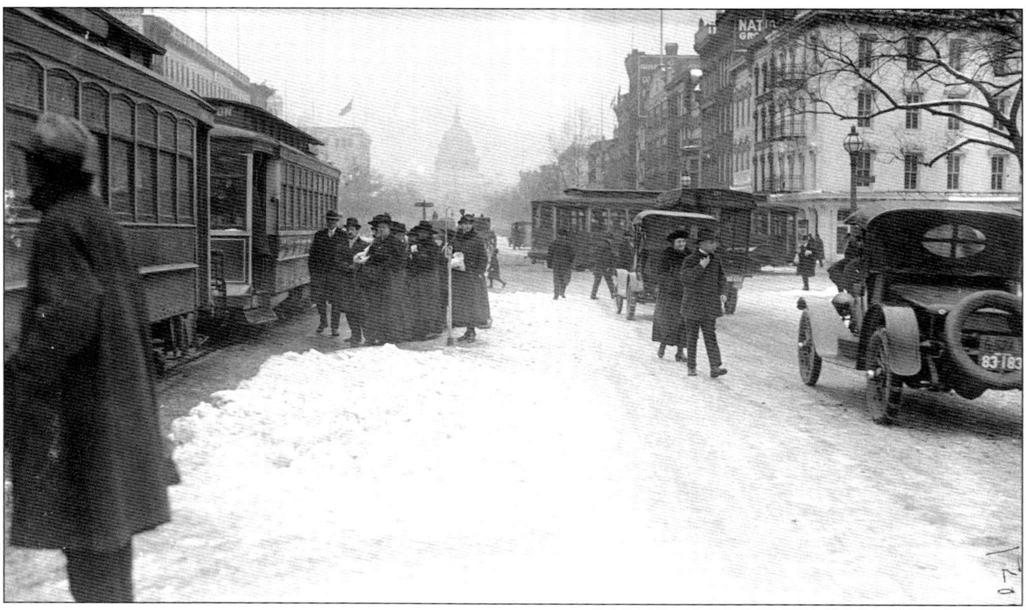

Another view from about the same location on Pennsylvania Avenue near Seventh Street shows three streetcars. Both automobiles and the truck at right have snow chains on their tires, a necessity in these conditions. Streetcar passengers were quite exposed to traffic when boarding the cars, and as the streets became more congested with autos, it could be quite risky getting on and off.

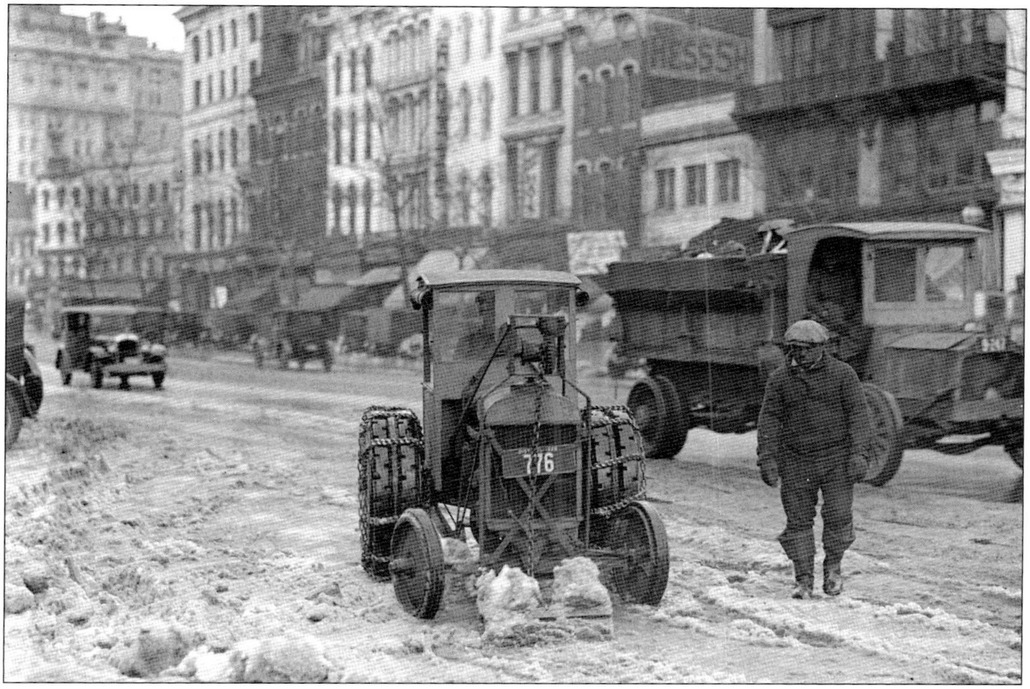

The city could employ all sorts of vehicles for snow removal work. In this scene from about 1924, a Fordson tractor is being used for snow removal on the avenue between Ninth and Tenth Streets. One has to wonder just how effective such a vehicle was in this work.

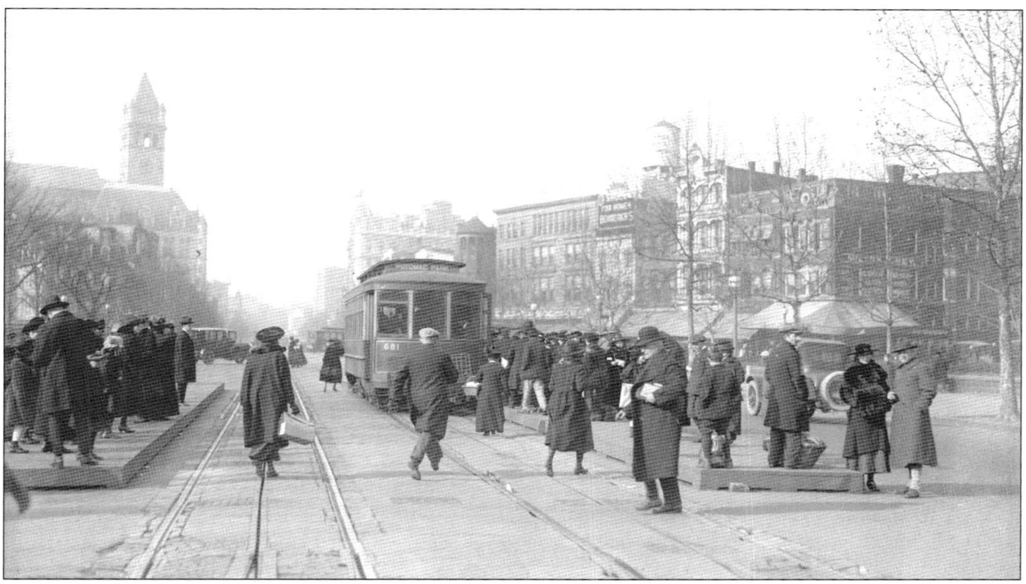

This streetcar scene from about 1919 shows a major improvement: the installation of boarding stands that not only made it easier to step aboard streetcars but also set aside a physical space for passengers in the middle of the increasingly busy streets. The electric cars got their power from rails laid in conduits in the street between the tracks. The system was quite safe, as shown by the woman at left center walking directly over the conduit.

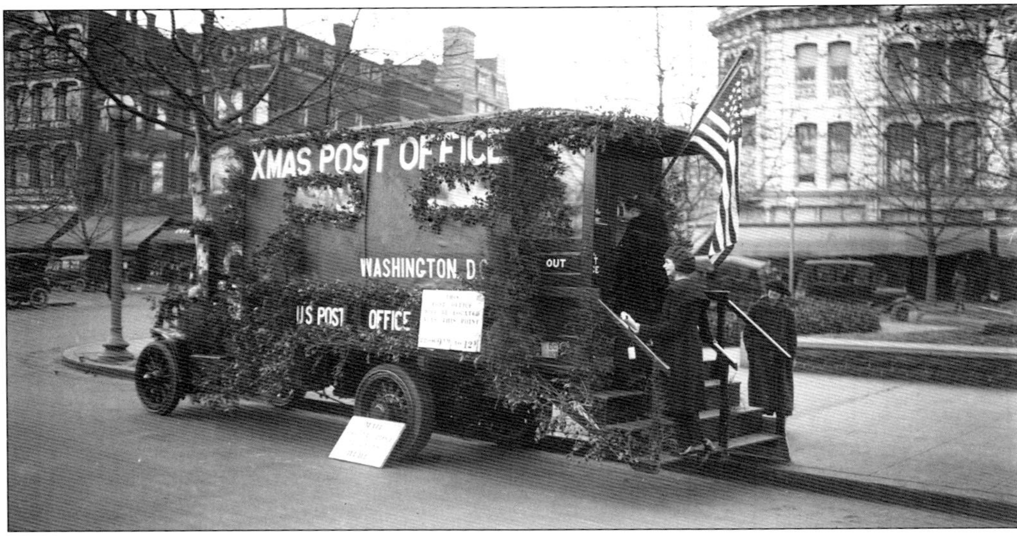

A fully functioning and gaily decorated mobile US Post Office is seen parked on the avenue in front of Kann's Busy Corner in December 1920. It was able to handle the parcel post needs of Christmas shoppers who have just walked out of nearby stores. As an official post office, the truck properly displays the US flag just like its nonmobile brethren.

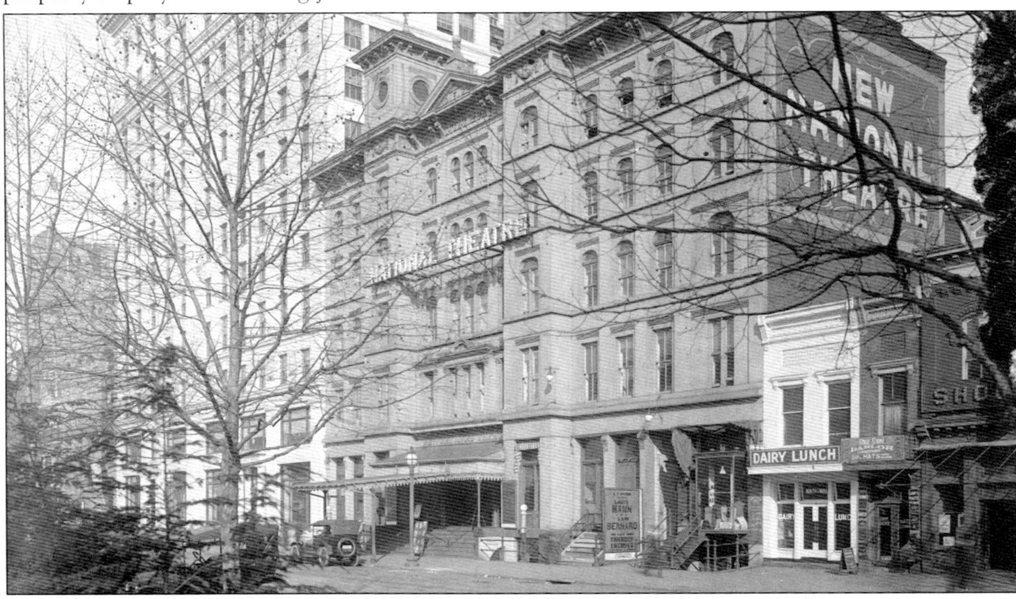

By the 1840s, theaters of varying sizes and quality could be found along the length of the avenue. One of the earliest was the National Theater, which opened in 1835 on E Street facing Pennsylvania Avenue just off Thirteenth Street. It was destroyed by fire in 1845, and a second was built only to be destroyed by fire again. The same fate befell two more buildings. A fifth, larger and grander, rose in 1885 and was more enduring. Known as the New National Theater, it could seat 1,900 and featured a fireproof asbestos stage curtain. The Italianate design, seen in March 1918, featured two distinctive towers that stood out even after the adjacent Munsey Building was rebuilt to 12 stories. New building codes enacted in 1922, after the collapse of the Knickerbocker Theater in a snowstorm, led to a major reconstruction of the National, but the sixth building kept the same basic form.

Vaudeville and burlesque theaters abounded in Washington for many years, and the Cosmos Theater at 921 Pennsylvania Avenue was a typical example. Built in 1907 as a vaudeville house, the theater was enlarged two years later and added a movie screen by 1913. The Cosmos is seen in early March 1917 decorated for Woodrow Wilson's second presidential inauguration and offering "refined entertainment" running continually from 1:00 p.m. to closing. The theater turned to burlesque before closing in the late 1920s.

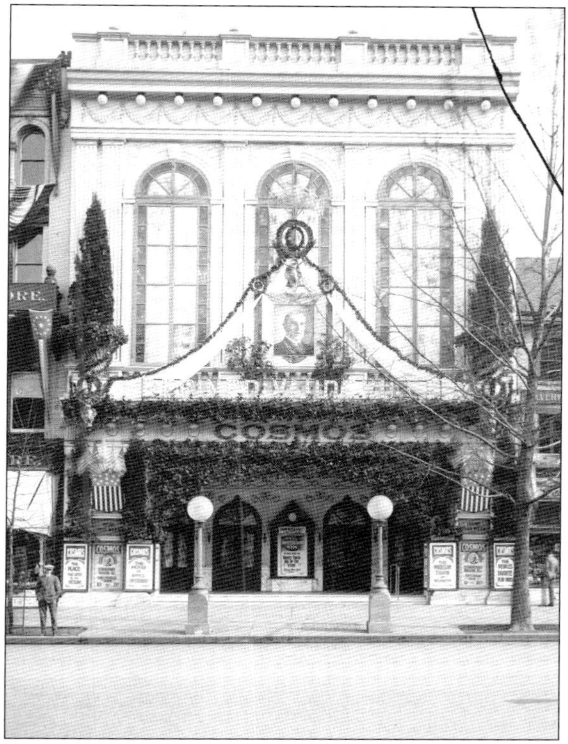

Poli's Theater, in the 1400 block of Pennsylvania Avenue, stood directly south of the Willard Hotel and across from the Treasury Building. The theater offered a series of vaudeville acts, movies, and even lectures. In 1920, the silent film *Keep to the Right* is showing, starring Edith Taliaferro. The entire block was demolished in 1930 for what is today Pershing Park.

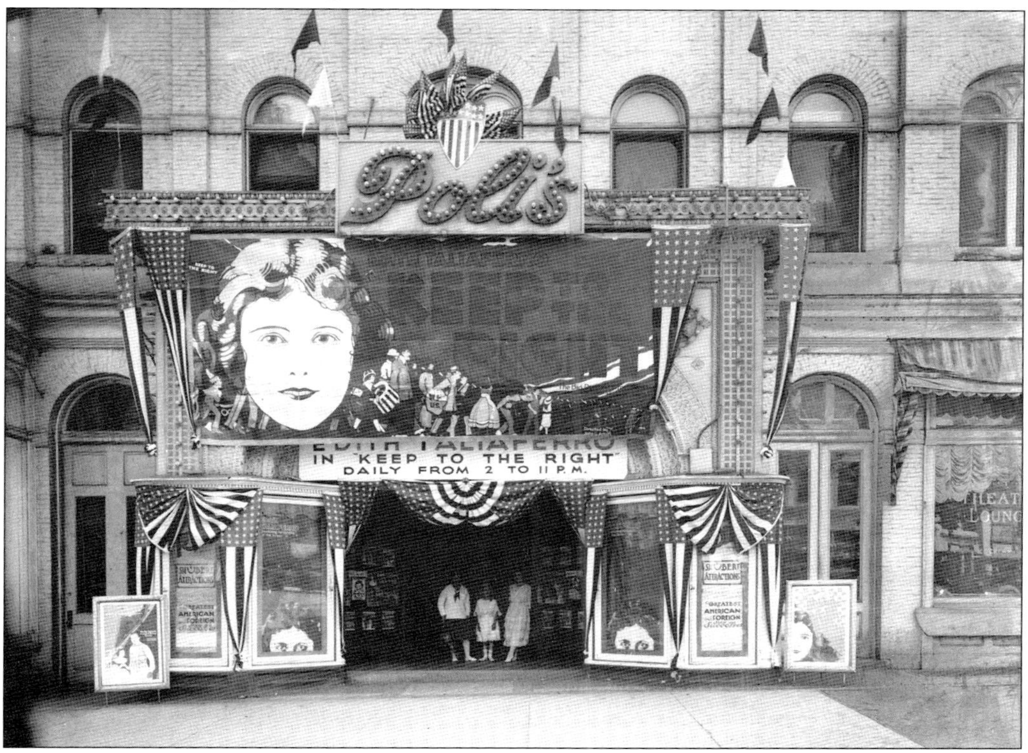

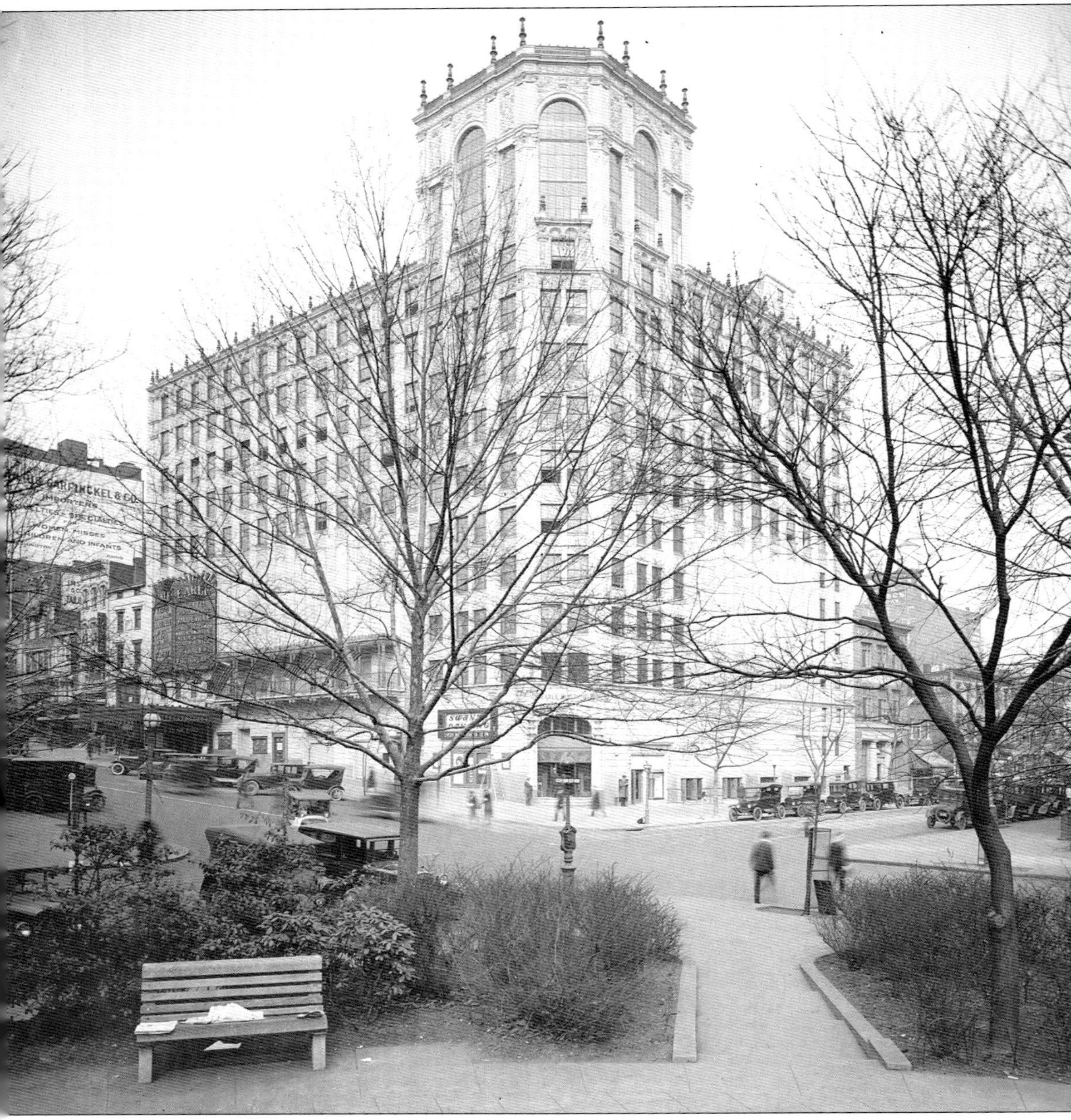

The brand-new Earle Theater towers over the intersection of Thirteenth and E Streets and Pennsylvania Avenue in this view from January 1925; the Earle opened as a major movie palace on December 27, 1924. The facility, which includes an office building, originally featured the Neptune Room restaurant, a ballroom, and a rooftop garden. The theater's owner, Harry Warner of Warner Bros. film fame, changed the name in 1947 to the Warner Theater.

Five

Hotels and Restaurants

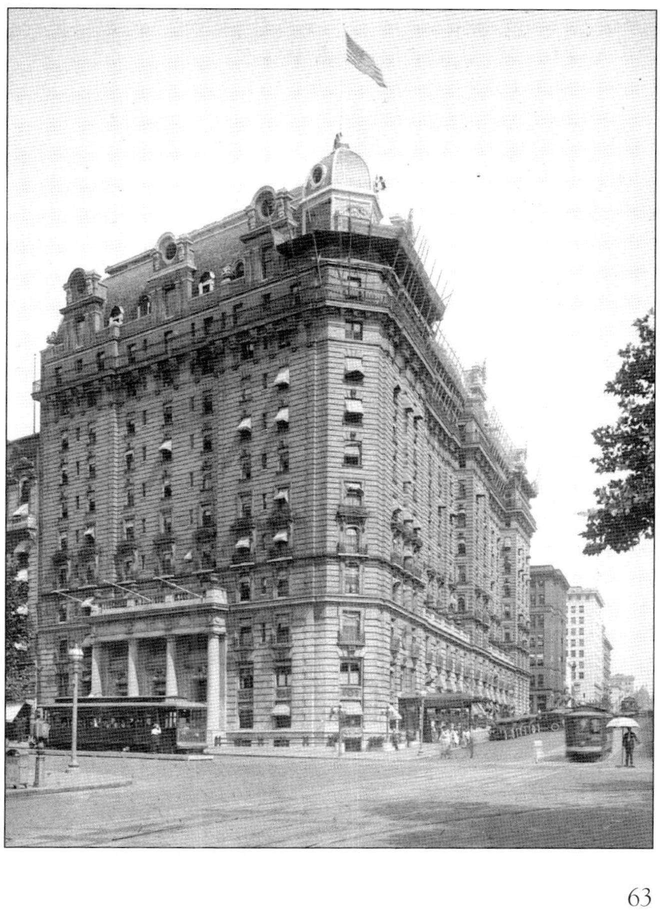

Rooming houses and hotels sprouted up on the avenue virtually from Washington's beginning, providing lodging for the hundreds of people coming to work in the new city. They ran the gamut from seedy to grand and everything in between. In the 1830s, the National and Metropolitan Hotels, across Sixth Street from each other, vied for top billing. After 1901, the Willard Hotel reigned supreme as the avenue's grand dame. The Willard's imposing Beaux-Arts structure, which replaced an earlier five-story building, is nearly at the head of the avenue, visible all the way from the Capitol and dominating a large open space. In this view from 1922, scaffolding has been erected outside the 12th-floor apartments and penthouse to convert a ballroom into a roof garden. The hotel stretched the entire length of its Fourteenth Street block.

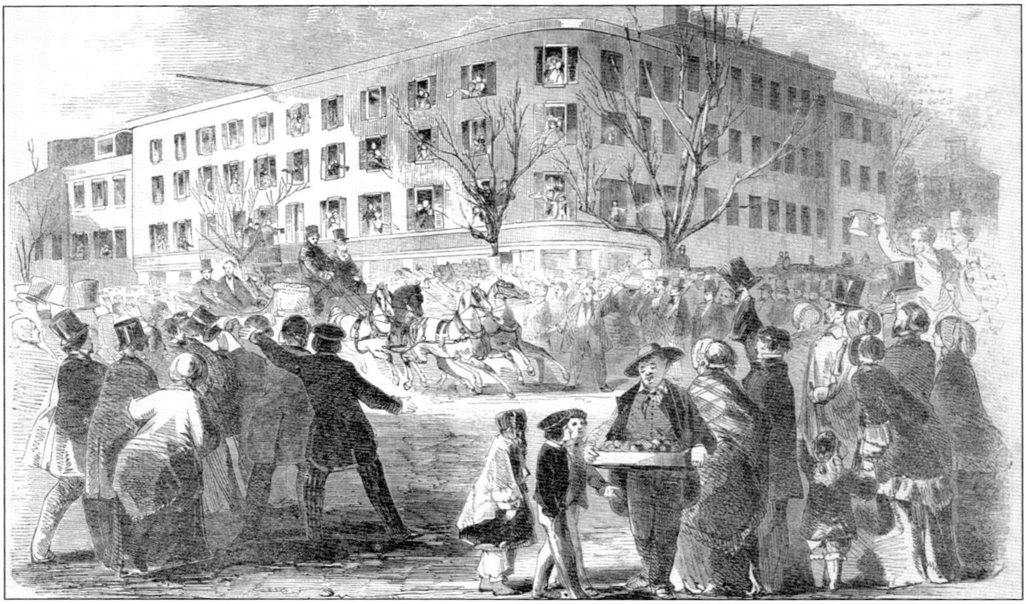

The Willard grew from six rowhouses built in 1816 on Pennsylvania Avenue between Fourteenth and Fifteenth Streets, the corner house operating as Tennison's Hotel. Henry Willard was hired as manager in 1847, greatly improving the hotel's operation and soon leasing the building himself. Eventually, Willard and his brothers acquired the enlarged hotel, and its reputation continued to improve, with a long list of well-known personalities among its patrons. This 1853 illustration shows Franklin Pierce leaving the hotel to be inaugurated as president at the Capitol.

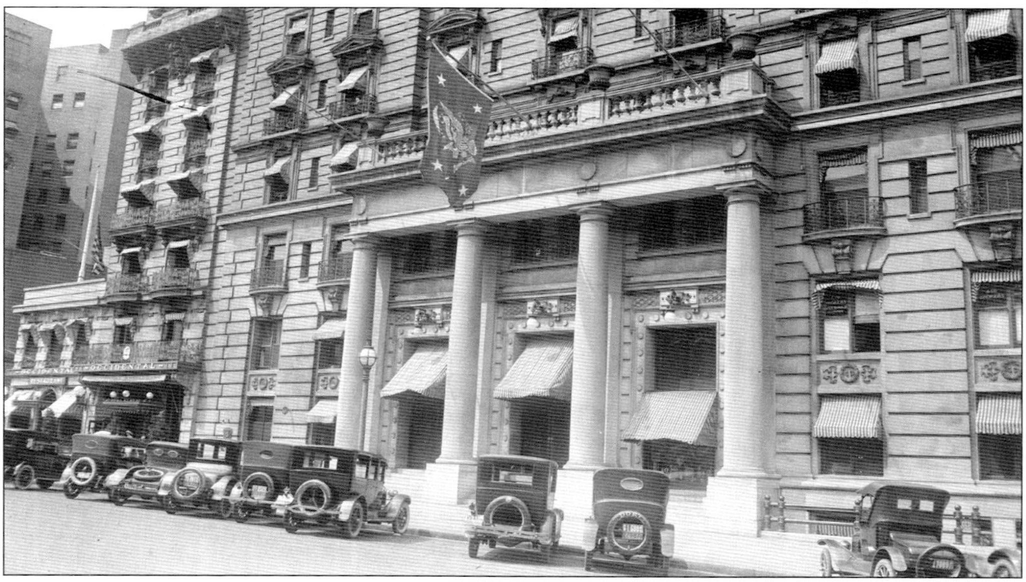

The president's flag hangs over the Willard's main entrance on August 4, 1923, indicating that Calvin Coolidge is inside. As vice president, Coolidge lived at the hotel in a suite costing $8 a day. After assuming the presidency on August 3, 1923, upon the death of Warren Harding, Coolidge continued his stay to allow Florence Harding time to move out of the White House. The design of the flag seen here was chosen by Woodrow Wilson and was in use from 1916 to 1946.

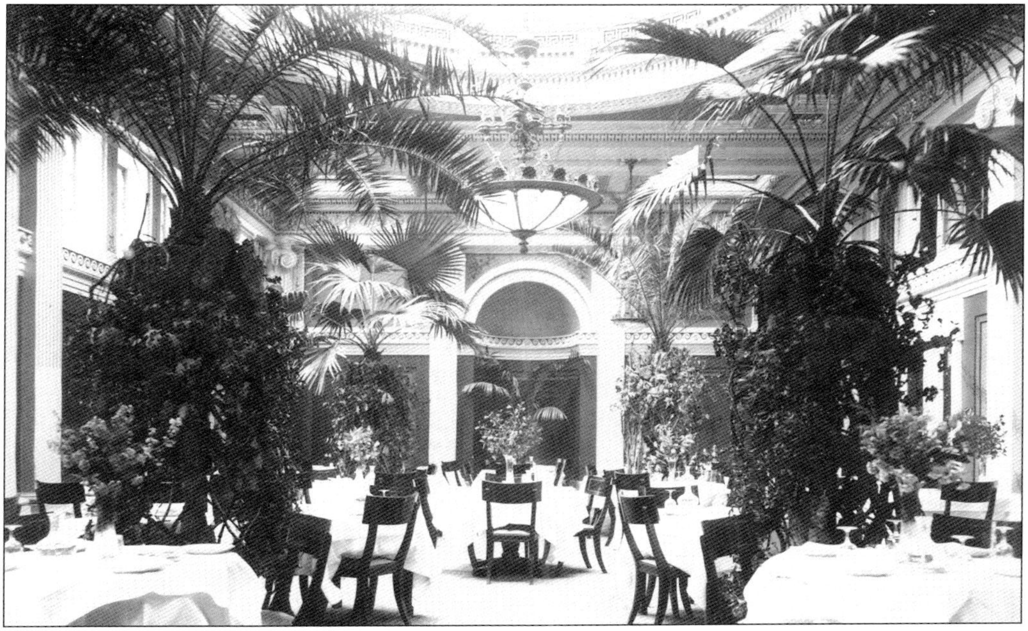

The Willard's upper dining room is seen in 1910, photographed by Frances Benjamin Johnston. Lit by a large skylight, the room is lavishly decorated with large palm plants, a popular style of the day. The hotel's dining rooms were considered some of the most exclusive eating spaces in Washington, charging prices few could afford.

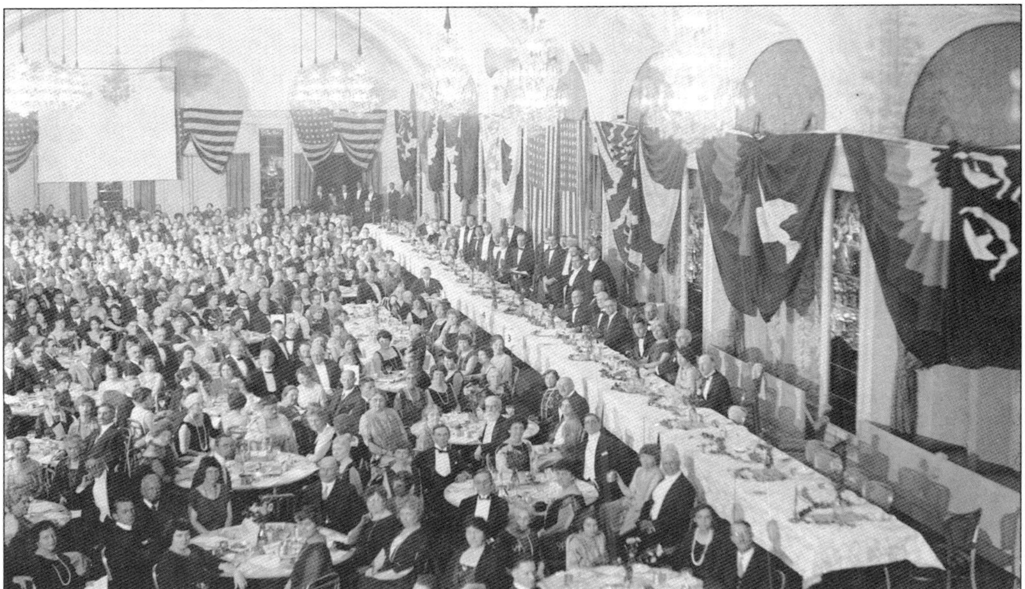

The Near East Relief Society, dedicated to helping those in need in the Middle East, holds its Golden Rule dinner in the Willard's huge banquet room on October 24, 1924. Pres. Calvin Coolidge stands at the center of the head table at right. The society asked families to substitute an "orphanage-style meal" on a Sunday and donate the money saved from a normal Sunday meal to the relief effort. The banquet was meant to endorse the effort.

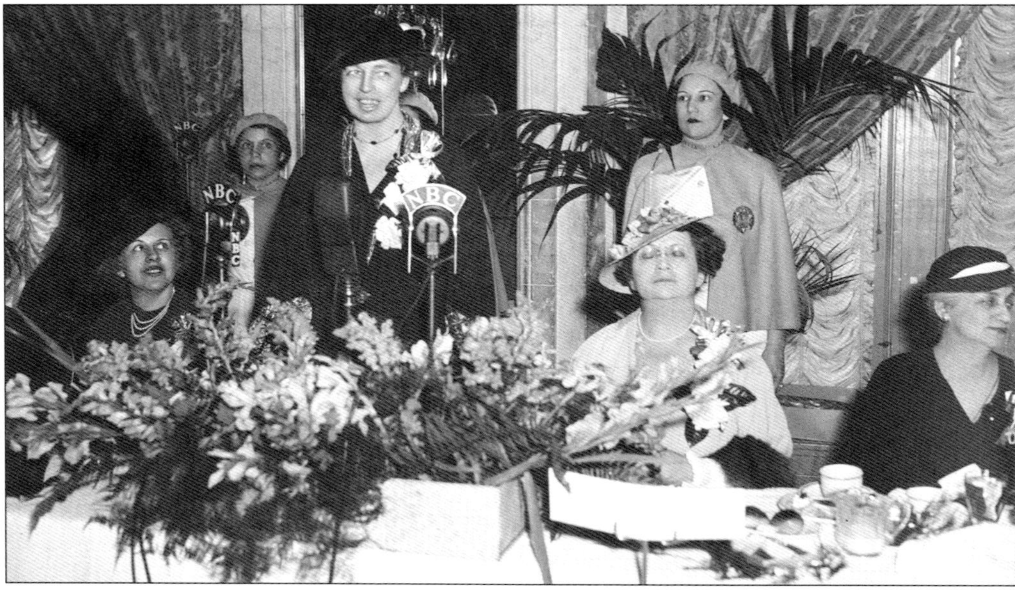

First Lady Eleanor Roosevelt addresses a luncheon at the Willard Hotel given by the Women's League of United Synagogues during its annual convention in 1936. As with most major hotels, significant gatherings such as conventions, dinners, and luncheons were a major source of income.

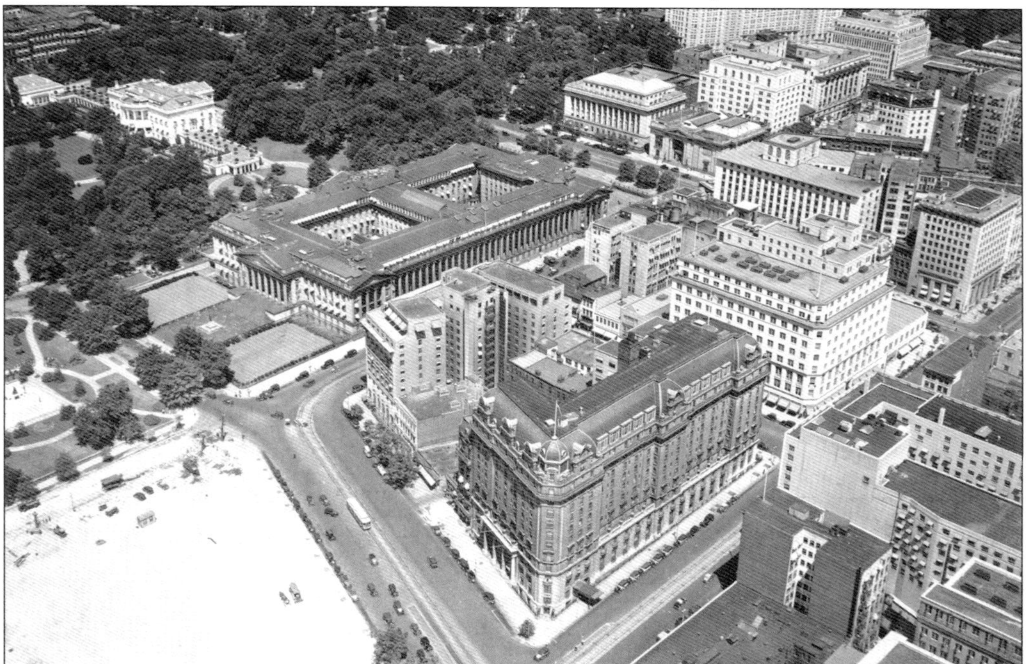

The Willard Hotel's prominent location is clear in this aerial view from July 1931. It is at lower center, marked by its large mansard roof and corner cupola and occupying an entire block along Fourteenth Street. The Treasury Building is at left center at the intersection of Pennsylvania Avenue with Fifteenth Street, while the White House is at upper left. The open area at lower left has been newly cleared of buildings and will soon become a park. (National Archives.)

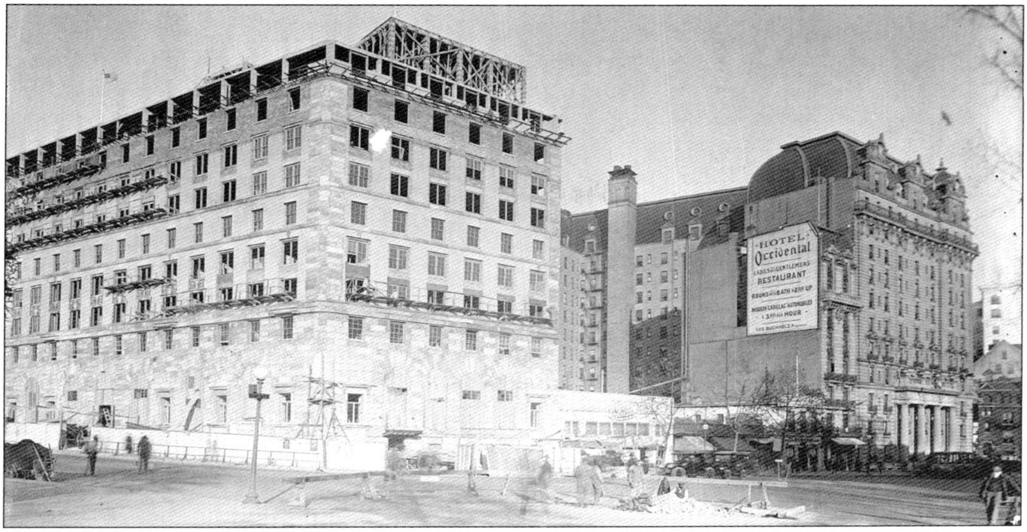

The Hotel Washington is under construction on the corner of Pennsylvania Avenue and Fifteenth Street during 1917. Built on the site of the Corcoran Building, the new hotel opened in 1918 as a competitor to the Willard, seen at far right. The small Hotel Occidental is nestled against the Willard, while a Child's restaurant is next to the new hotel. Only slightly smaller than the Willard, the Hotel Washington was modern and elegant in its own right.

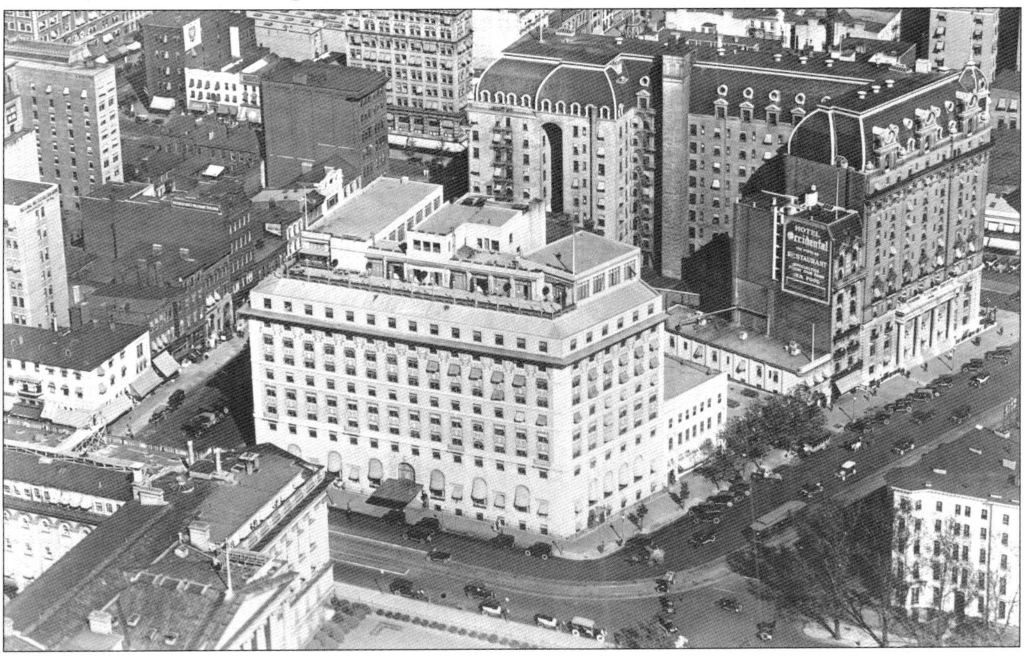

One of the Hotel Washington's most famous features was its rooftop terrace, clearly visible in this aerial view from 1921. The rooftop café and restaurant afforded magnificent views of Washington and especially of sunsets over the Potomac River. The small, three-story, light-colored building at far left on the corner of Fifteenth and F Streets is Rhodes Tavern, one of the oldest commercial buildings in Washington. The southeast corner of the Treasury Building is at lower left. (National Archives.)

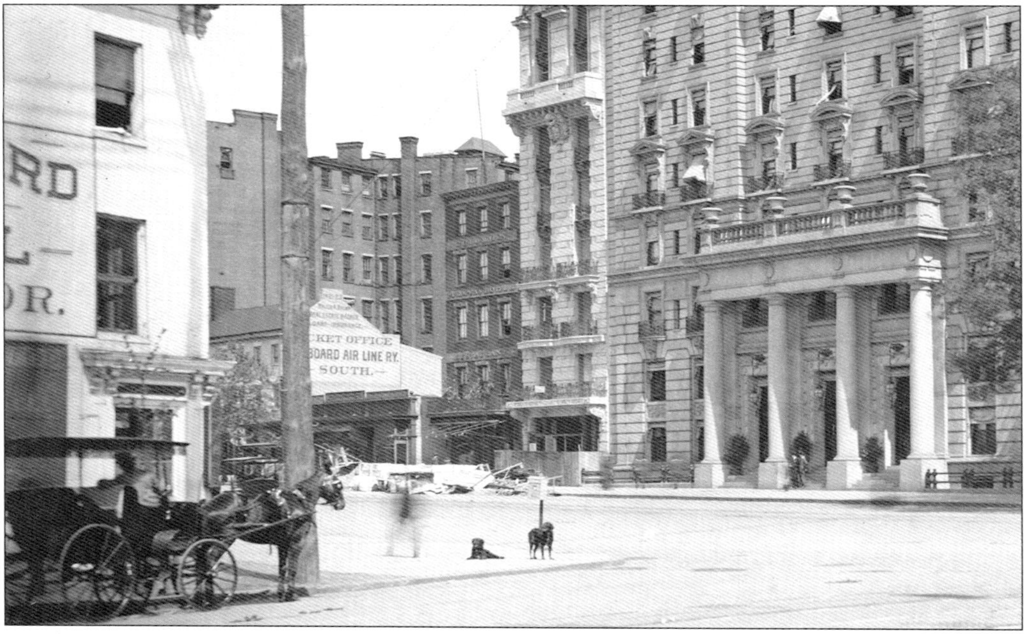

Barely noticeable next to the massive bulk of the Willard Hotel, the narrow Columbia European Hotel and Restaurant and the taller Hotel Occidental are seen in 1904. The Occidental was built after the Civil War by Henry Willard, who sold his interest in the Willard Hotel to his brother Joseph. The building was extensively rebuilt, as seen here, and reopened in 1906 after acquiring the next door Columbia, which was partly demolished and converted into the two-story Occidental Restaurant.

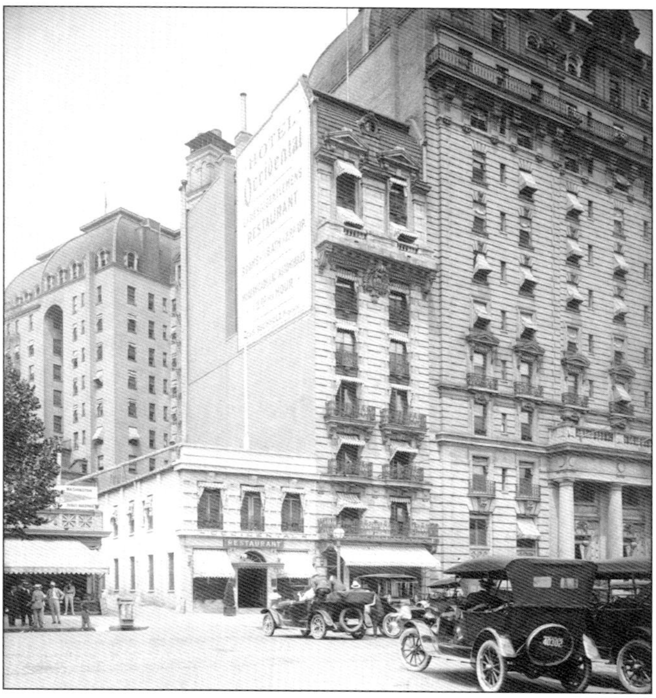

German immigrant Gustav Buchholz, former head waiter of the Willard, managed the Occidental when the hotel and restaurant opened in 1906. He bought the business in 1912 and sought to make the operation a power center, frequented by politicians, athletes, authors, and celebrities. The Occidental prospered under the slogan "Where Statesmen Dine." During World War I, Buchholz declared his loyalty to America and strongly supported the war effort. This scene is from 1916.

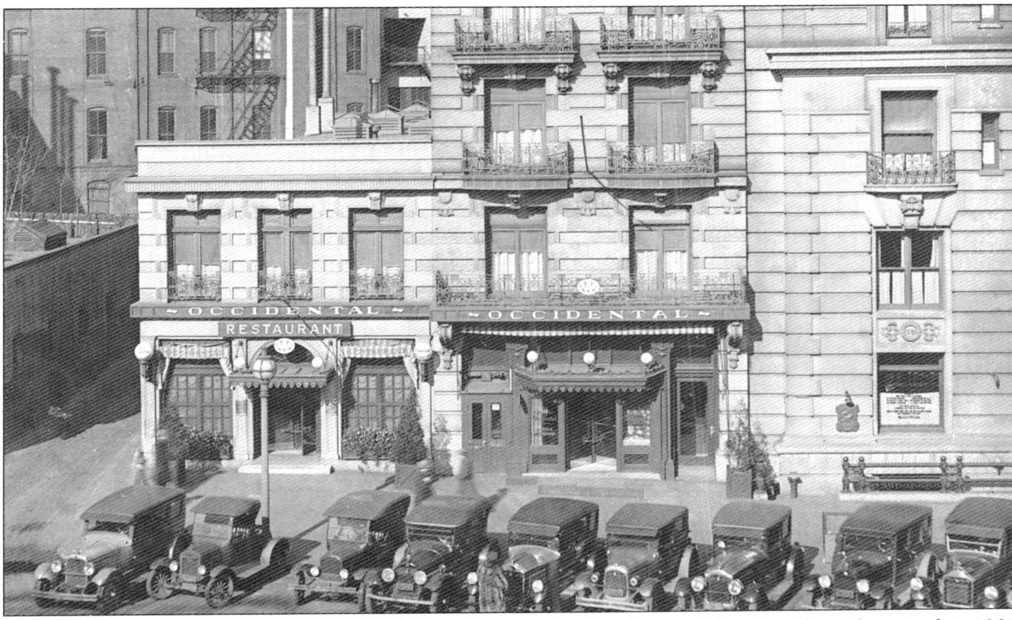

Photographs nearly always show a solid line of cars parked in front of the Occidental, as in this 1926 view with someone in a full-length fur coat by the cars. Well-known personalities of all kinds were routinely seen coming and going from the Occidental, and the 1924 world champion Washington Senators held their celebration there after their World Series victory. The sign in the restaurant's window reads "Ladies Restaurant," reflecting a special effort to attract women patrons.

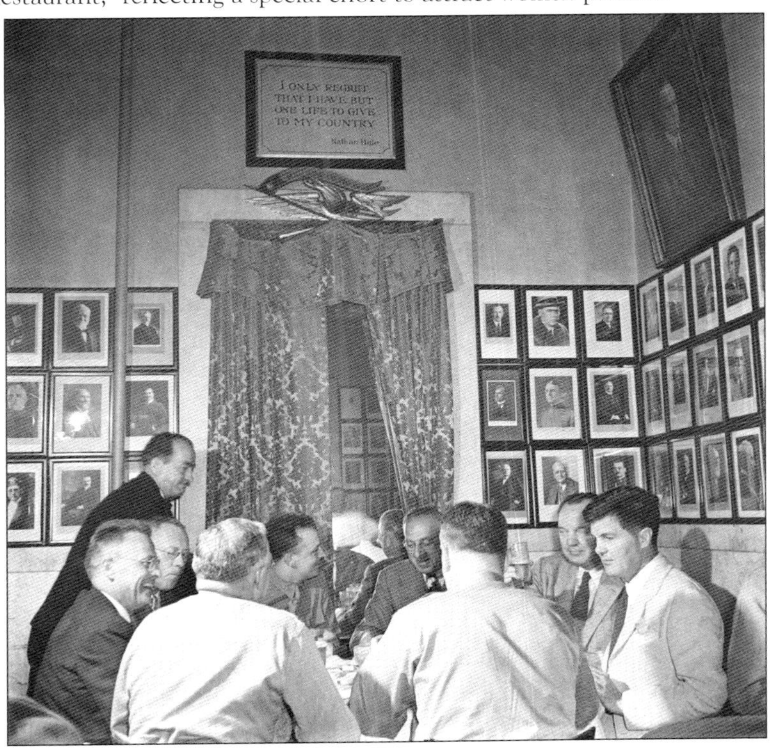

The Occidental's walls, like all good power restaurants, were covered with portraits of customers, many of them autographed. Furnishings in the dining room included a huge black stove, the first electric stove in Washington. The restaurant prospered through Prohibition and throughout World War II. Here, a group of men dine at the Occidental in June 1942.

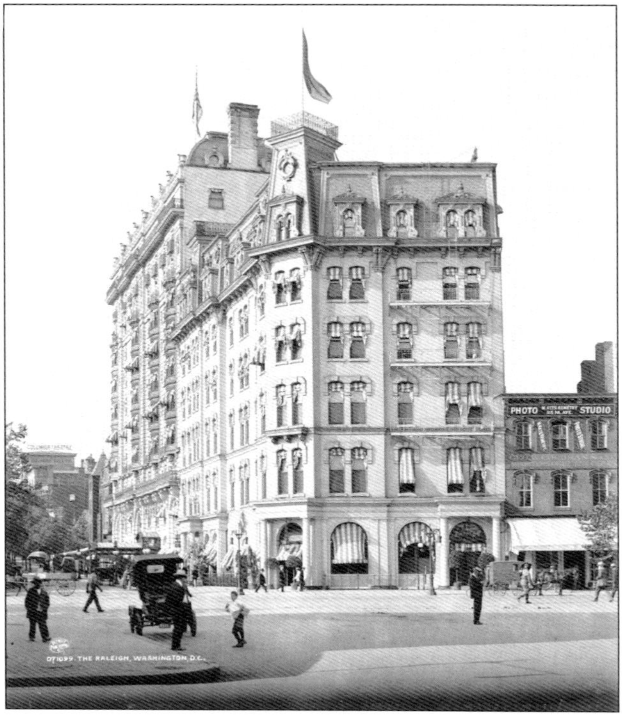

Just across from the Post Office Building at Twelfth Street and Pennsylvania Avenue stood the Raleigh Hotel, seen in 1906. The structure was built in 1875 by Alexander Shepherd as the Centennial Building, at the time the finest office building in Washington, replacing an earlier hotel, Kirkwood House. The Second Empire–style building was converted in 1893–1894 to become the Raleigh Hotel, and in 1897, a major addition designed by Henry Janeway Hardenbergh was built along Twelfth Street. Hardenbergh also designed the new Willard Hotel, which opened in 1901.

The 12-story addition of 1898 vaulted the Raleigh into the top tier of Washington hostelries. Competition from the Willard spurred a further expansion in 1911, when the original Centennial Building was demolished and replaced by a huge 13-story structure capped by a prominent cupola. Lobbied by the builders, Congress modified the city's 130-foot height restriction for the avenue to 160 feet to accommodate the design. Hardenbergh designed the new Raleigh in the same Beaux-Arts style as the Willard, two blocks up the street.

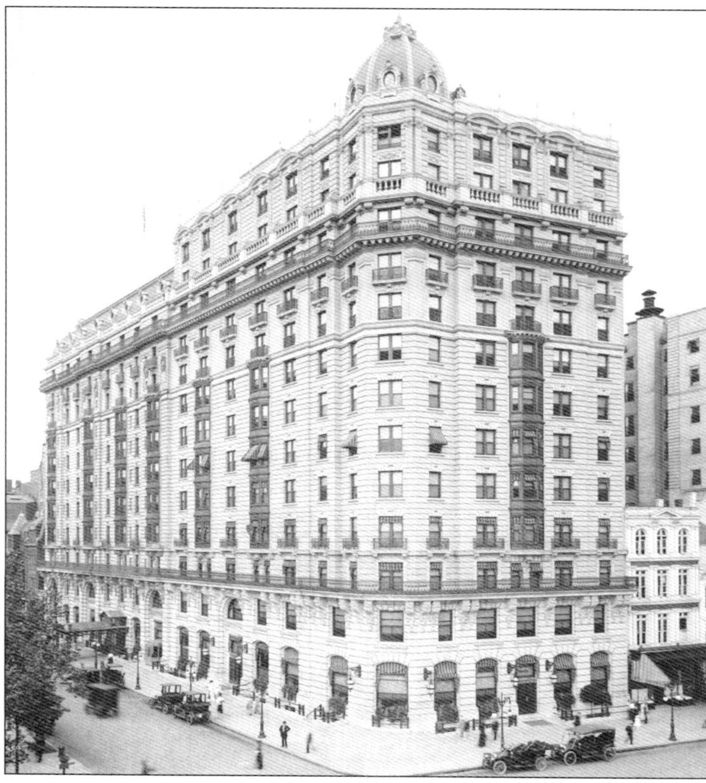

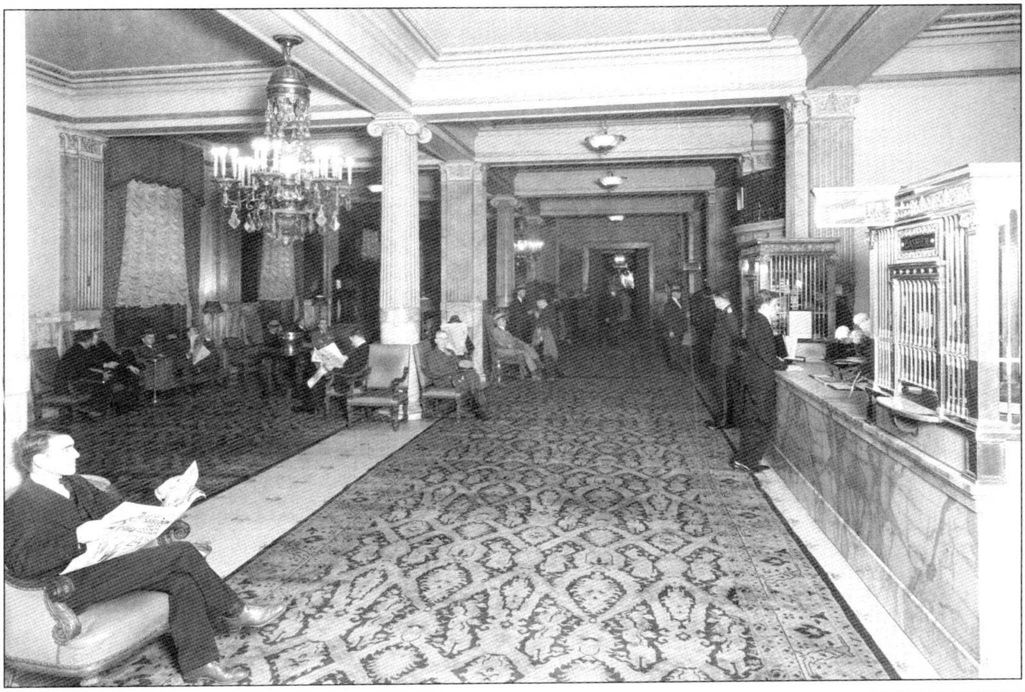

Patrons occupy nearly every chair in the lobby of the Raleigh in 1930. The hotel was famous for its rich architectural detailing and for the artwork displayed throughout its public spaces. While the Raleigh vied with the Willard for top honors on Pennsylvania Avenue, business was being lost to the Mayflower Hotel, which opened in 1925 some blocks away on Connecticut Avenue. The older hotels fought back with restyled decor and increased entertainment.

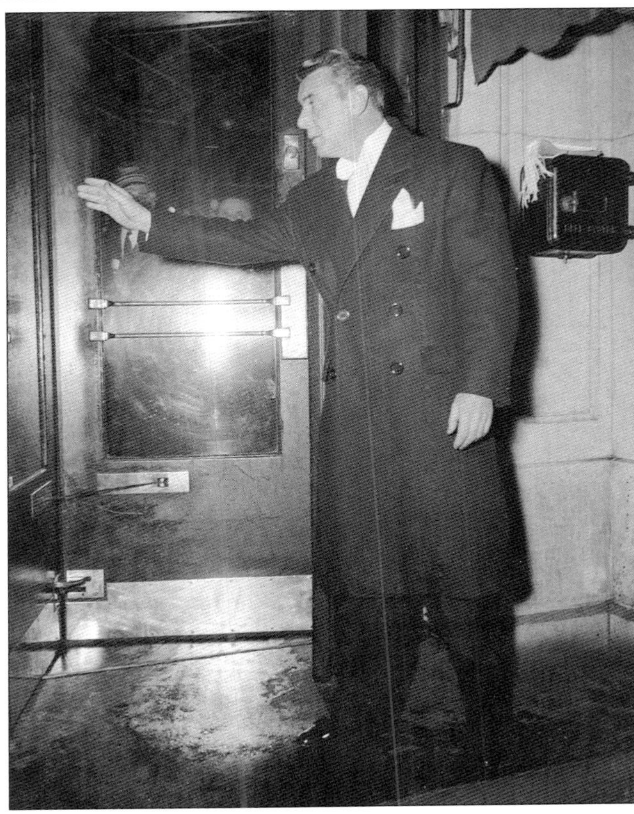

The Raleigh regularly attracted actors, musicians, and other entertainers. Here, actor George Brent arrives at the hotel on January 30, 1939, to attend a birthday ball given for Pres. Franklin Roosevelt. Brent was a major Hollywood leading man of the 1930s and 1940s, costarring 13 times with Bette Davis.

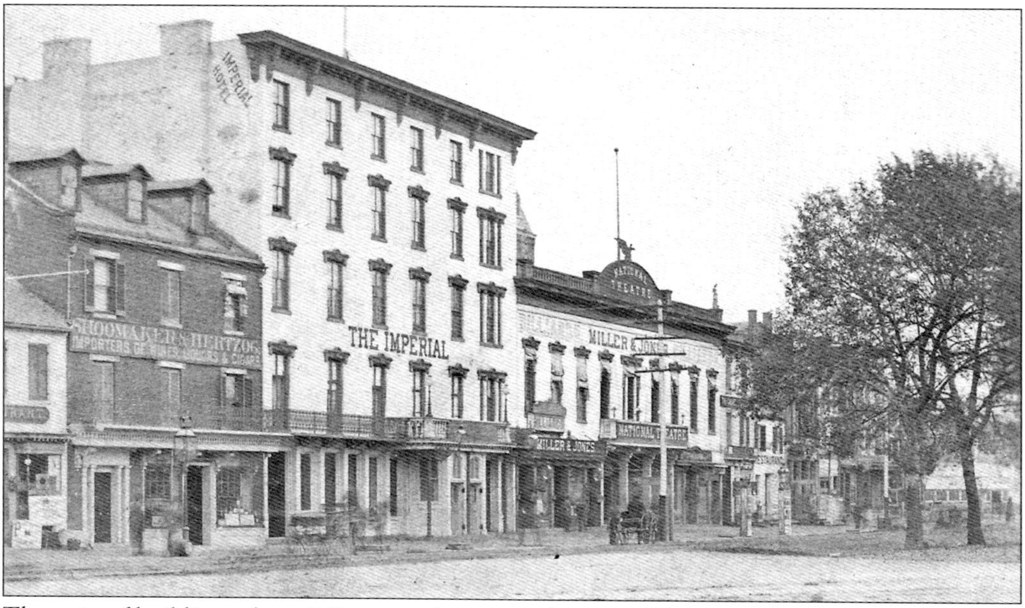

The strip of buildings along E Street at the avenue between Thirteenth and Fourteenth Streets was known for about 60 years as "Rum Row" or "Newspaper Row." Newspaper and telegraph offices crowded the northwest end of the block, the National Theater stood at the other end, and saloons filled spaces in between. Stuck in the middle was the Imperial Hotel, opened in 1869 as Jenness House. The hotel passed through a succession of owners before being demolished in 1905 for the Munsey Building. (John DeFerrari.)

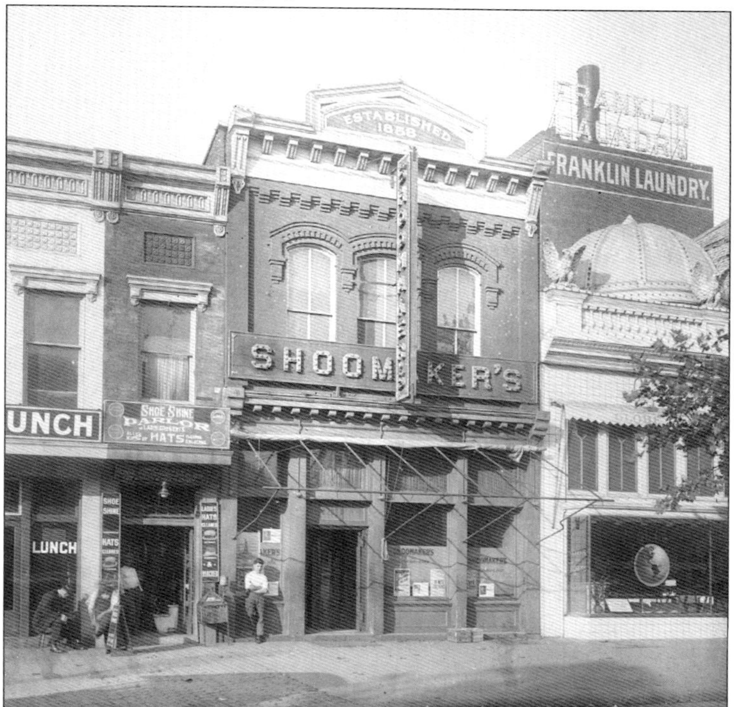

Shoomaker & Hertzog's saloon began operating in 1858 on the ground floor of the National Theater but moved in the early 1870s to the west side of the Imperial Hotel, as seen in the previous image. The saloon was dingy, dirty, and very popular, becoming well known for its liquor selection and the ebullient personality of William "Shoo" Shoomaker, who eventually bought out his partner. Shoomaker's building was purchased in 1915 by Frank Munsey to expand his office building, and the saloon moved to the western end of the block, as seen here.

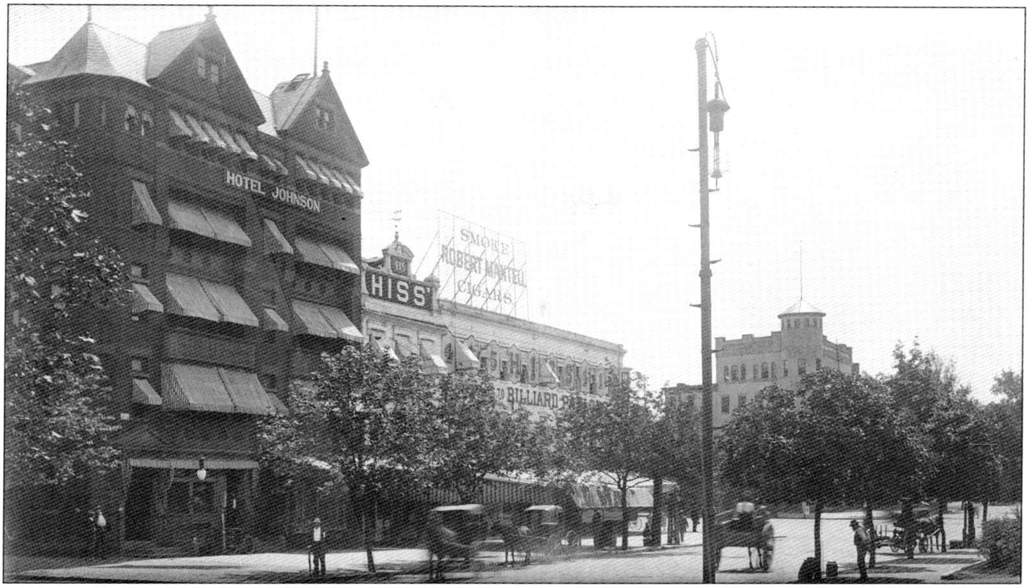

Shaded by window awnings, the Hotel Johnson sits on Thirteenth Street just up from Pennsylvania Avenue at right in this 1901 view. The hotel grew out of a gambling house specializing in faro games, an immensely popular card game in the second half of the 1800s. The Johnson was sold in 1912 and extensively remodeled as the Sterling Hotel. After a series of ownership changes, it was demolished in 1932 for a parking lot, eventually becoming the site of the Pennsylvania Building.

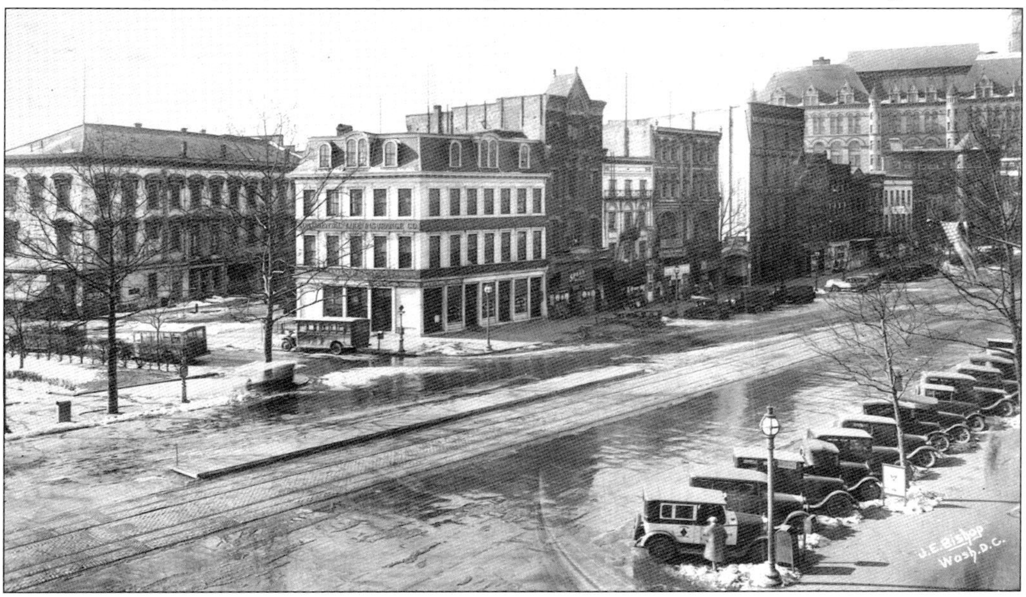

An eclectic mix of businesses occupies the south side of Pennsylvania Avenue at Ninth Street in this view from 1928. Nestled in the center of the block is the Main Hotel, the four-story light-colored building with fire escape ladders. The Main was typical of small, cheap hotels catering to tourists. Other stores include the James F. Oyster cheese shop, an auto supply company, a furniture storage building, and an Army-Navy goods store. All of this would be swept away within a few years. (National Archives.)

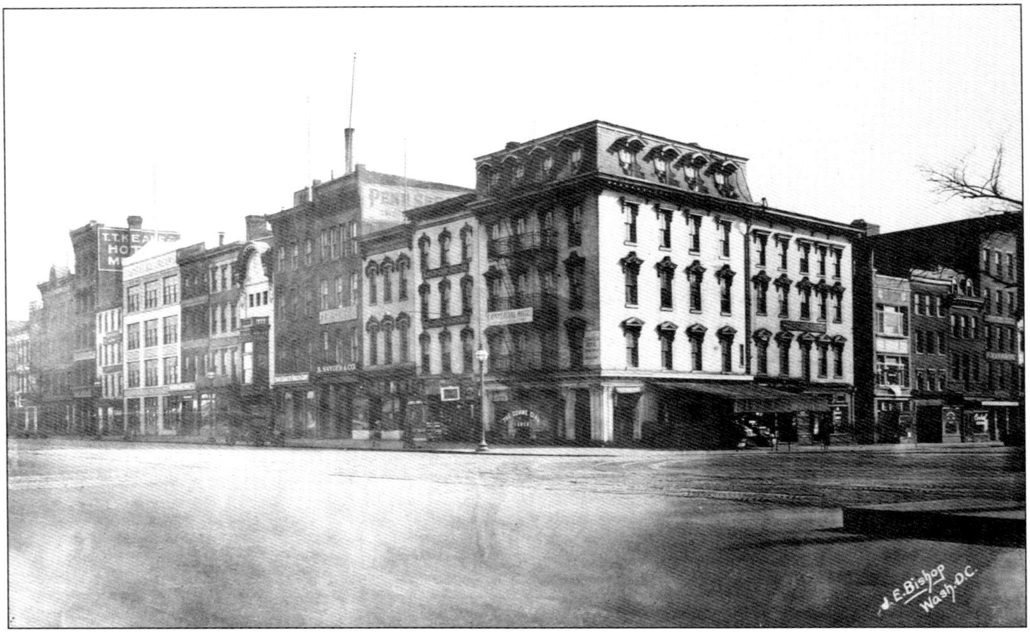

Another low-cost hotel, the Commercial Hotel and Lunch Room, sits at the corner of Seventh Street on the south side of Pennsylvania Avenue in 1928. Next door is the American House, proudly proclaiming "For Ladies and Gentlemen," with more small businesses down the street. All of these buildings were slated for demolition for the new Federal Triangle project. In a decade, the Federal Trade Commission Apex Building would occupy this block. (National Archives.)

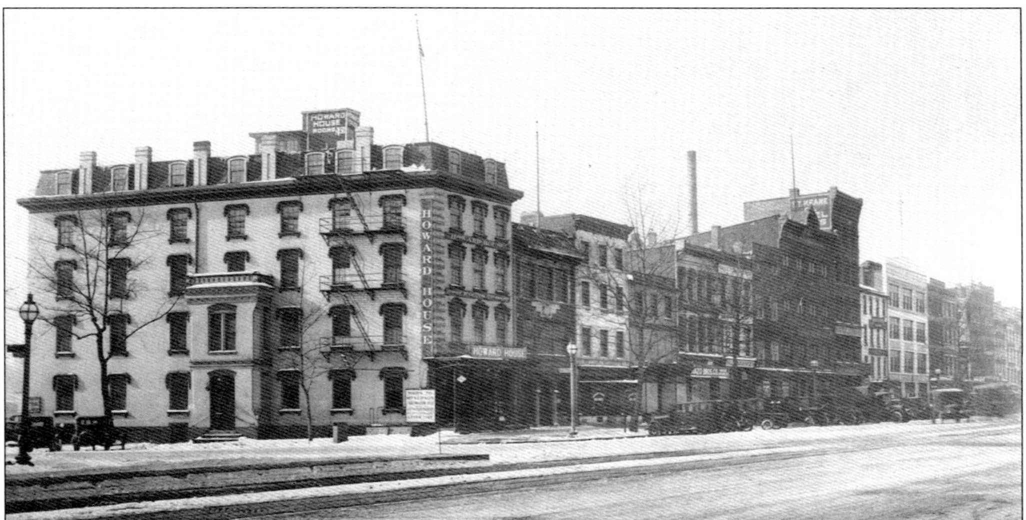

The Howard House, on the southwest corner of Pennsylvania Avenue and Sixth Street, offered rooms for $1.50 a day in 1928. Even in this winter view, a sign offers motor bus tours to Mount Vernon, Arlington, and the National Zoo via the Green Line, a sightseeing service. The Gray Line and the Royal Blue Line were among the Green Line's competitors, all available along the avenue. (National Archives.)

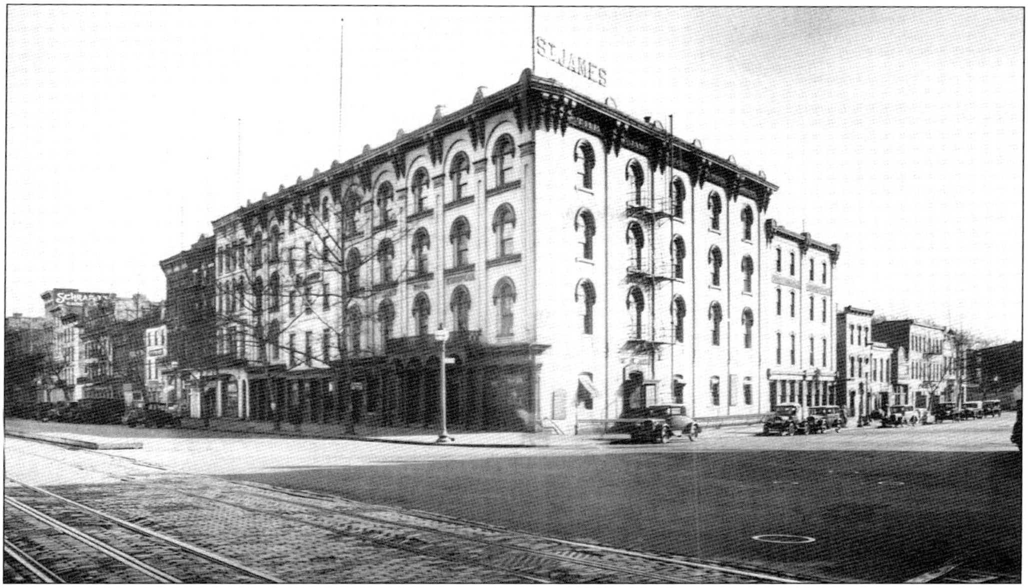

The St. James Hotel, another midlevel hotel on the avenue, sits on the southeast corner at Sixth Street. While a hotel operated at this spot at least by the 1830s, the location turned strategic when the B&P station opened in 1873 a block down Sixth Street, and the St. James became one of the first hotels newly arrived travelers from the south encountered. This view is from 1928. (National Archives.)

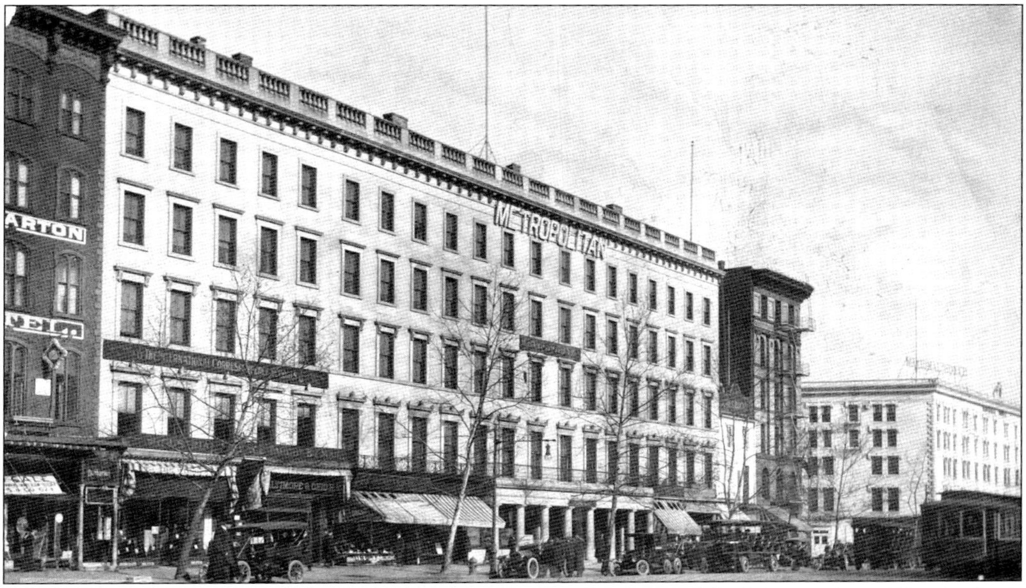

Between Sixth and Seventh Streets on the avenue's north side stood the Metropolitan Hotel, which for much of the 19th century vied with the next-door National Hotel as Washington's finest hostelry. The Davis Hotel occupied the spot beginning in 1802. Hotel manager Jesse Brown purchased the property, rebuilt it, and reopened in 1821 as the Indian Queen Hotel. Another major reconstruction in 1850 resulted in the enlarged Brown's Marble Hotel, which becoming the Metropolitan in 1865. This February 1913 view shows the National at right. (National Archives.)

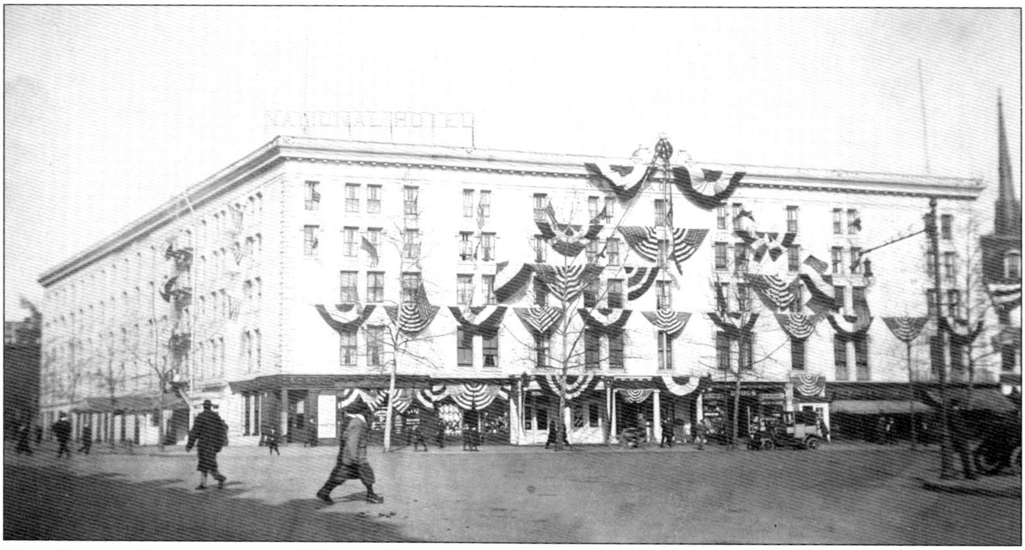

On the northeast corner of Pennsylvania Avenue and Sixth Street, the National Hotel was remodeled in 1826 from six rowhouses into a 200-room hotel, Washington's finest. Among its guests were English novelist Charles Dickens. The hotel was enlarged twice again into this structure, seen in 1909, possibly decorated for the upcoming inauguration of Pres. William Taft. A major fire in 1921 sent the establishment into decline, and it was purchased by the city in 1929. Used as the DC Armory, it was demolished in 1942. (National Archives.)

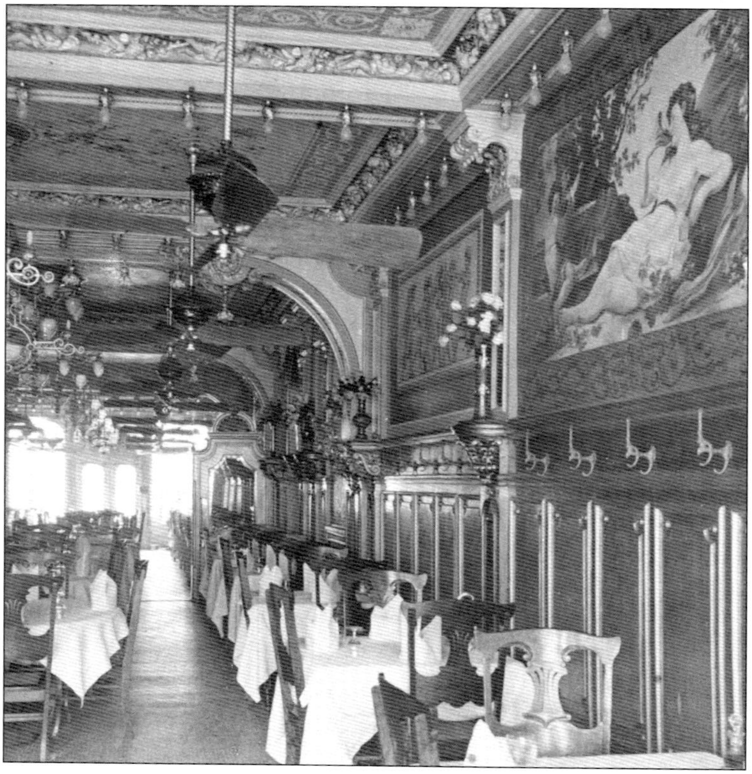

The opulent yet comfortable interior of Fritz Reuter's café is pictured in 1900. German immigrant Reuter converted a boardinghouse on the northwest corner of Pennsylvania Avenue and Four and a Half Street into the Hotel Fritz Reuter, an inn and restaurant offering "the best dinner in the city for the money." The business operated from 1889 to 1914, first as a German-styled *gashaus* and later with a rathskeller. Reuter suffered from depression and killed himself in the hotel in January 1906, although his partner continued the business.

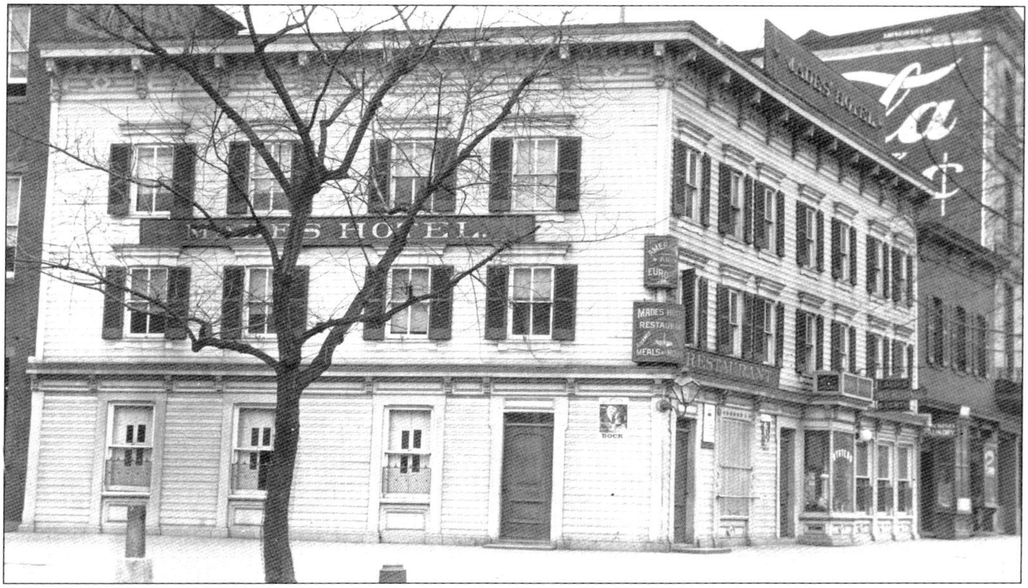

The unassuming Mades Hotel opened in 1858 on the southwest corner of Pennsylvania Avenue and Third Street. Owned by Prussian-born Charles Mades, the hotel featured a frog pond where customers could select their meal. The hotel stood at the east end of what was Washington's Chinatown, concentrated on the avenue's south side between Third and Fourth Streets. While few signs proclaimed it as such, Chinatown remained there until the late 1920s, when it was relocated by the federal government to H Street NW.

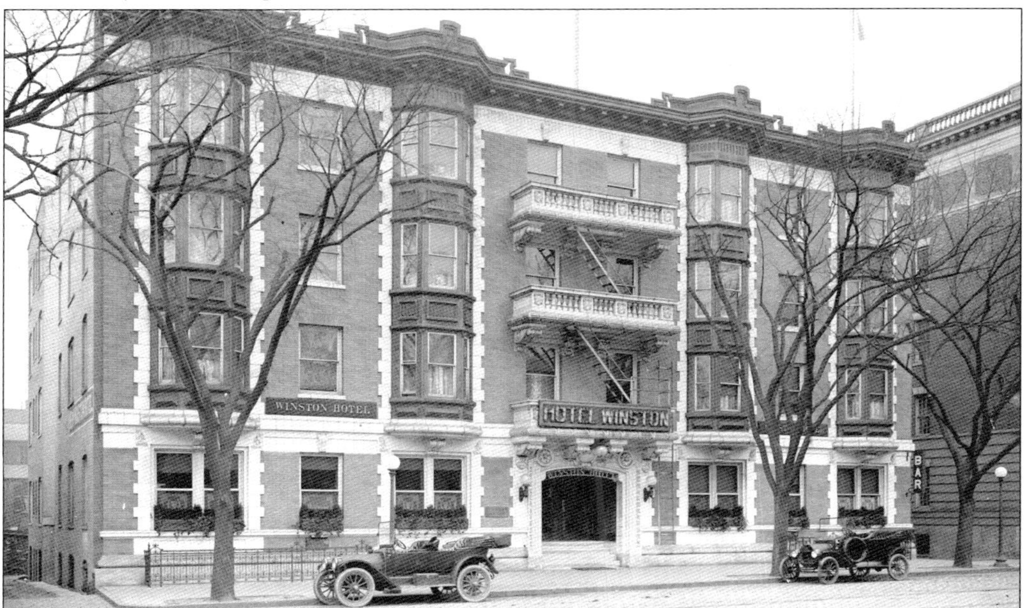

The Winston was another small but comfortable hotel on the avenue. It was at the corner of First Street by the Peace Monument, close by the Capitol as well as the nearby Baltimore & Ohio Railroad station and, after 1908, Union Station. The entire block was razed around 1930 to clear the grounds and today is a landscaped park.

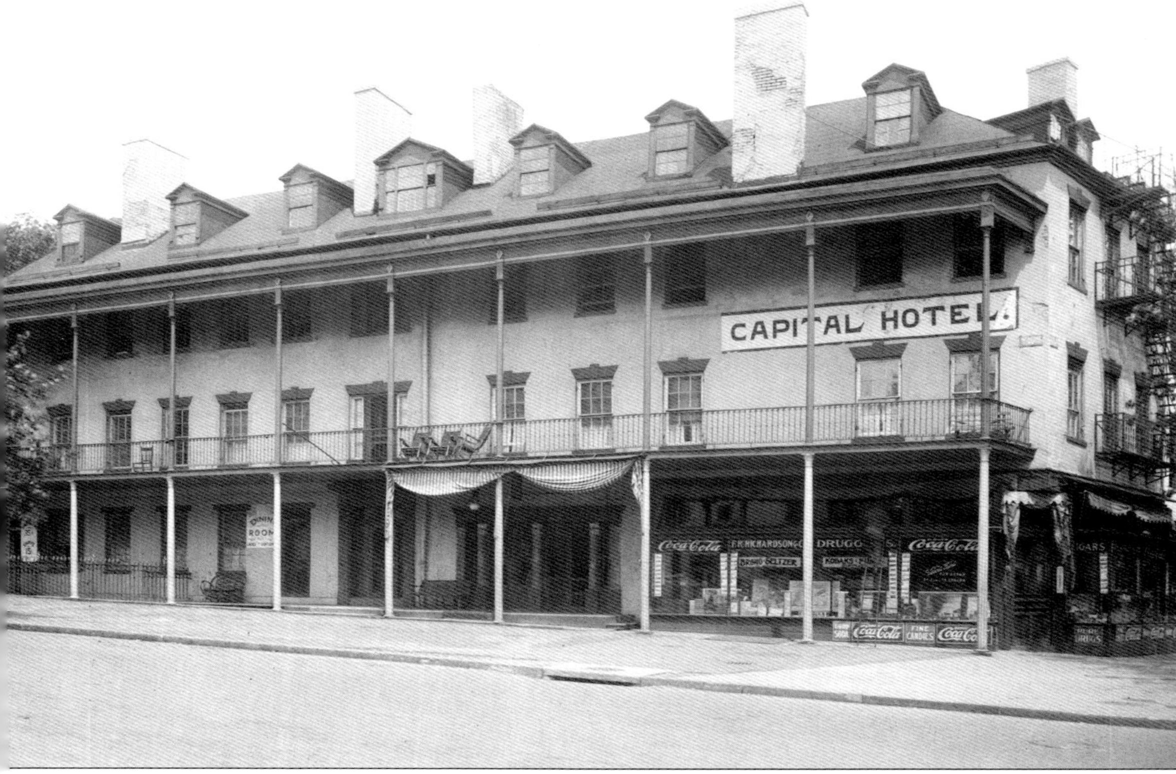

A hotel with a darker history stood at the northeast corner of Third Street and Pennsylvania Avenue. The St. Charles Hotel opened in 1820 featuring an extensive slave pen in its basement. Six 30-foot-long cells extended under the streets; grilles in the sidewalks provided light and air, and slaves were confined behind iron doors, with iron rings set into the walls for chains. The hotel provided a guarantee, offering to reimburse owners should any slave escape. The St. Charles was considered an upscale hotel, popular with Southern landowners and politicians. The pens remained in use even after the slave trade was outlawed in Washington in 1850, and traveling owners kept their property in the pens during their stays in the city. After the Civil War, the hotel lost much of its upscale clientele to competitors but was often used by Native Americans in Washington to negotiate with the federal government. A fire in the 1890s resulted in a name change to the Capitol Hotel; later it was renamed the Hotel Belvedere and lastly it was the New Capital Hotel, as seen in this view from about 1920. The building was finally demolished in 1924.

Six

Presidents, Parades, and Protests

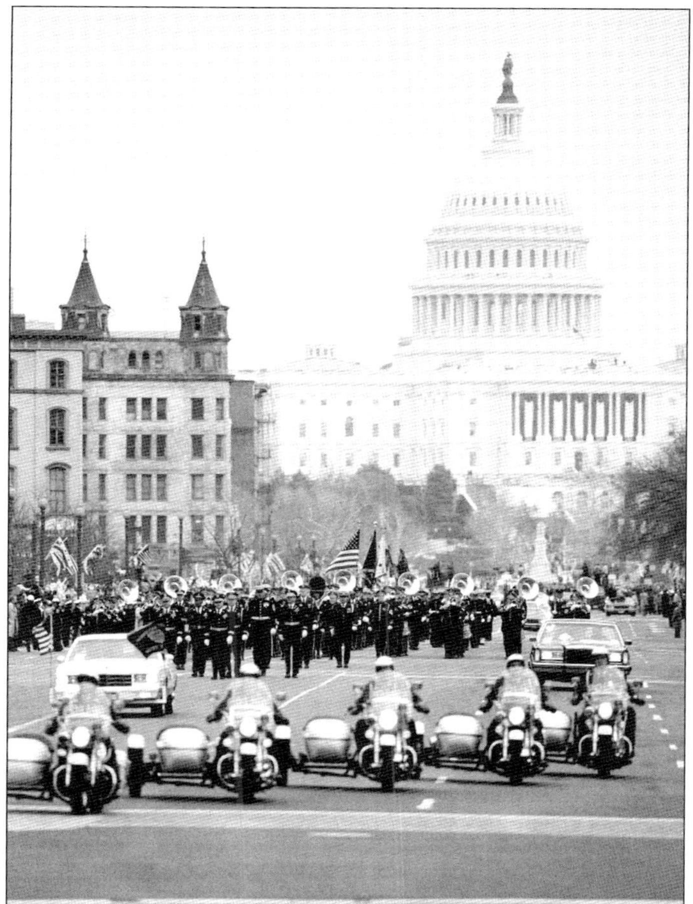

District of Columbia motorcycle police lead Pres. Ronald Reagan's first inaugural parade on January 20, 1981, passing the dilapidated Central National Bank building. The inaugural parade is the best-known regular event on the avenue. The first presidential parade happened somewhat by accident in March 1805 when friends, congressmen, and strangers joined Thomas Jefferson on his ride back to the White House after his swearing-in ceremony. The parade became an official event in 1809 after James Madison's inauguration. The avenue has also hosted presidential funerals, as former heads of state were borne from the White House to the Capitol to lie in state. Patriotic parades to prepare for war and victory parades to celebrate their end marched down the avenue, as did protesters seeking political change.

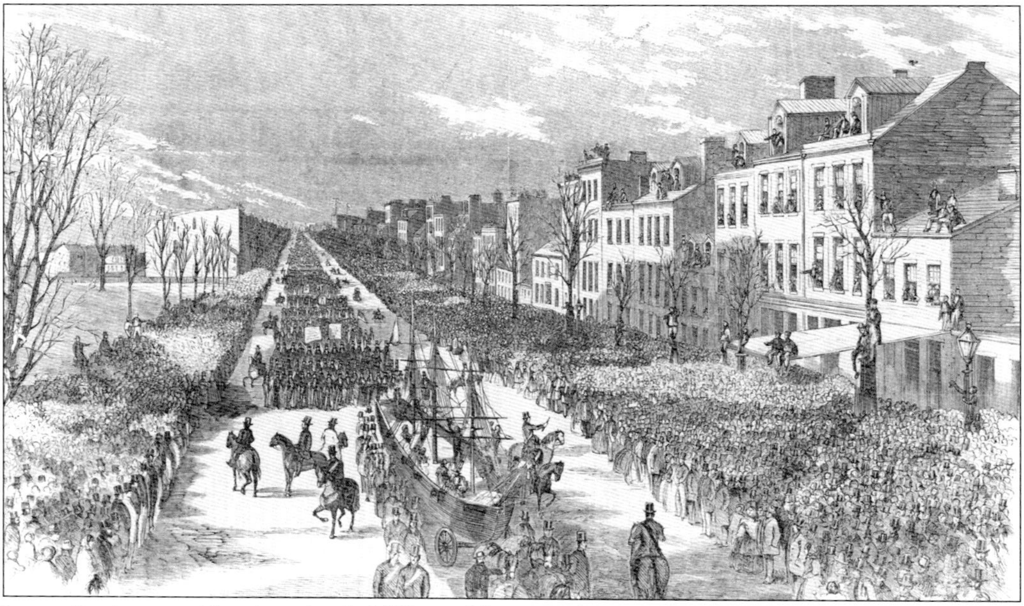

James Buchanan rides the wheeled "Ship of State" as his parade approaches the Capitol for the inauguration on March 4, 1857. Buchanan's inaugural was marked by violence in the streets of several US cities as the slavery issue increasingly polarized the country. This illustration from *Frank Leslie's Illustrated Newspaper* appears to show the parade reaching the foot of Capitol Hill at First Street.

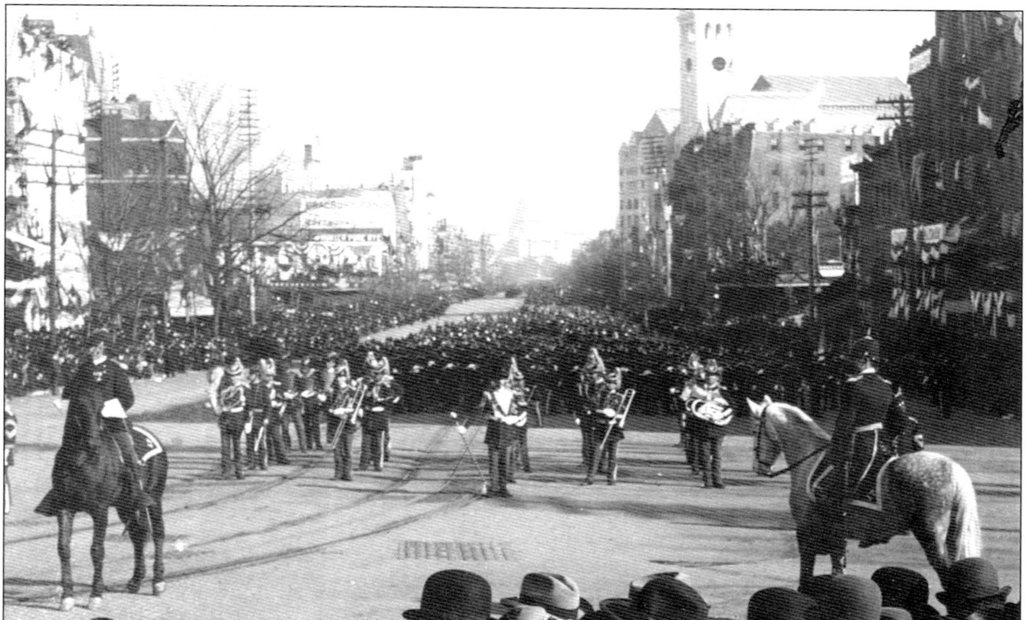

The inaugural parade for William McKinley pauses on Pennsylvania Avenue on March 4, 1897, before swinging to its right onto Fifteenth Street. The Post Office tower at right lacks its clocks, as the building was still under construction and would not be completed until 1899. Notice the spiked helmets worn by the Army officers on horseback.

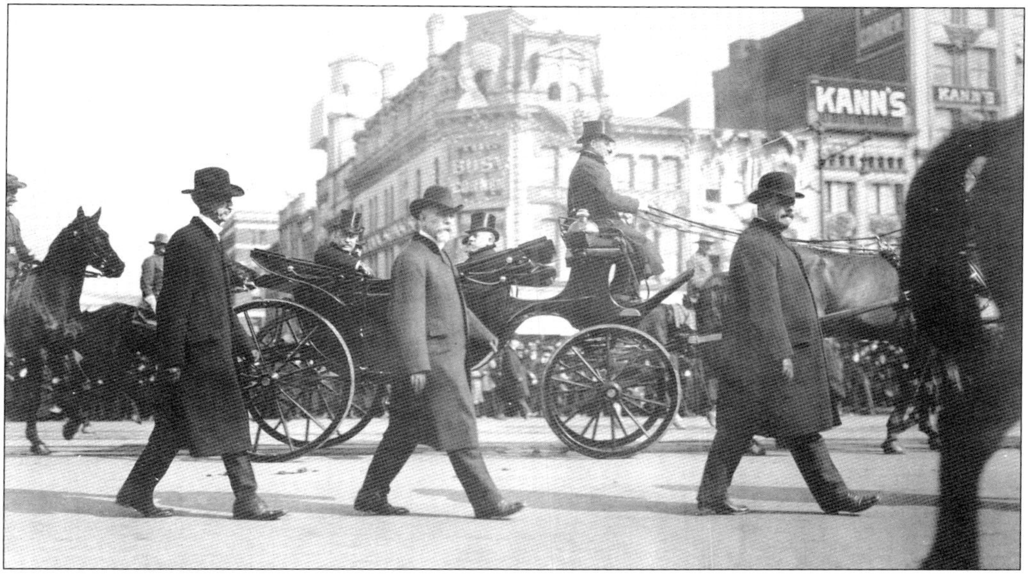

Wearing a formal top hat, Theodore Roosevelt sits in the rear of an open horse-drawn carriage as he rides past the Busy Corner and Kann's department store to his swearing-in ceremony at the Capitol on March 4, 1905. The men walking alongside the carriage are probably Secret Service agents. The Treasury Department agency began protecting the chief executive after the September 1901 assassination of William McKinley, which led to Vice President Roosevelt's first term in office.

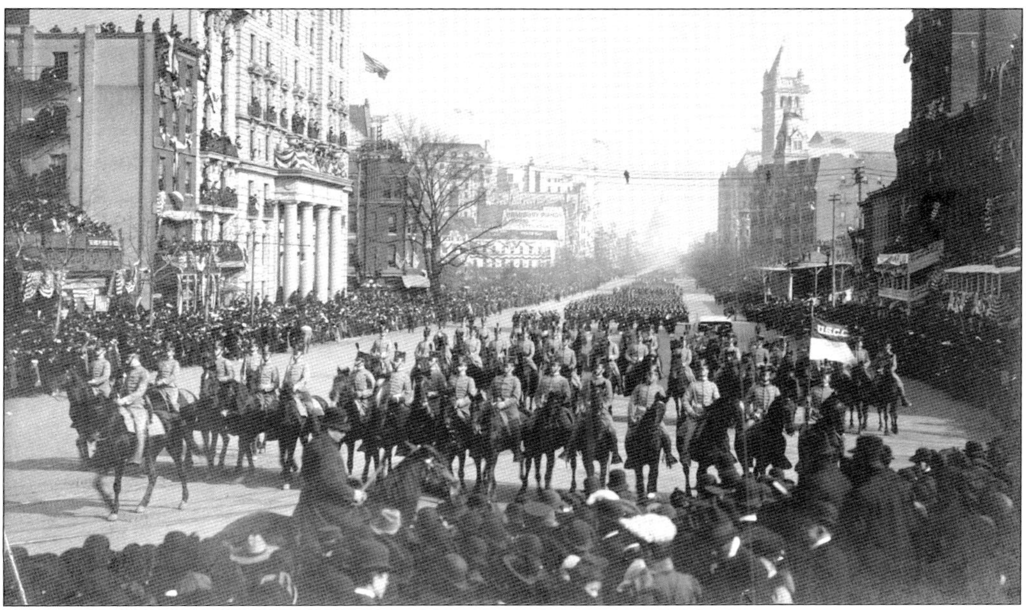

Army cadets from the US Military Academy at West Point pause on their mounts during Theodore Roosevelt's parade on March 4, 1905. Their banner, reading "U.S.C.C." for the US Corps of Cadets, is displayed at right. Many of the buildings feature temporary wooden viewing stands erected for the parade, and at least two photographers perch precariously above the avenue on telephone wires. The Occidental and Willard Hotels are at left.

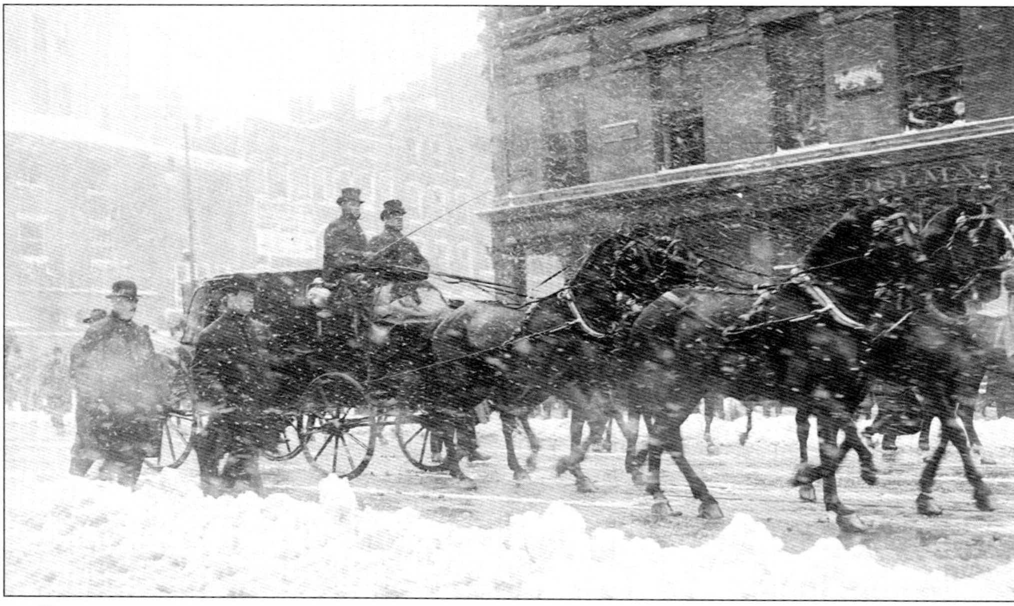

William Howard Taft stayed inside his coach with predecessor Theodore Roosevelt on March 4, 1909, as the two headed to the Capitol in a blizzard. Even in these conditions, the Secret Service agents stood close by, but the swearing-in ceremony that was to have taken place on the Capitol steps was moved indoors to the Senate Chamber. The storm brought most of the city to a standstill, stalling trains and making streets impassable with snow and toppled trees and telephone poles.

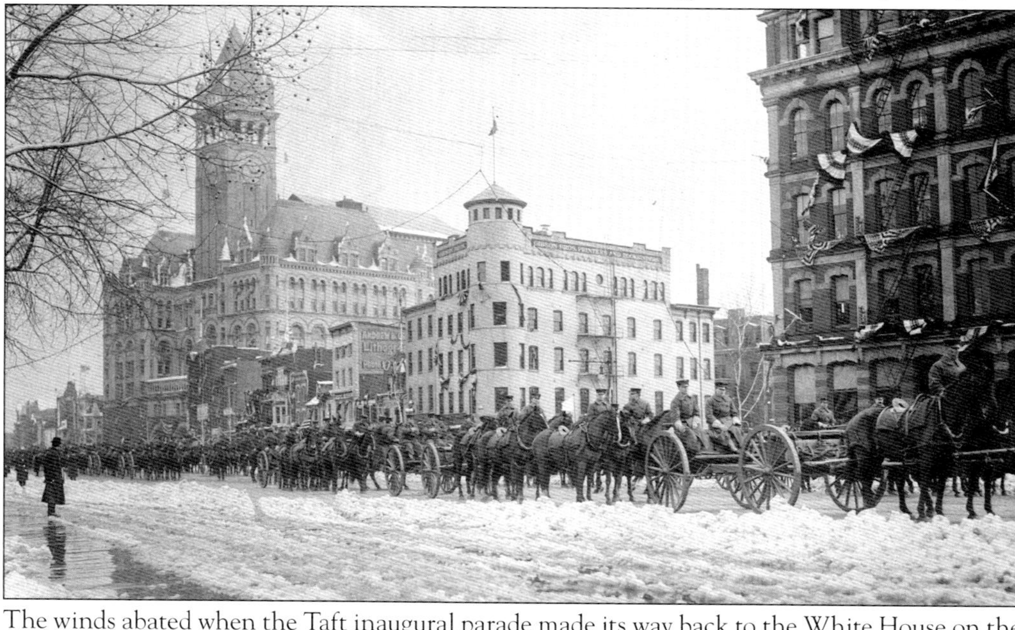

The winds abated when the Taft inaugural parade made its way back to the White House on the afternoon of March 4, 1909. The parade route was passable due to the efforts of more than 6,000 men who, working through the night, used about 500 wagons to clear an estimated 58,000 tons of snow and slush from the parade route. Here, Army cavalry pauses at Thirteenth Street by the towered Gibson Brothers Printers and Bookbinders building.

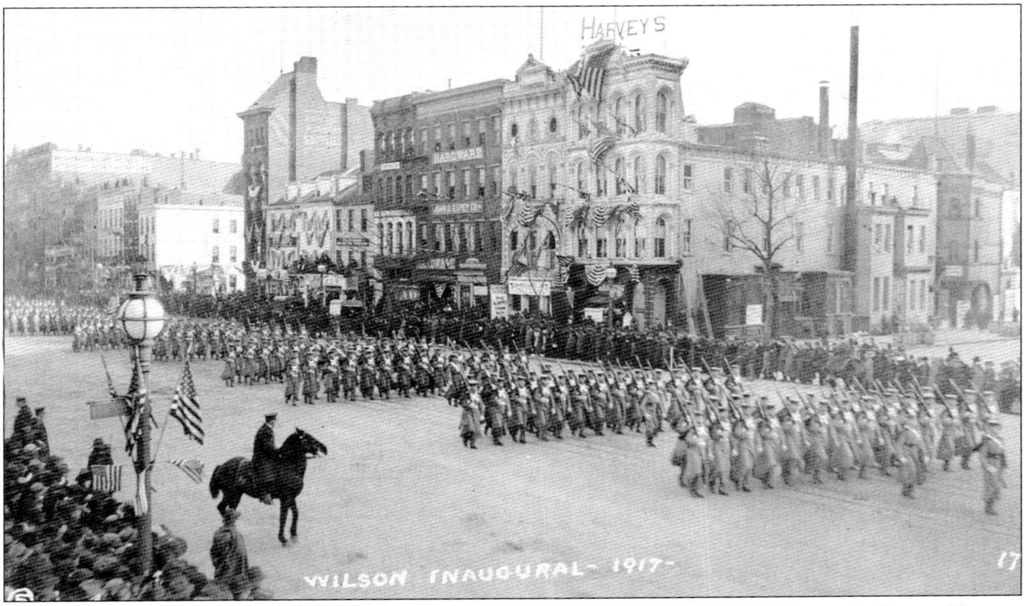

Woodrow Wilson's second inaugural parade, on March 4, 1917, passes by Harvey's Oyster House, one of Washington's best-known eating establishments. The restaurant began operations in 1858 and moved to this location at Eleventh Street and the avenue in 1866. Here, it grew into an elegant eating establishment, all the while claiming eye-opening records for the number of oysters it dished out, such as serving a billion oysters in one season. Forced to move in 1931 by the Federal Triangle project, Harvey's remained in business until the early 1990s.

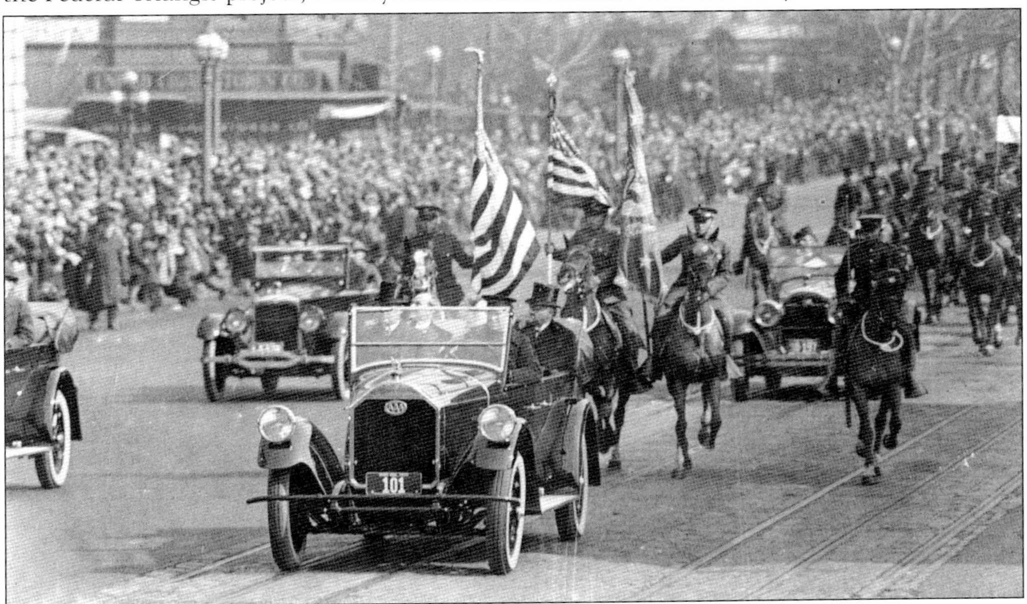

Pres. Calvin Coolidge rides down the avenue in an open-topped Pierce-Arrow automobile during his inaugural parade on March 14, 1925. Coolidge is in the back seat without a hat, sitting with his wife, Grace, and William Howard Taft, who became the first former president to administer the oath of office as chief justice of the Supreme Court.

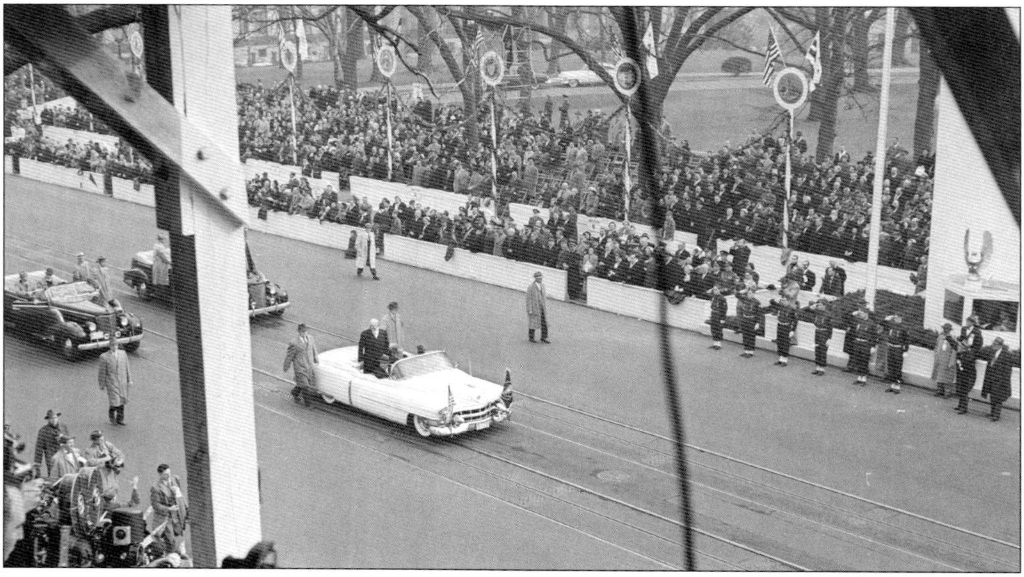

News cameras focus in as Pres. Dwight Eisenhower stands in a Cadillac convertible approaching the grandstands at the head of the parade route on January 20, 1953. The elaborate inaugural procession included 22,000 service members, 5,000 civilians, 50 floats, 65 musical groups, 350 horses, an Alaskan dog team, and three elephants, along with an atomic cannon. To shorten the time between election and inauguration, the date of the swearing-in ceremony was moved forward from March to January beginning with Franklin Roosevelt's second inaugural in 1937.

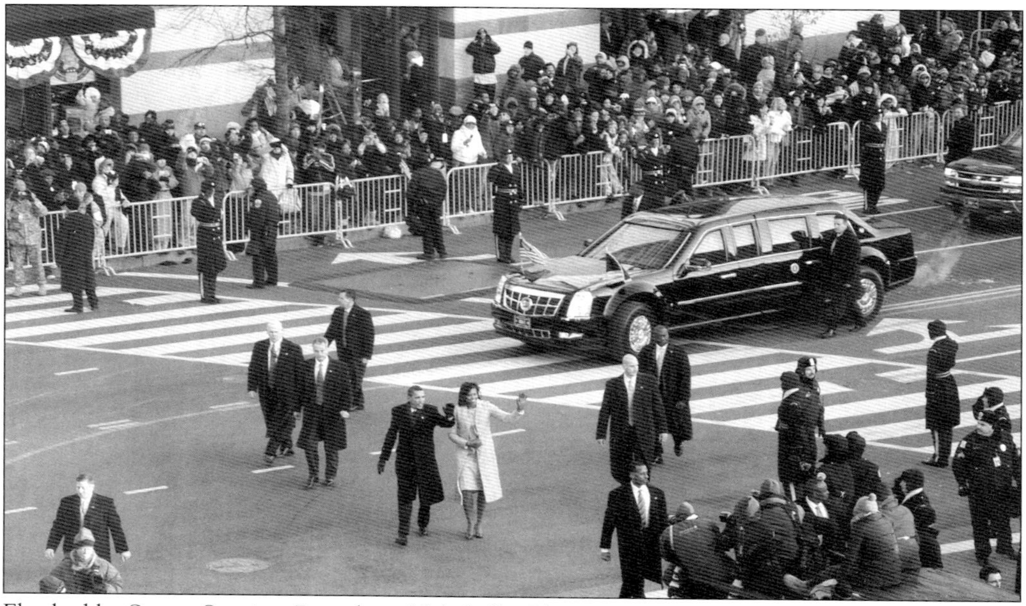

Flanked by Secret Service, Barack and Michelle Obama wave to photographers along Fifteenth Street during the inaugural parade of January 24, 2009. The first couple walked most of the 1.2-mile route from the Capitol rather than ride in the new presidential inaugural car, following behind them. Jimmy Carter in 1977 was the first president to exit the limousine and walk the avenue back to the White House.

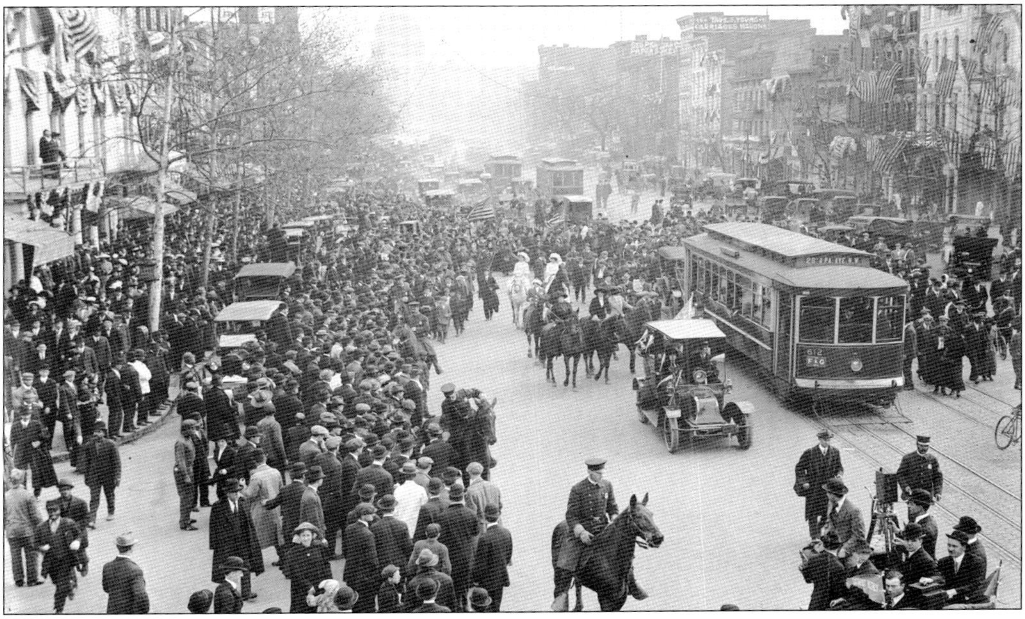

The rise of the suffrage movement to secure voting rights for women spurred a series of protests in Washington beginning in 1913. The first major event was the Woman Suffrage Procession on March 3, 1913, the day before Woodrow Wilson's first inauguration. Led by Alice Paul of the National American Woman Suffrage Association, the parade featured nearly 8,000 marchers. Here, leaders of the parade are on horseback coming up the avenue, which was not closed for the event despite the granting of a parade permit, allowing hostile male onlookers to close in.

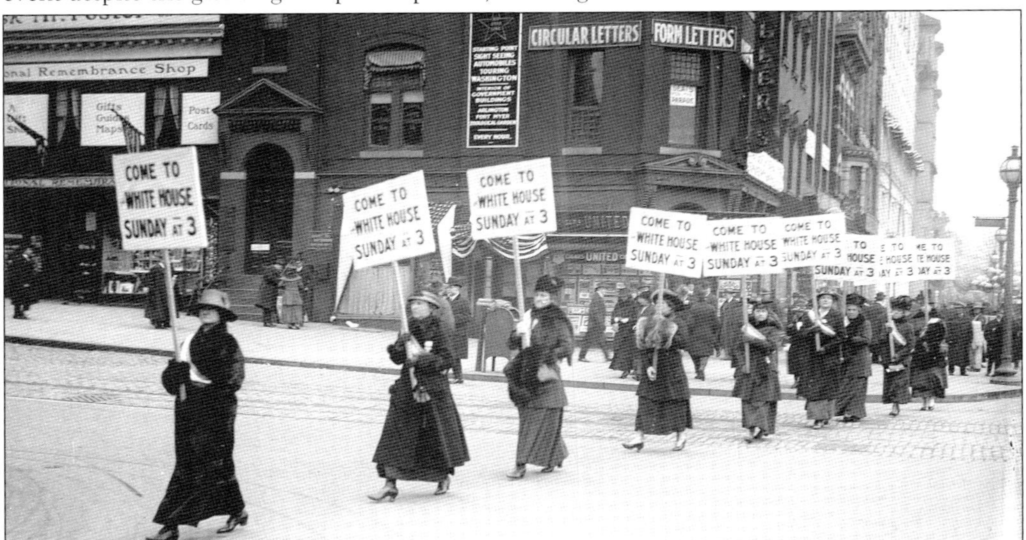

The suffrage movement continued to be a presence on Washington's streets in 1917, when these women marched across Fourteenth Street at the avenue to advertise a coming rally. Protesters maintained a vigil outside the White House gates in all weather, trying to shame President Wilson into supporting their cause, which emerged victorious with the ratification of the 19th Amendment on August 18, 1920. Ask Mr. Foster, the store at left, served the tourist trade.

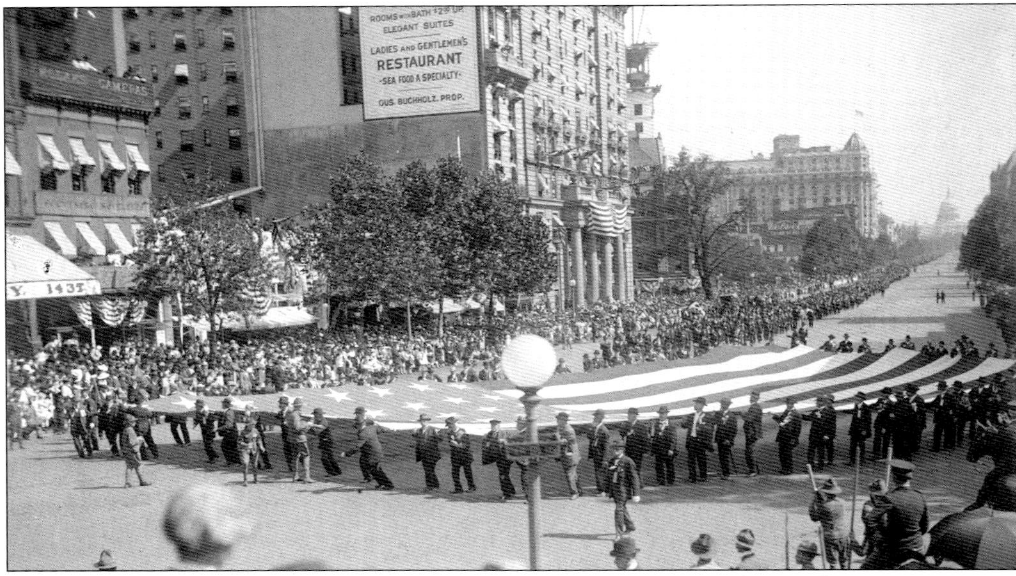

The Civil War ended in 1865, but its parades continued as long as the conflict's veterans were able to march. The Grand Army of the Republic's (GAR) annual national encampments allowed veterans of the Union Army to meet up each year in locations around the country, with the 49th encampment taking place in Washington on September 30 and October 1, 1915. For their parade, GAR veterans carried an enormous US flag down the avenue. The last GAR encampment was in September 1949 in Indianapolis, Indiana.

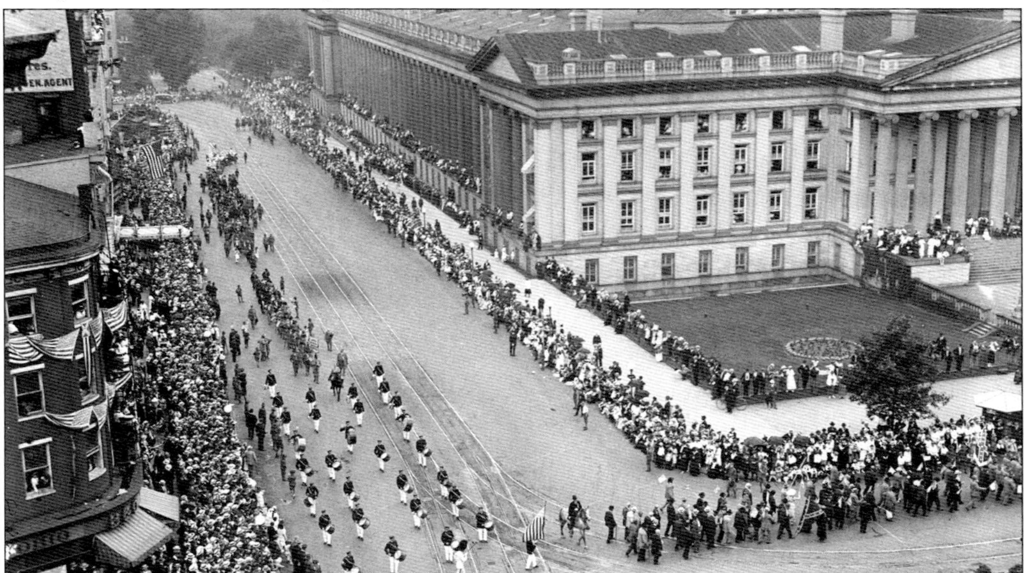

Confederate Civil War veterans held their first reunion in 1884, but not until the 1890s did the southern side's meetups take hold nationally. The 27th national reunion of the United Confederate Veterans (UCV) took place in Washington from June 5 to 7, 1917, and featured a parade, seen here coming up Fifteenth Street from Pennsylvania Avenue and passing the Treasury Building. The final UCV national reunion took place in June 1951 in Norfolk, Virginia.

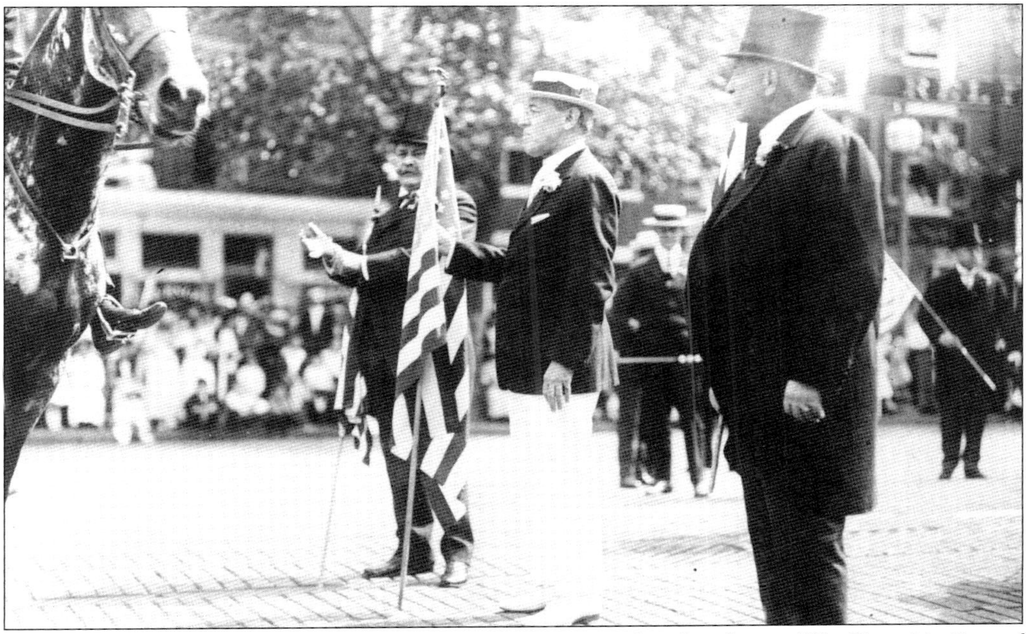

Woodrow Wilson campaigned for reelection in 1916 under the slogan "He Kept Us Out of the War," and the question of whether to join the Great War then raging in Europe—later to become World War I—divided the country. A major Preparedness Day parade on June 14, 1916, was organized by groups urging the United States to ready itself for war. Two weeks before the event, Wilson himself asked to take part in the procession. Here, he stands ready to lead 60,000 marchers up the avenue.

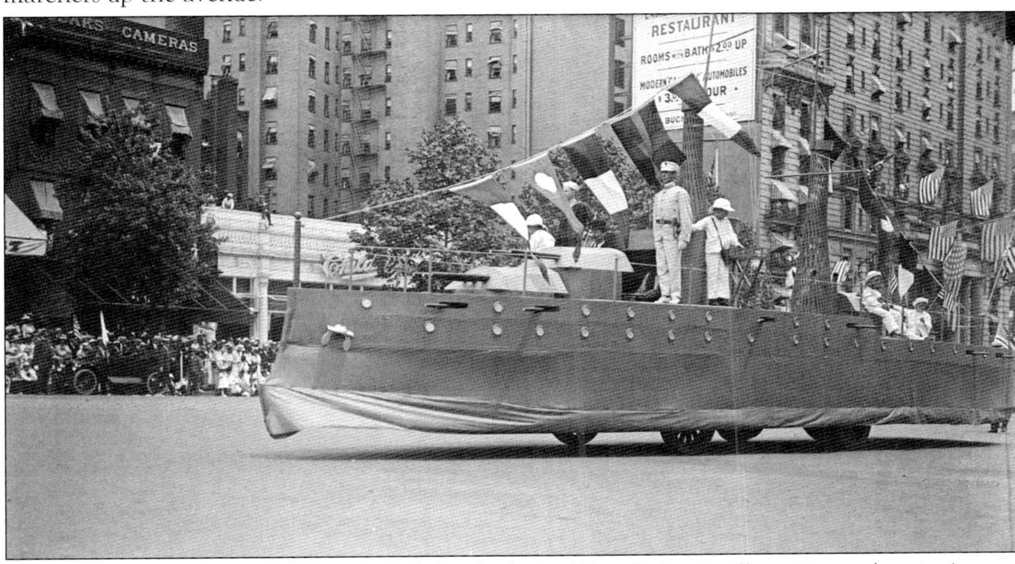

USS *Preparedness*, an elaborate wheeled, flag-bedecked "battleship," rolls up Pennsylvania Avenue past the Willard Hotel during the June 14, 1916, Preparedness Day parade. Battleships were the most expensive military items any nation could build, and each ship reflected great national pride. The float's driver, near the feet of the standing officer, cannot see ahead and is taking directions from the man in a bowler hat looking out over the turrets.

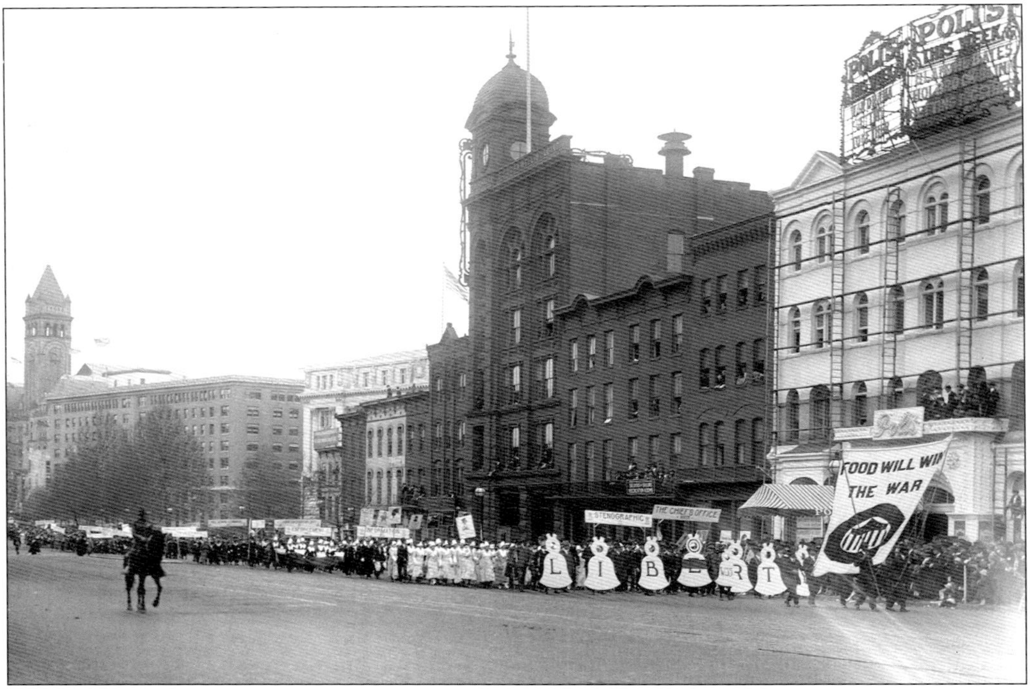

Wartime parades were not always military affairs. In 1918, a procession sponsored by the US Food Administration (USFA) readies to march. The USFA managed support for US military forces overseas and for the food reserves of allied nations. The domed building at center in the block between Fourteenth and Fifteenth Streets is the C.C. Cornwell Building, which housed the GAR's Washington offices. Poli's Theater, at far right, is showing *Getting Together*, a stage play showcasing US-Allied military cooperation.

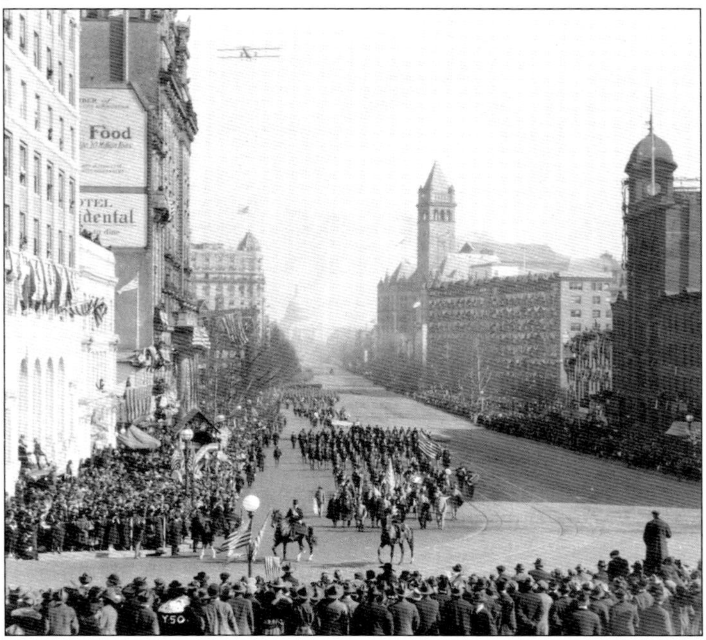

US troops in Europe began returning home within weeks of the November 1918 armistice with Germany, and by February 1919, a series of victory parades marched up Pennsylvania Avenue. This procession is turning up Fifteenth Street past the Hotel Washington just as a Martin biplane bomber passes overhead. The larger flag-bedecked building at right center is the Southern Railway Building of 1917, a new structure built after the earlier Southern Railway Building with its distinctive tower burned in 1916. (National Archives.)

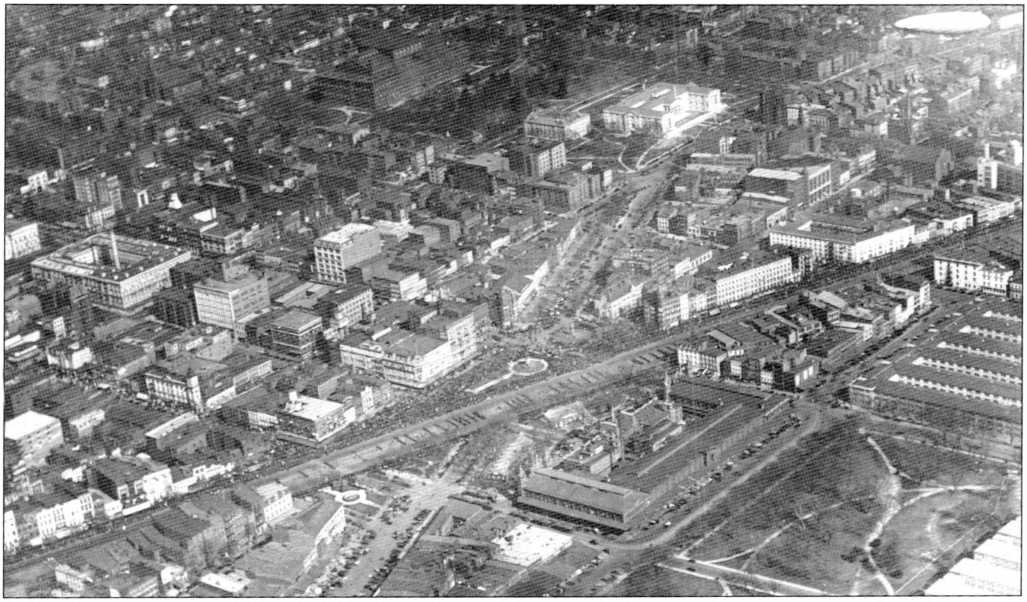

The US Army's 1st Division marches up Pennsylvania Avenue in the victory parade of February 27, 1919. This view focuses on Market Square at center, with the sprawling expanse of Center Market at lower right center. Louisiana Avenue crosses Pennsylvania Avenue leading up to the light-stone former Washington City Hall at upper right. The lower portion of Louisiana Avenue was obliterated by the Federal Triangle project, when the upper portion was renamed Ohio Avenue. Note the blimp at upper right. (US Naval History and Heritage Command.)

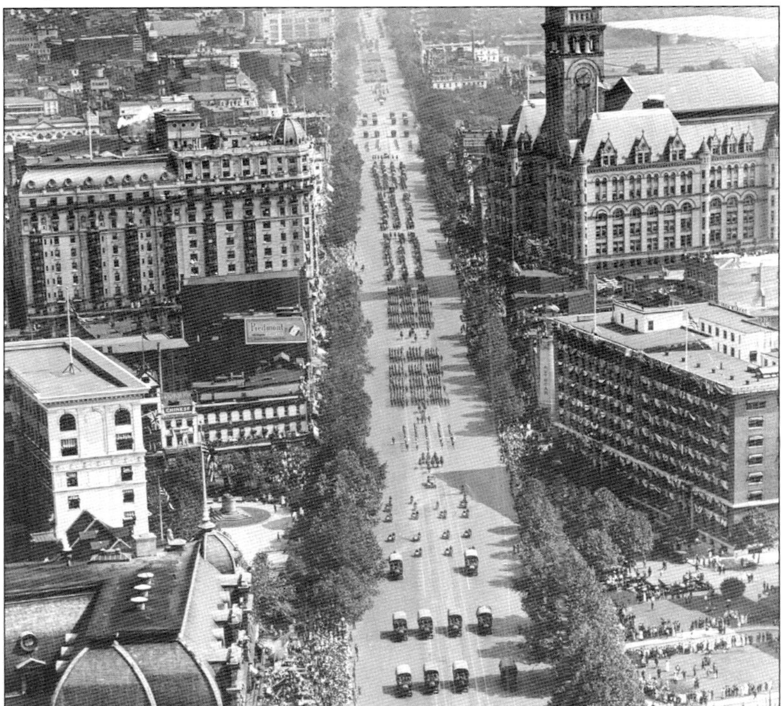

Another major military parade took place on September 17, 1919, honoring returning Gen. John Pershing, commander of US forces in Europe during World War I. Here, the procession passes between the Raleigh Hotel, at left with its distinctive cupola, and the old Post Office and Southern Railway Buildings on the right. The domed roof of the Willard Hotel is at lower left. (National Archives.)

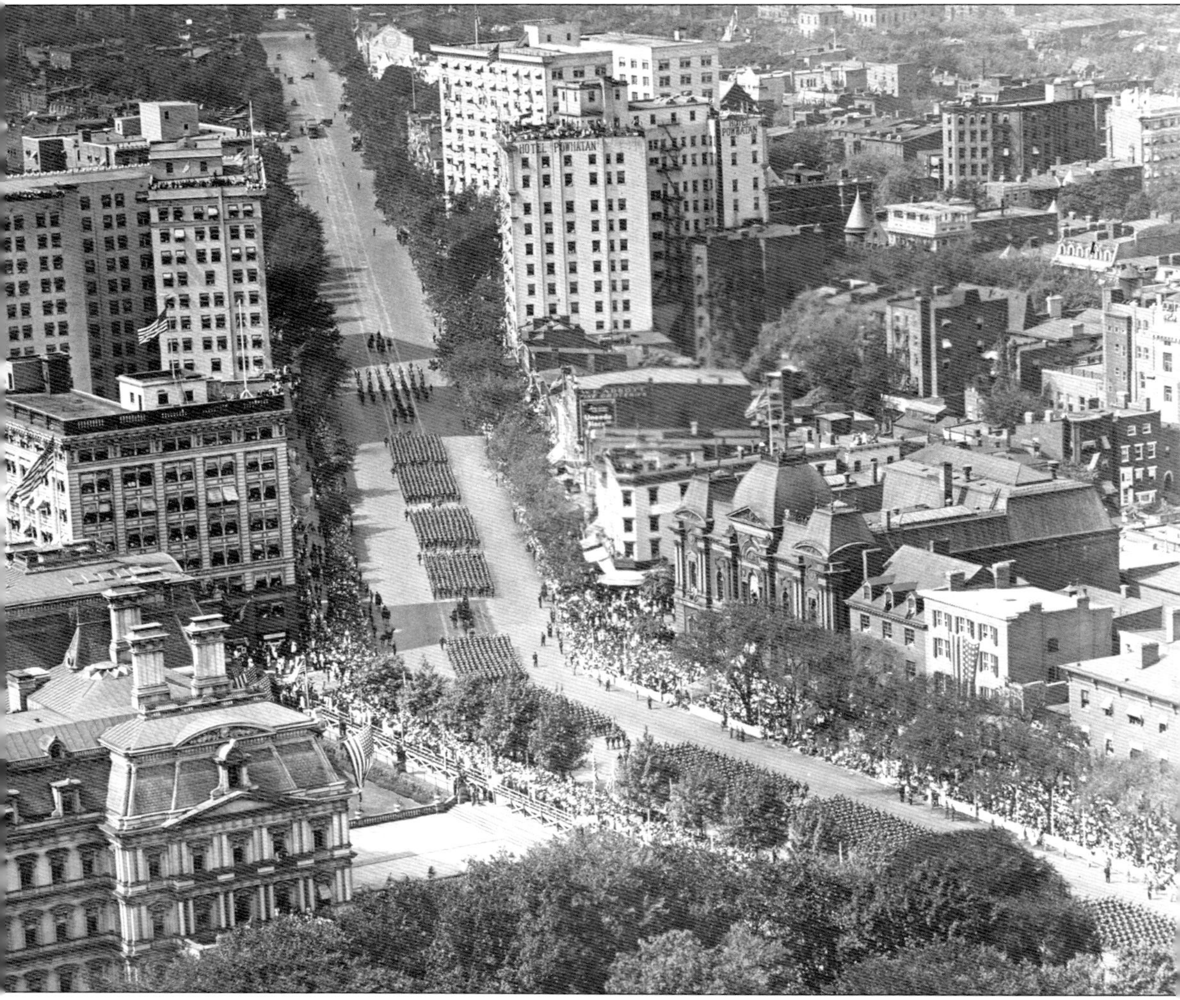

This view of the September 17, 1919, parade for General Pershing looks northwest up Pennsylvania Avenue past the White House. The portion of the avenue at lower left directly in front of the executive mansion is today known as Executive Drive. The avenue turned northwest at Seventeenth Street past the distinctive Renwick Building at right center, which opened in 1863 as the first purpose-built art museum in America. The Powhatan Hotel, at center, was built in 1911. Renamed the Roger Smith Hotel in 1938, it was razed in 1977. (National Archives.)

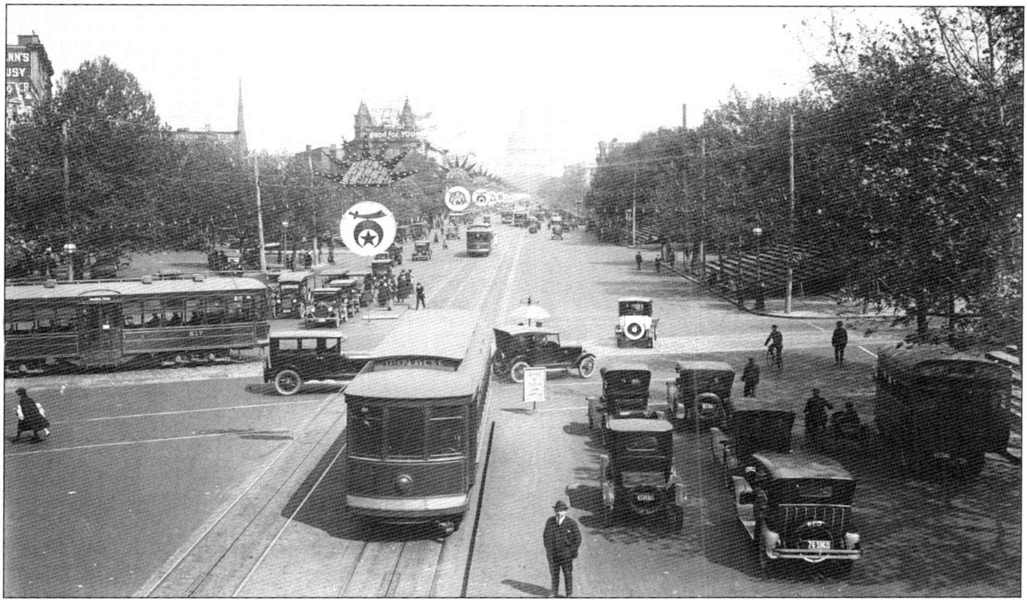

Shriners parades were for many years an annual staple on Pennsylvania Avenue. The Shriners were an outgrowth of the Freemasonry movement of fraternal organizations with an emphasis on fun, fellowship, and support for a network of children's hospitals. The Washington parades were sponsored by the Almas Temple, the Shriners lodge in the city. As seen above in 1923, the Shriners decorated the avenue for its entire length from the Capitol to Fifteenth Street and produced a festive light display in the evening. Pres. Franklin Roosevelt, himself a Mason, reviewed the 1935 parade from a special stand fitted with a brass bar FDR could use to steady himself. The Shriners have no connection to the Middle East, Egypt, or any religious group, but they regularly use Mideastern and Muslim imagery and styles, including wearing fez caps.

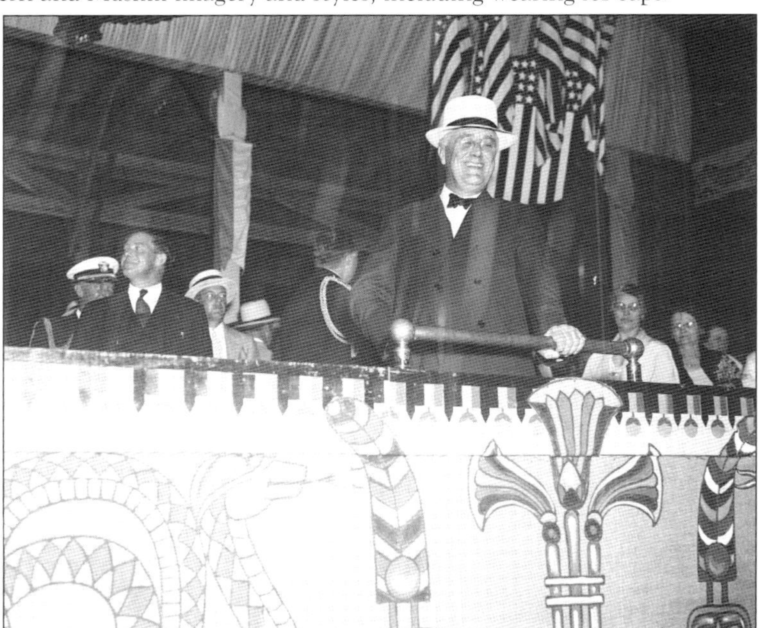

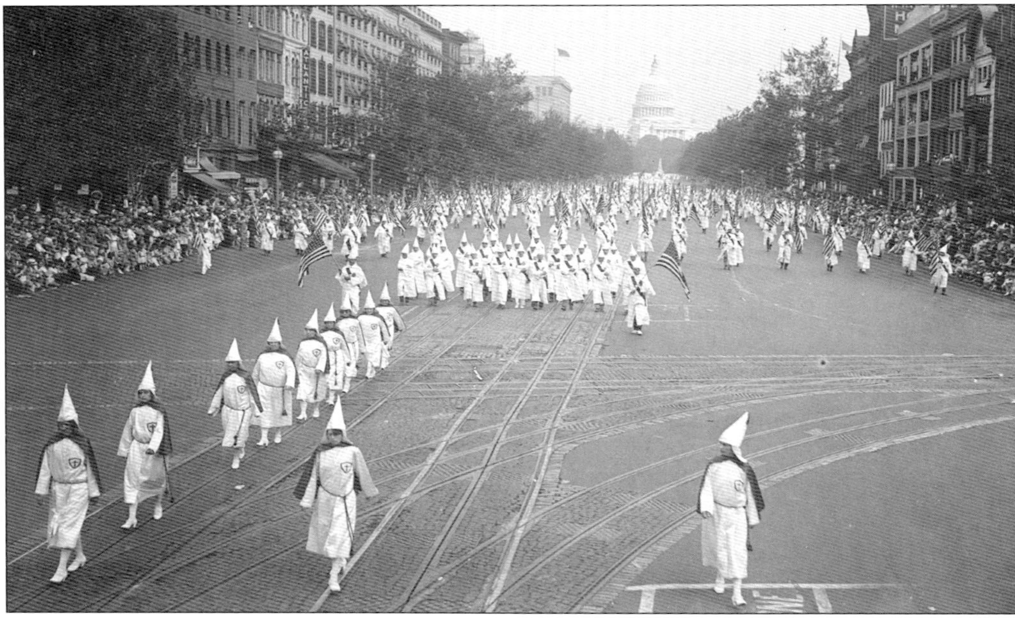

The Ku Klux Klan march down the avenue on August 8, 1925, one of the most infamous public events ever to take place in Washington. At perhaps the height of its power with well over five million members nationwide, the Klan put on a major demonstration when members uncharacteristically appeared without covering their faces, an expression of confidence that struck fear in some onlookers. More than 30,000 people took part in the demonstration—some estimates ran as high as 50,000—cheered on by a huge crowd of onlookers. The event marked a growing fear of immigrants and the urban migration of minorities from rural areas, and targeted blacks, Asians, Catholics, Jews, and other groups. African American residents of the city largely stayed out of sight during the weekend of KKK events, including a fireworks show in Arlington. Presidents Warren Harding and Calvin Coolidge each spoke out against the Klan and warned of its darker sides even as the group sought to portray itself as just another fraternal organization.

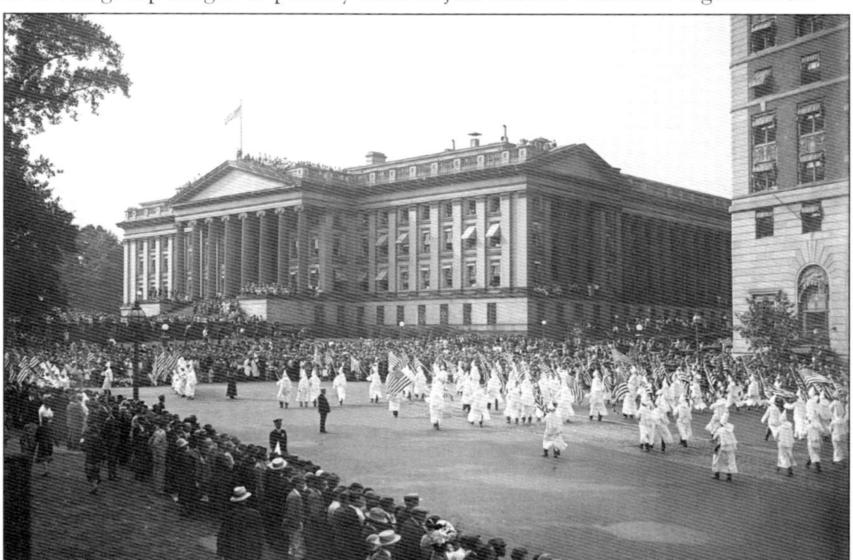

Crowds surge at Fourteenth Street and Pennsylvania Avenue on June 18, 1945, to welcome home Gen. Dwight Eisenhower, supreme commander of Allied forces in Europe, a month after the German capitulation in World War II. A huge flag and welcome banner are set up over the avenue. The gabled Washington Post Building is at center left, with the larger Munsey Building just above, and a corner of the Willard Hotel at lower left. Eisenhower would get another parade in about eight years when he moved to the White House.

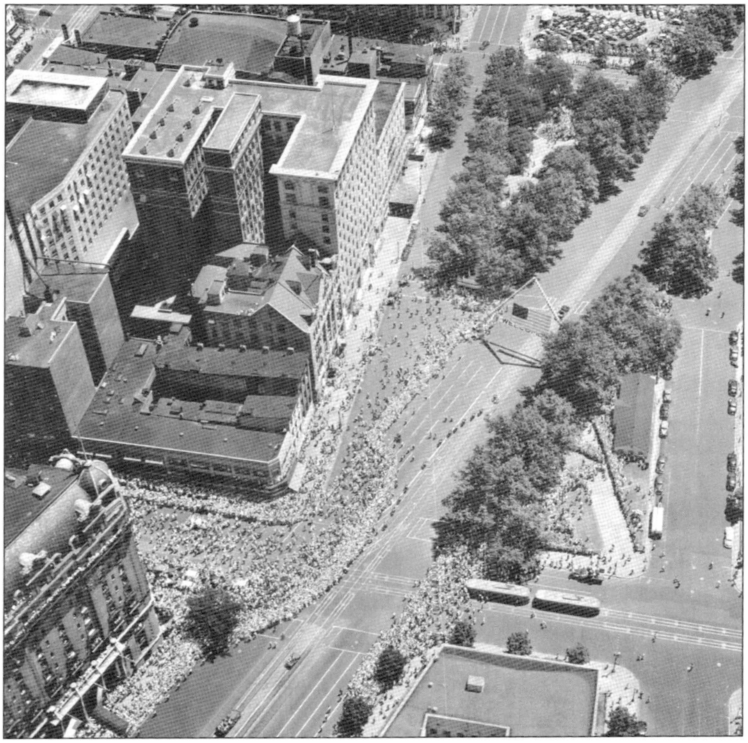

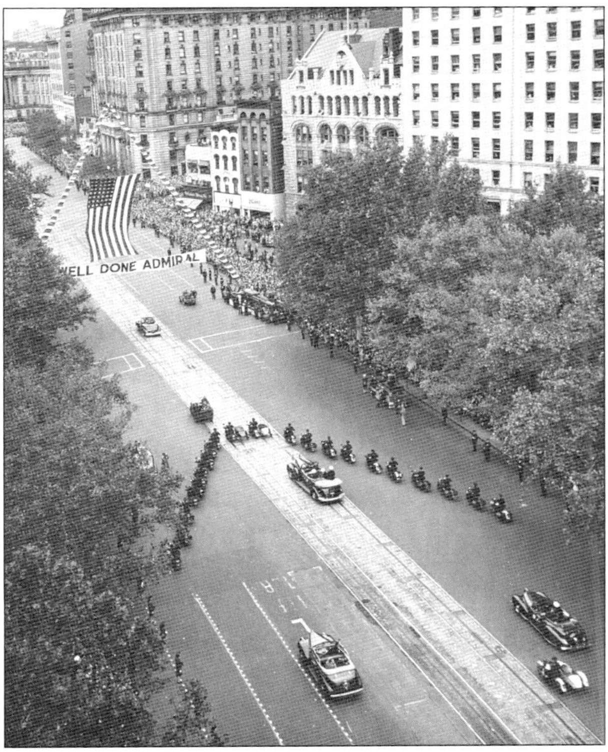

Another victory parade took place on October 5, 1945, to thank Adm. Chester Nimitz, the US Navy's overall commander in the Pacific during World War II. Nimitz was given the keys to the city and, like Eisenhower in June, passed under a large flag with a "Well Done Admiral" banner. This view shows the admiral's car passing the Munsey Building at right. The parade included many captured Japanese weapons, including tanks, vehicles, and aircraft.

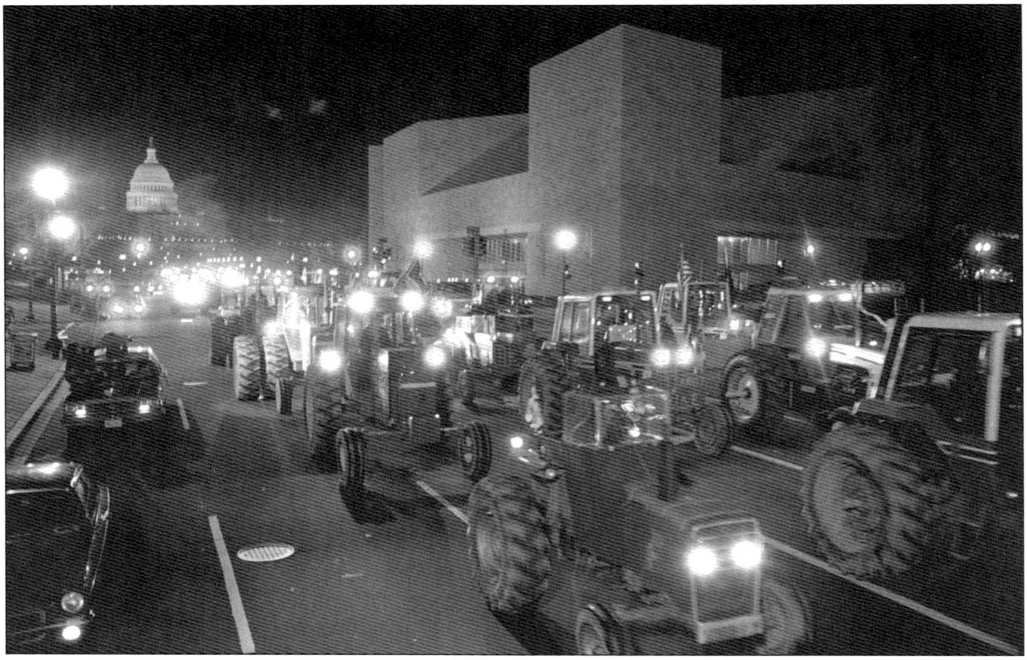

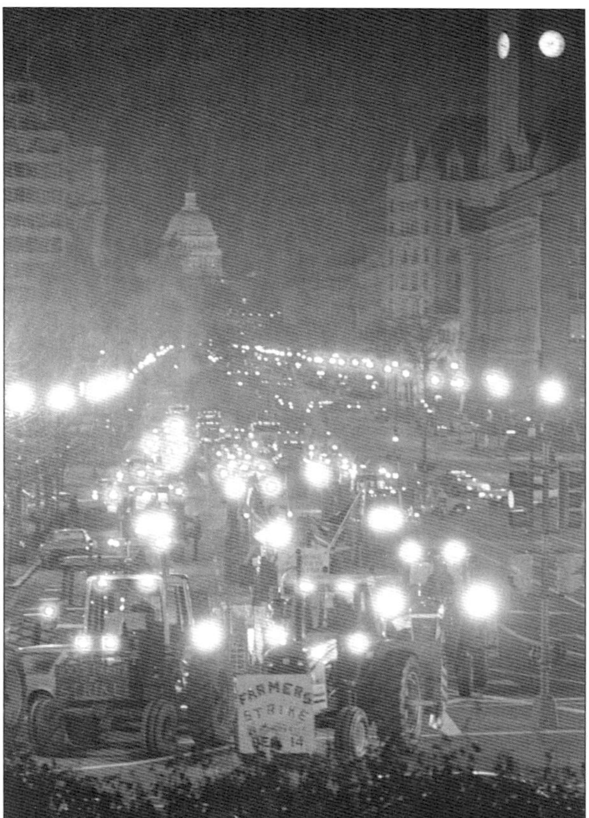

A memorable series of protests was carried out in the 1970s and 1980s by the American Agriculture Movement, which sponsored a series of farmers' demonstrations. At the heart of the issue was the future of the family farm, threatened by ever-growing corporate farms that were putting the individual farmer out of business. Hundreds of farmers drove their tractors from all over the United States to Washington to demand legislative relief from Congress. One of the early protests took place in December 1977, when several hundred tractors paraded at night down Pennsylvania Avenue to the White House. Emotions ran high as the urban city was suddenly filled with decidedly rural vehicles, highlighting what many felt was a growing disconnect between city and country dwellers. The farmers returned to protest in February 1979 but garnered immense local good will when they used their tractors to clear roads and free trapped motorists when a major blizzard struck Washington that month.

Seven

The Division, also known as Murder Bay

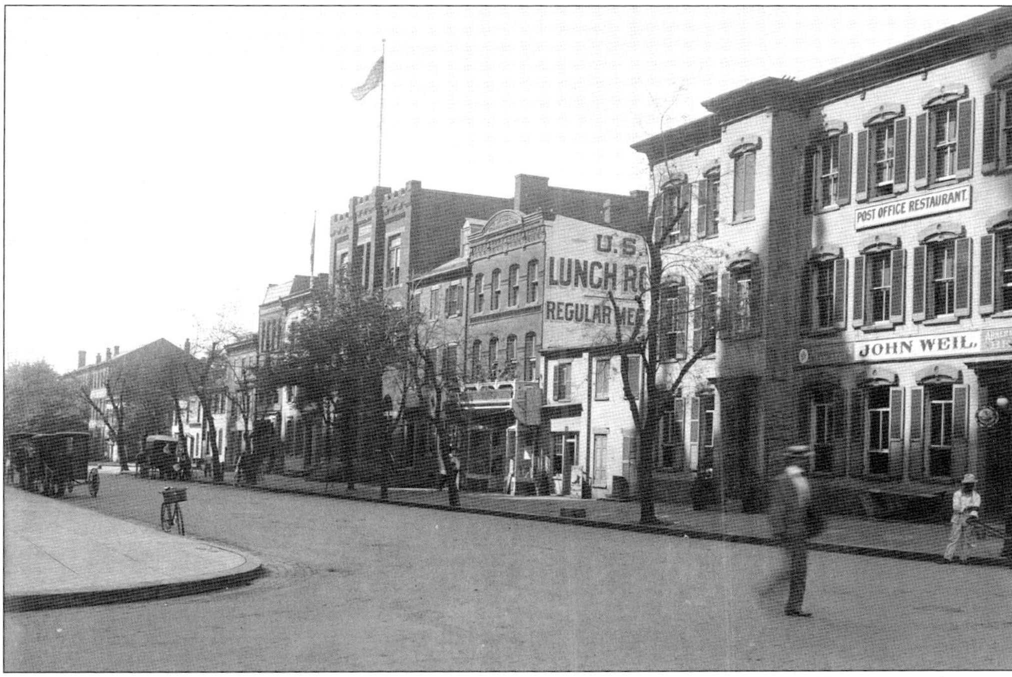

Tucked behind Pennsylvania Avenue's south side in a triangular area bounded by Fifteenth Street on the west and the Washington Canal on the south was a densely packed neighborhood that, for a time, had a well-deserved reputation as one of the most notorious red light districts in the nation. A hotbed of crime, prostitution, gambling, and drinking, "Murder Bay" thrived for about 80 years, resolutely defying periodic attempts to impose law and order. During the Civil War, the area took on another name, "Hooker's Division," when Gen. Joseph Hooker, commander of the Army of the Potomac, herded thousands of sex workers from elsewhere in the city to the strip along Fifteenth Street. Ultimately, the area became known simply as "the Division," a name that outlasted the Murder Bay moniker. The myth that women of easy virtue acquired their nickname from the general is not true—the term came into use in New York years prior to the war—but Hooker's actions heightened the neighborhood's reputation. This 1901 view looks south down Twelfth Street from the avenue. Virtually every building housed some sort of semi-illicit activity.

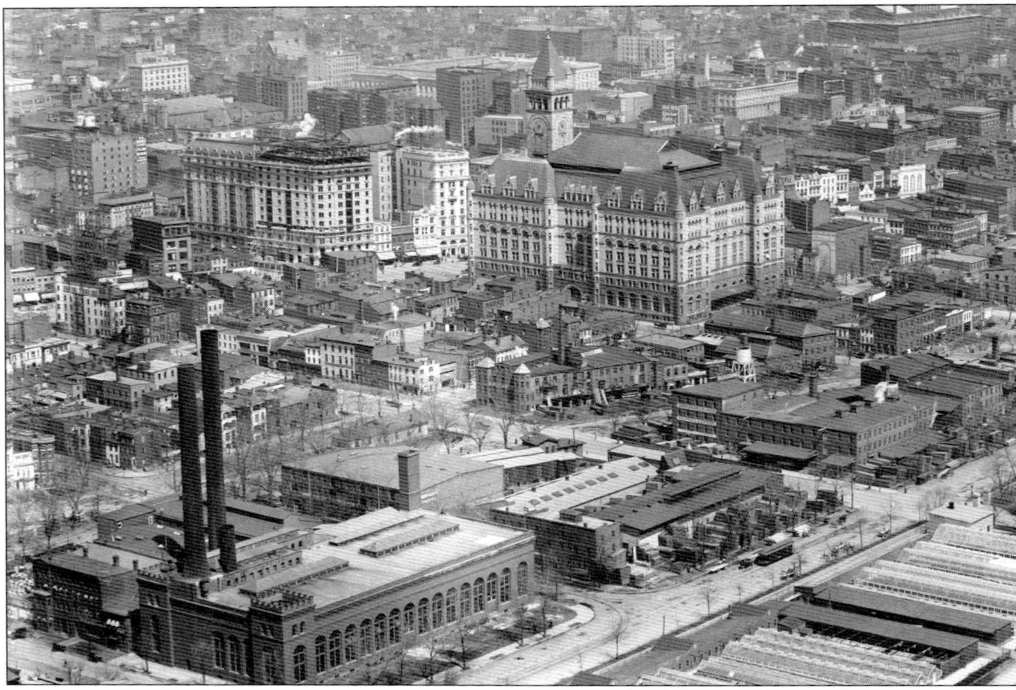

The Division neighborhood is at center in this view from the Washington Monument in about 1911. The Post Office is at center top, with the Raleigh Hotel directly across the street nearing the completion of its major rebuilding. In the foreground is an electric power plant at the corner of Fourteenth and B Streets, formerly the site of the Washington Canal and later Constitution Avenue. The neighborhood's low buildings were tightly packed in along Ohio Avenue, which ran parallel to Pennsylvania Avenue.

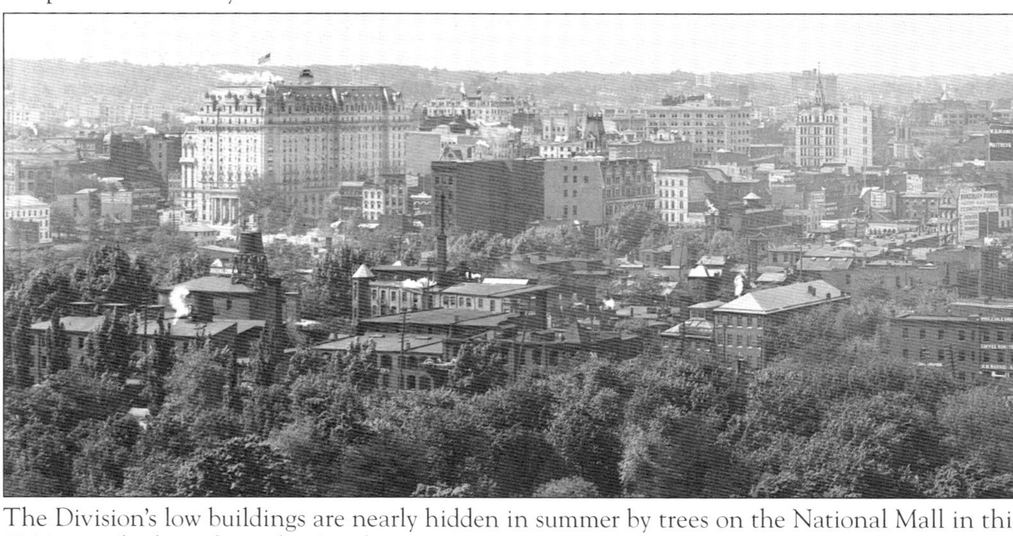

The Division's low buildings are nearly hidden in summer by trees on the National Mall in this 1904 view looking from the Smithsonian Institution's castle, with the Willard Hotel towering over its surroundings at left. By day, the Division looked like most city neighborhoods, but in the evening, its lights remained lit well into the night, and contemporary writers noted the din of hundreds of pianos belting out ragtime tunes.

WITHIN SIGHT OF THE WHITE HOUSE.

Section of Washington, D. C., Known as "Hooker's Division," Which Contains 50 Saloons and 109 Bawdy-Houses—List of 61 Places Where Liquor Is Sold With Government But Without City Licenses.

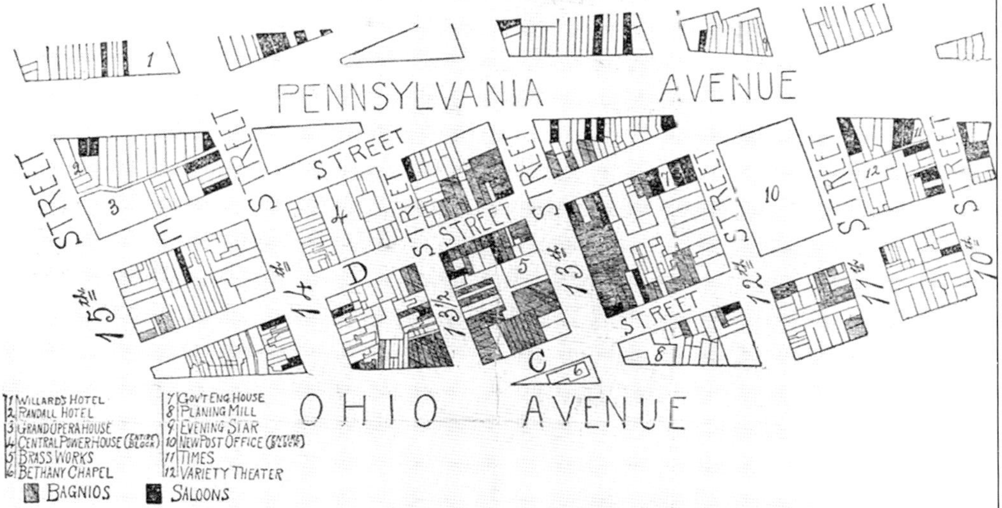

The territory indicated by the accompanying diagram is in Washington, D. C., and is known as "Hooker's Division." During the Civil War it was occupied by the camp of General Joe Hooker's troops in their defense of Washington. Since then it has become the plague spot of Washington, a center of vice, liquor-selling, and prostitution, such as is characteristic of all High-License cities. It is in the very heart of the city, extending along Pennsylvania avenue to the United States treasury. The four daily papers of the city, *Post*, *Star*, *Times*, and *News*, are published in this teritrory. Within its borders are the leading banks, opera-houses, and hotels.

This district alone contains 109 regular houses of prostitution, exclusive of assignation-houses, 31 of which are in the single block surrounded by C, D, 13th and 13½ streets northwest. Besides this there are an even 50 saloons, most of them run directly in connection with bawdy-houses.

Each one of these 109 houses of prostitution sells liquors openly and freely every day, and not a single one pays the $400 local license. There are 61 bawdy-houses in this district which hold Federal permits, while the other 48 pay no license whatever. They not only defy every provision of the High-License law, but they refuse to pay the Government license as well.

Grover Cleveland can sit in his bedroom window at the White House and survey this entire territory. He is within sight and gunshot of each of these 109 dens which defy the laws which he is supposed to execute through his commissioners. The following is a list of 61 persons in this district and their addresses who are selling liquor under Federal permits and who do not pay the $400 High-License:

Kate Anderson, 1431 D, N. W.; Mrs. May Albert, 300 11th; Ray Astor, 406 13th, N. W.; Ida Bronson, 217 10th N. W.; Kate W. Brown, 1208 D; Lulu Burke, 214 11th; Mrs. K. T. Crowley, 313 13th; Nannie Coles, 1207 C; Alice Curry, 1215 C.; Sarah Carter, 325 13th; Maud Conant, 305 13½; Sarah Chesley, 311 13th; Emma Coleman, 309 13th; Maud Duval, 404 13th; Ida Drury, 1222 D, N. W.; Bessie Edmondson, 310 13th; Grace Emerson, 1353 Ohio; Grace Furguson, 1309 C; May Fitzpatrick, 1340 14th; May Fitzgerald; Willie Gilmore, 401 13th; Cora Graham, 401 15th, removed to 1428 C street; Mary Gray, 326 13th, N. W.; Daisy Grey, 321 13th; Annie Hester, 1317 D; Mabel Haynes, 1307 C; Fannie Hill, 314 13½, N. W.; May Howard, 1222 C, N. W.; Jennie Javins, 1225 C, N. W.; Lizzie Jones, 1106 C, N. W.; Kate Lott, 1209 C; Josie Jong, 1315 D, N. W.; Nellie Larue 412 13th; Alice Linden, 312 13th; Mary Milovich, 1313 C; Edith Bertha May, 1304 D; Gertie Peterson, 1357 Ohio; Lou Roberts, 301 13½; Ellen Reynolds, 307 13th; Belle Saville, 1213 C; Gussie Smith, 1214 C; Blanche Mc Coy, 1310 D, N. W.; Ella Monroe, 1433 D, N. W.; Victoria McClellan, 1355 Ohio; Rosie Moore, 1116 C.; Anna Murphy, 1219 C; Dora L. Marion, 326 13, N. W.; Ida Nightingale, 322 13½; Bell Norris, 1424 C, N. W.; Lena Ordway, 1223 D.; Lizzie Peterson, 1309 D.; Sadie Street, 1226 D; Blanche Snow, 1114 C; Miss H. Stewert, 328 13th; Bertie Stokes, 301 13th; Mellie Turner, 305 13th; Minnie Thompson, 1217 C.; Lottie Tilford, 212 11th; Josie West, 1220 C; Nellie Wallace; 1211 C; Eva White, 306 13th.

A newspaper account and map from 1893 shows the Division jammed with brothels and bars at a time when prostitution in the District was not illegal. This article was in conjunction with an effort to clean up the neighborhood by requiring $400 "high-licenses" to sell alcohol, an effort that did not meet with much success. The story notes that in the Division alone, there were 109 houses of prostitution and 50 saloons, and it mentions that Pres. Grover Cleveland was "within sight and gunshot" of the neighborhood.

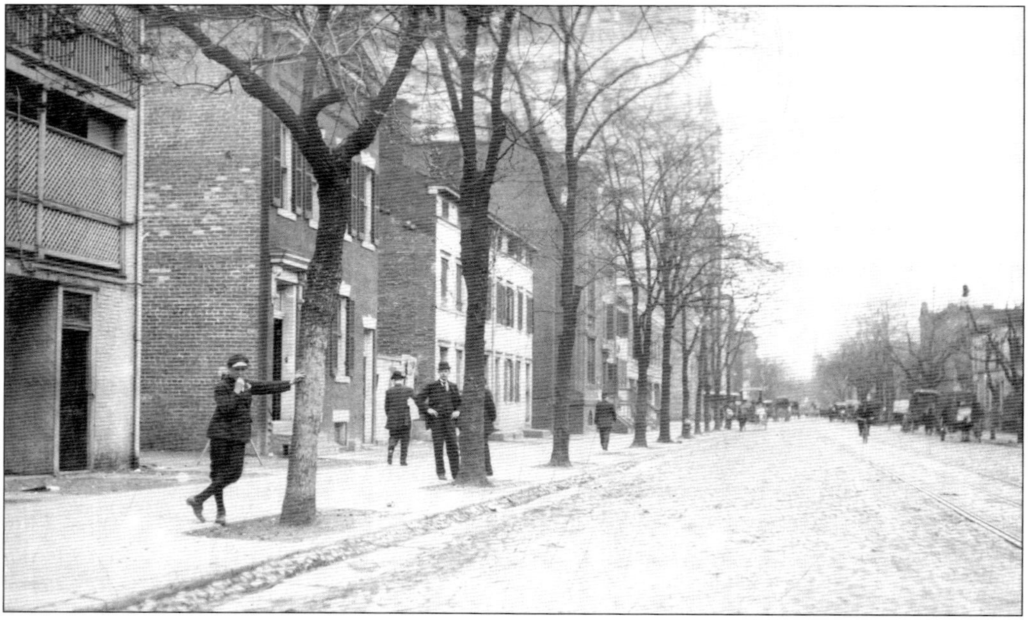

In the foreground of both of these photographs taken by Lewis Wickes Hine in April 1912 is Griffin Veatch, a bicycle messenger claiming to be 17 years of age. Hine, who advocated against child labor and worked to document young workers in the city, said Veatch told him he had been working as a messenger since age 11. He is seen above along C Street in the Division, with the Post Office Building looming down the street. The view below is along Ohio Avenue near Fourteenth Street. In addition to brothels and saloons, the Murder Bay neighborhood also featured dozens of gambling houses offering faro games. Much more popular than poker in the 19th century, faro was often referred to as "bucking the tiger," and many of these buildings advertised the game simply with a picture of a tiger in the window. A Bicycle playing cards history noted that during the Civil War, there were more than 150 gambling houses in Washington, "and Faro was the principal attraction in every one of them."

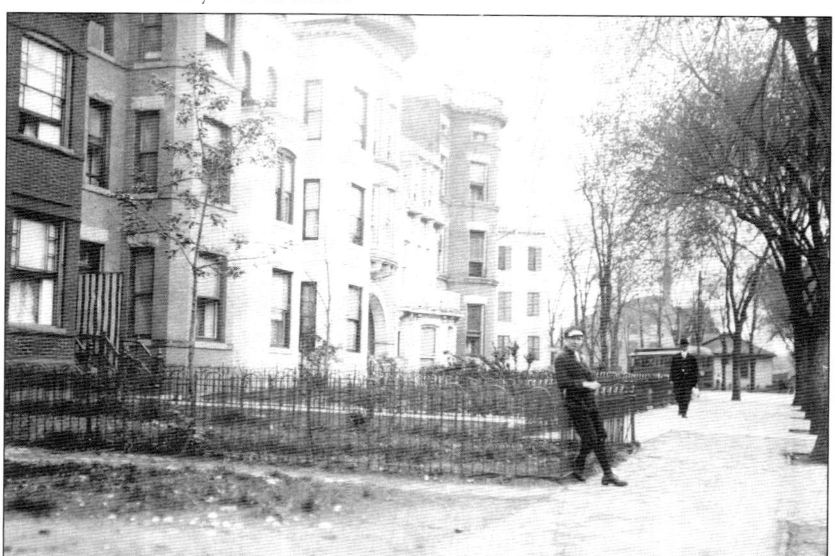

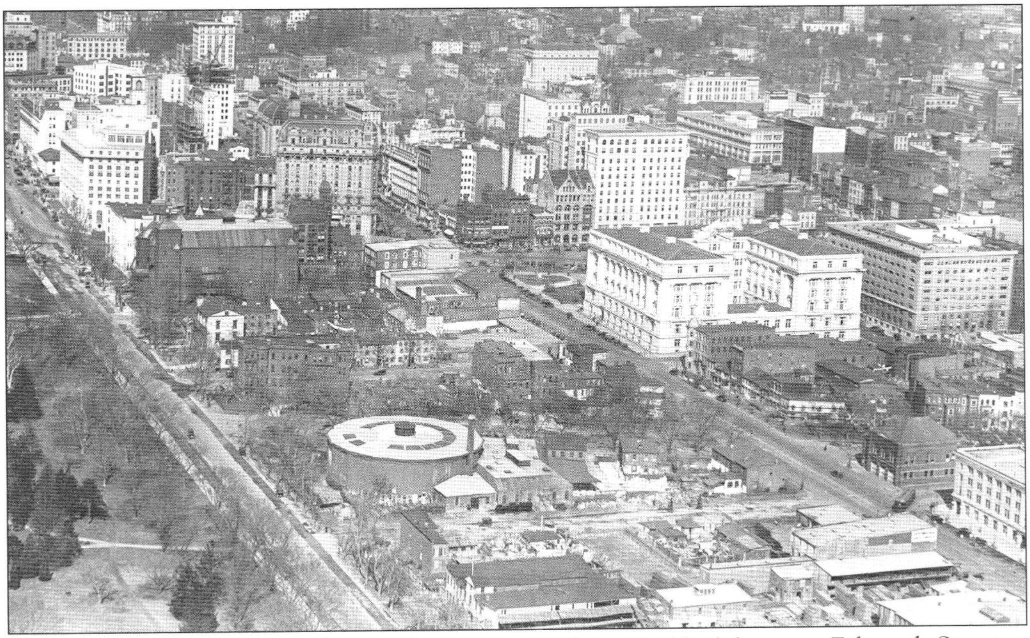

This 1918 view from the Washington Monument looks at the block between Fifteenth Street at left and Fourteenth Street. Ohio Avenue runs diagonally through the Division just above the circular wooden cyclorama building at Fifteenth and C Streets. When General Hooker created the Division during the Civil War, both sides of Fifteenth Street were populated, but the west side was cleared in the 1870s to create what became the Ellipse.

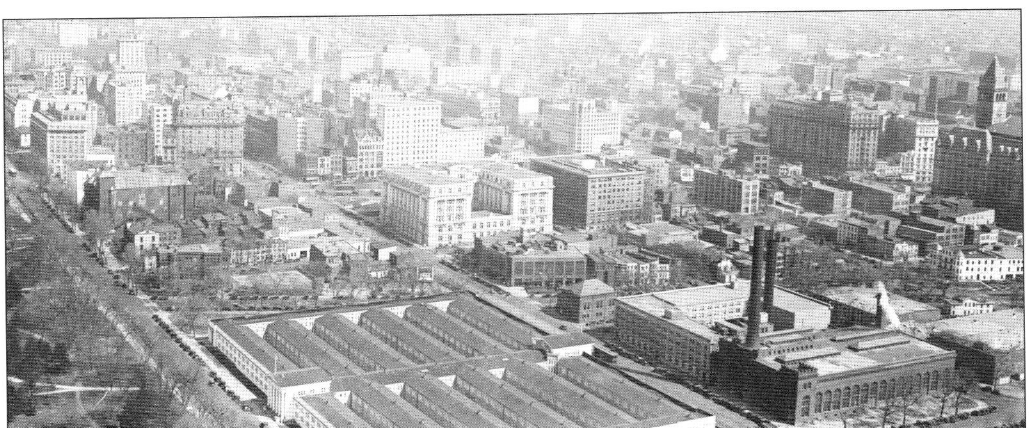

A similar view from 1925 shows the cyclorama building and the structures around it replaced with a series of temporary office buildings erected during World War I. Prostitution, always semi-illegal, was finally outlawed in the District of Columbia in 1914, and when alcohol consumption was outlawed in the city in November 1917, the Division's days were numbered. The neighborhood was virtually a slum by the time of this photograph.

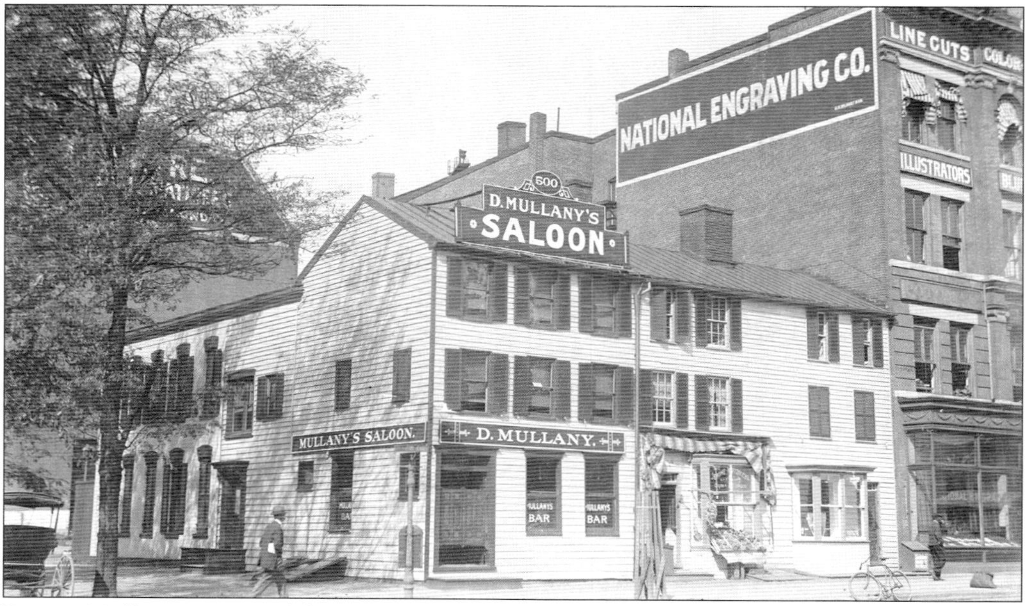

Dennis Mullany ran one of the most famous saloons in Washington on the corner of Fourteenth and E Streets in the Division. Despite its modest size, the establishment drew a wide variety of government and public men, journalists, writers, artists, theatrical actors and producers, and racing enthusiasts, crowding into a place where half the floor by the bar was filled with barrels of liquor. One of the saloon's many creations was the Mamie Taylor cocktail, named for a famous opera singer.

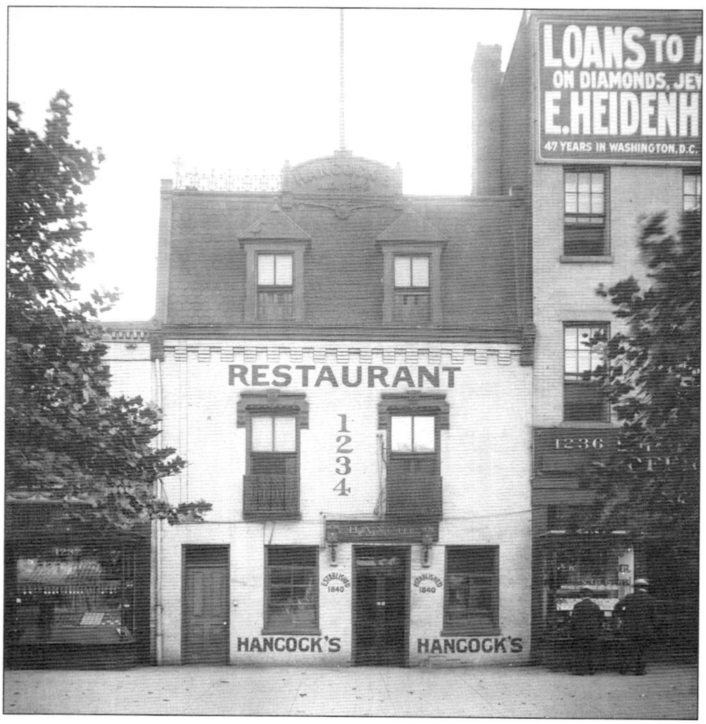

Another modest establishment with a national reputation was Hancock's Restaurant, on Pennsylvania Avenue between Twelfth and Thirteenth Streets, seen in 1913. Three generations of Hancocks ran the business at this location beginning in 1840. Author George Rothwell Brown wrote, "there never was a place in all the world where the art of making cocktails and frying chicken was raised to a higher perfection." The interior was filled with quirky yet authentic memorabilia, including a promissory note from Alexander Hamilton and the shoes Abraham Lincoln wore when he was assassinated.

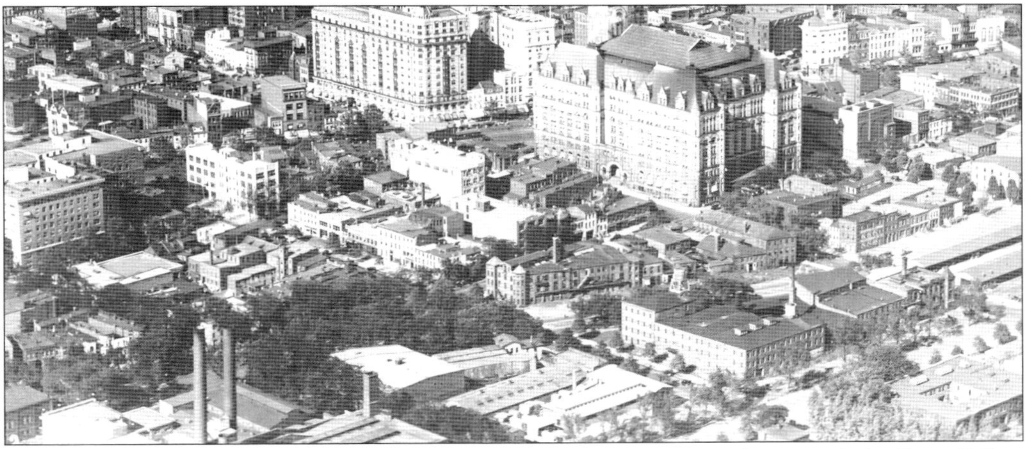

This aerial view from 1921 looks down at the Division's eastern side around the Post Office Building. With only a few exceptions, the jumble of low buildings in Murder Bay withstood serious development for 60 years following the Civil War, but with an economy largely fueled by alcohol consumption, its many business owners warily watched the national debate over Prohibition. Alcohol consumption was made illegal in the District on November 1, 1917, and most of the neighborhood's saloons were already out of business by the time the rest of the nation went dry on January 17, 1920. (National Archives.)

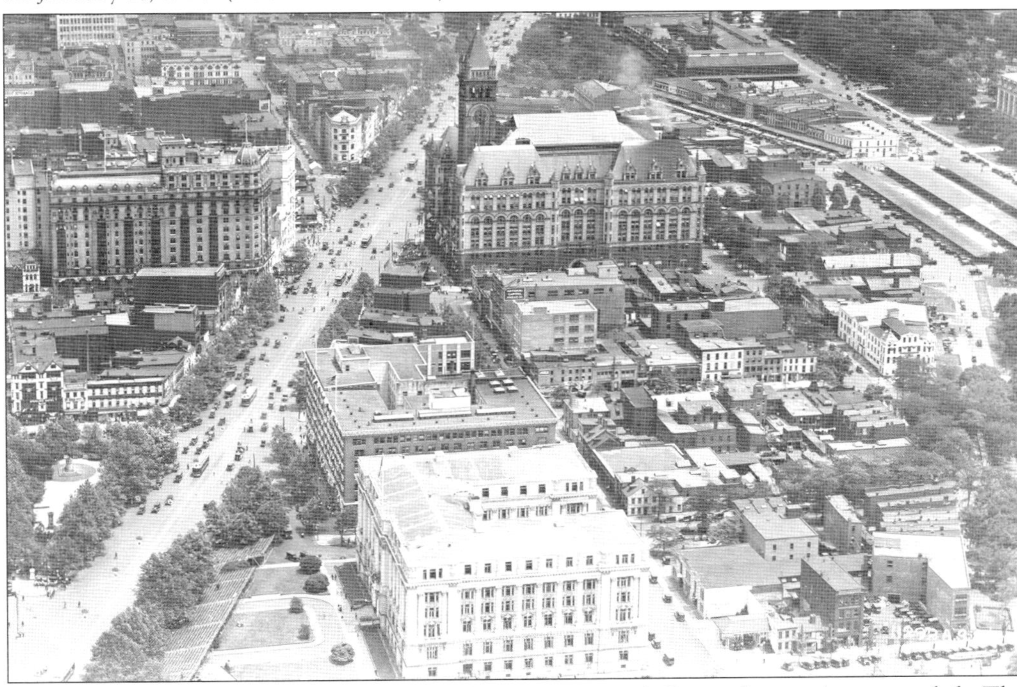

This view looks east over the District Building in 1923, with Pennsylvania Avenue at left. The diagonal street in the Division at far right is Ohio Avenue, leading to large commercial distribution sheds between Eleventh and Twelfth Streets along B Street (Constitution Avenue). At upper right, Louisiana Avenue reflects Ohio Avenue's angle and leads up past Center Market. This stretch of Louisiana Avenue and all of Ohio Avenue were obliterated when the Division was razed, and what was left of Louisiana Avenue was renamed Ohio Avenue. (National Archives.)

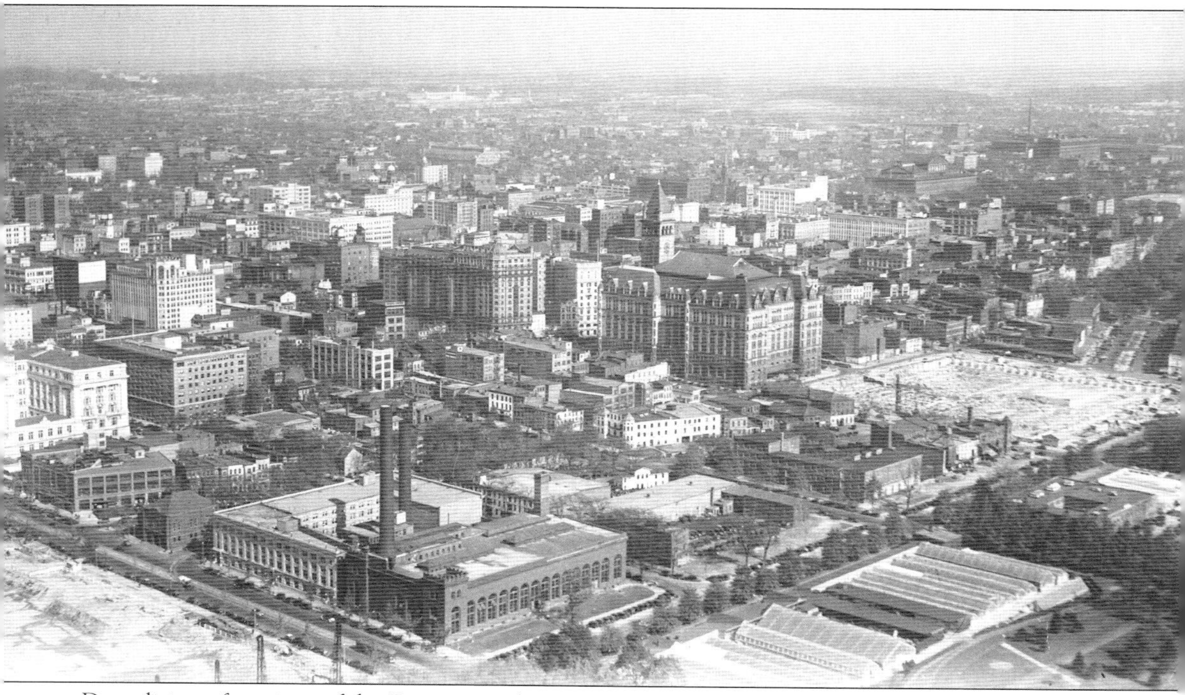

Demolition of sections of the Division and construction of the Federal Triangle had already begun when this photograph was taken in 1928. Land for the new Commerce Department Building has been cleared along Fourteenth Street at lower left, while at right, the foundation has been laid for the Internal Revenue Service Building in the space between Twelfth and Tenth Streets and C and B Streets. Within a few years, most of the buildings in the foreground would be gone. (National Archives.)

Eight

The Feds Take Over

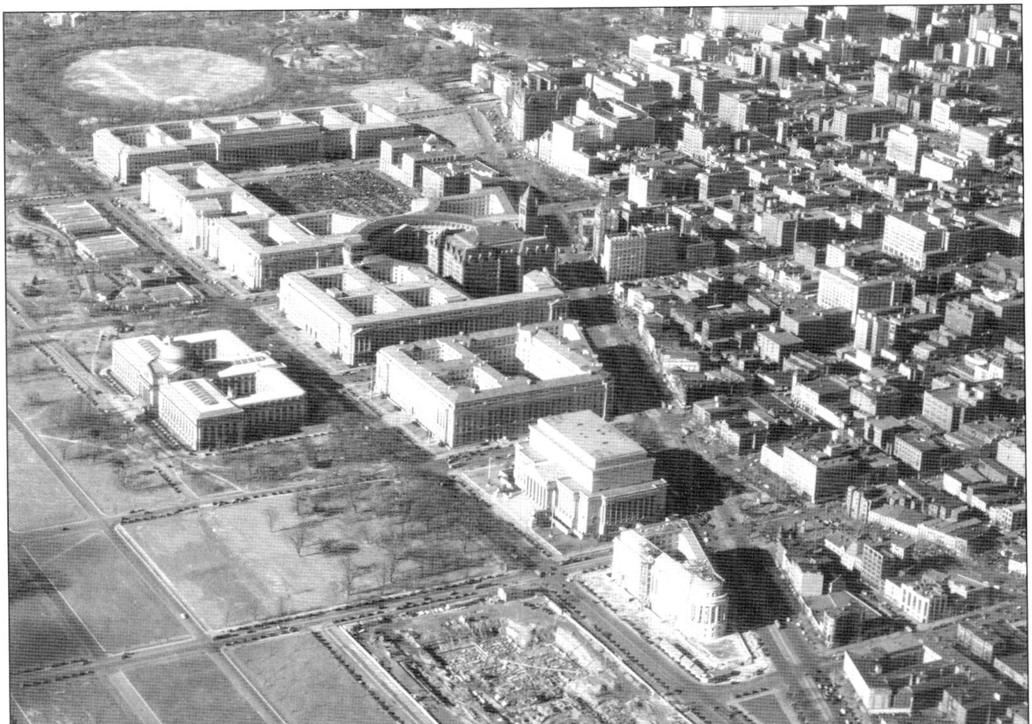

Creation of the Federal Triangle was perhaps the most dramatic change to hit Pennsylvania Avenue. In under a decade, all but three buildings on the avenue's south side were demolished, swept away and replaced by a wholly new complex of immense, monumental federal buildings. Gone were Murder Bay and the Division, Center Market, Chinatown, restaurants, hotels, theaters, and neighborhood stores. While much of the north side remained, the character of the street was permanently altered. The project was driven by several factors, beginning with a 1902 report from the Senate Park Commission, also known as the McMillan Commission, to clear the National Mall and bring order to the chaotic development around it. The enormous growth of the government during the war years of 1917 and 1918 pointed to the urgent need for more suitable housing for many federal departments. And the deteriorating slum of the Division had become an eyesore that many wished would go away. The 1926 Public Buildings Act paved the way for what became the country's largest public buildings construction program, seen here nearly complete in December 1937. (National Archives.)

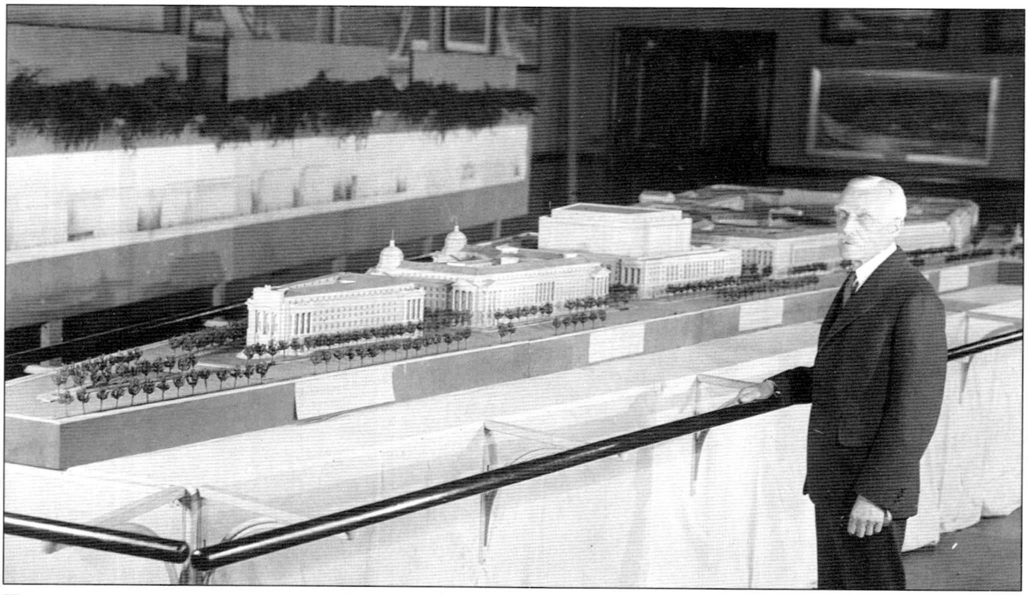

Treasury secretary Andrew Mellon, head of a government commission overseeing the Federal Triangle development, poses with a model of the project on April 27, 1929, ready for inspection by Pres. Herbert Hoover. The model shows many differences with the completed version and illustrates how the commission planned to raze all existing buildings in the triangle. In the end, the Old Post Office and Southern Railway Buildings were the sole survivors from pre-Triangle days.

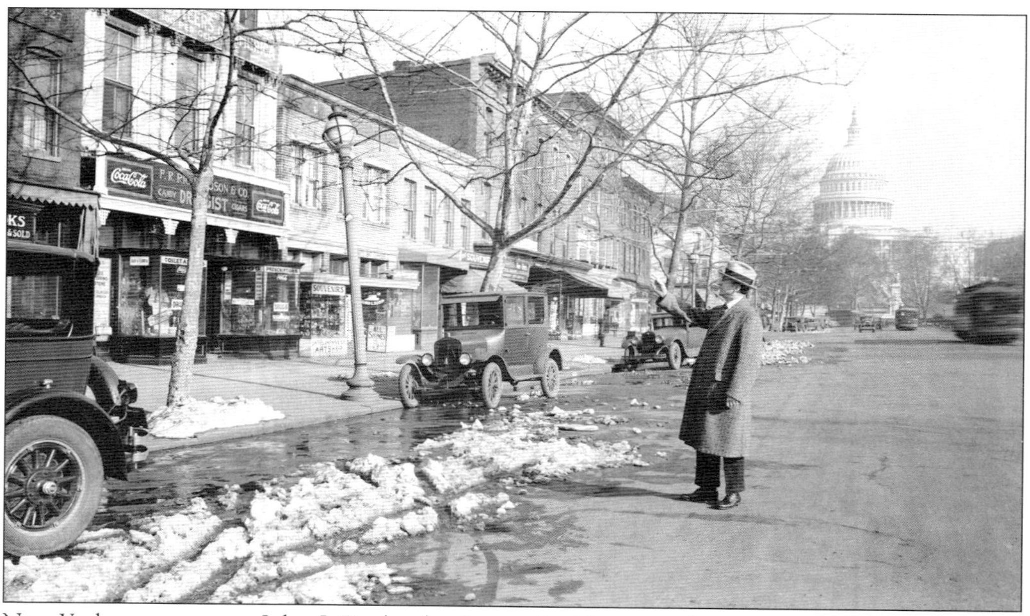

New York congressman John J. Boyland points to buildings on the avenue's north side between Second and Third Streets that would be razed as part of the plan to clear land close to the Capitol and next to the National Mall for the Federal Triangle. This view from February 16, 1926, shows the urban nature of the block, which was among the first to develop along the avenue. In a few years, all these buildings were gone, replaced by open land.

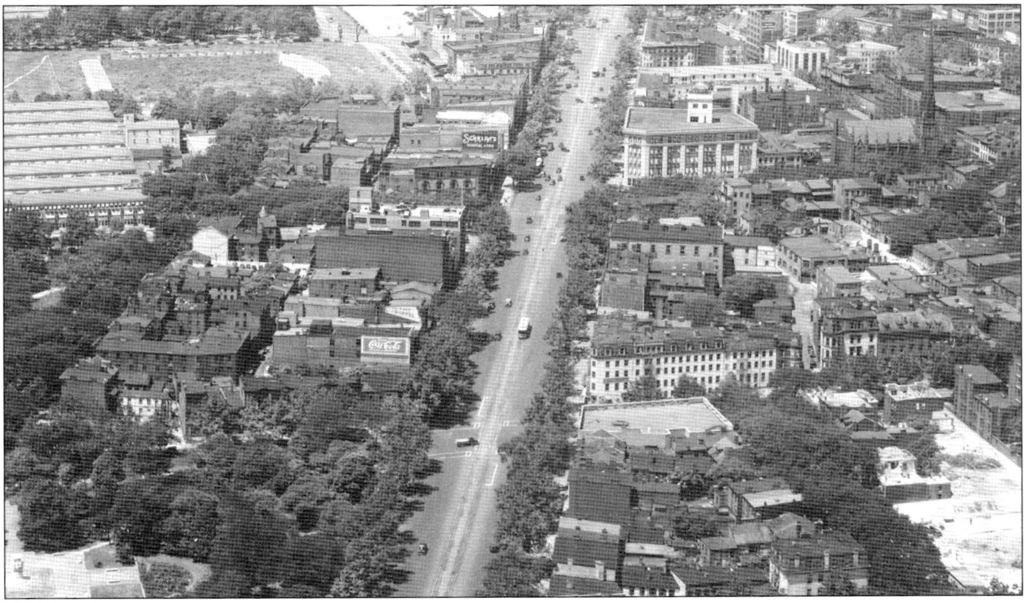

The lower avenue around Second and Third Streets is seen in July 1931 shortly before demolition. Washington's Chinatown was situated largely in the jumble of buildings at left. The community was greatly enlarged in the 1880s as Chinese immigrants fled anti-Chinese disturbances on the West Coast, and its residents operated many of the laundries, drugstores, and Chinese restaurants on the avenue. The community resisted relocation, but federal authorities negotiated a move to a formerly German neighborhood around Seventh and H Streets NW. (National Archives.)

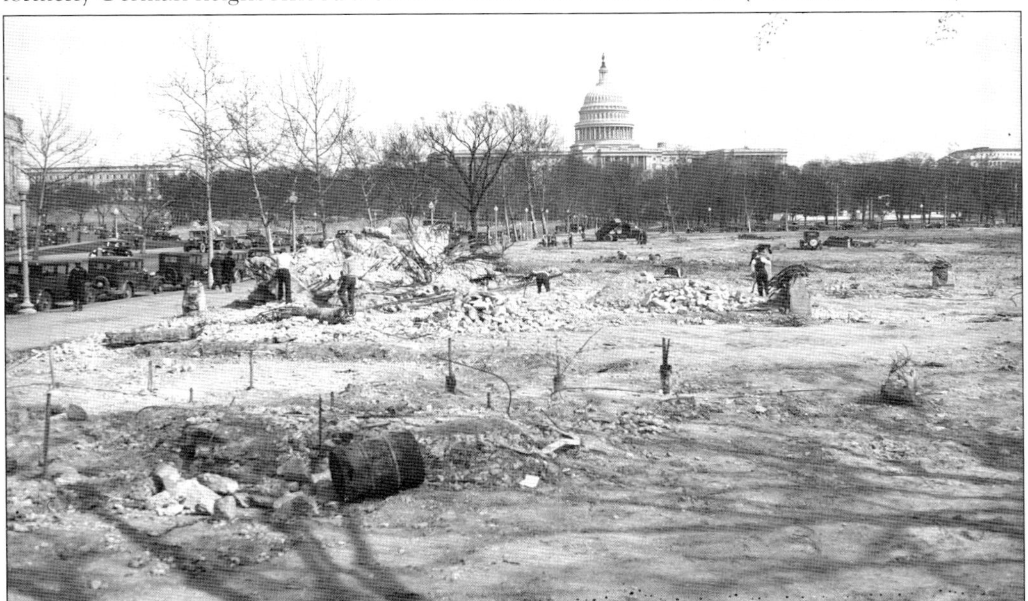

The remains of Chinatown are in the last stages of being hauled away in 1935. The north side of Pennsylvania Avenue at left is already clear. The space between Fourth and Seventh Streets became the site of the new National Gallery of Art, while the block between Third and Fourth Streets lay empty for some years before construction of the museum's trapezoidal East Building in the 1970s.

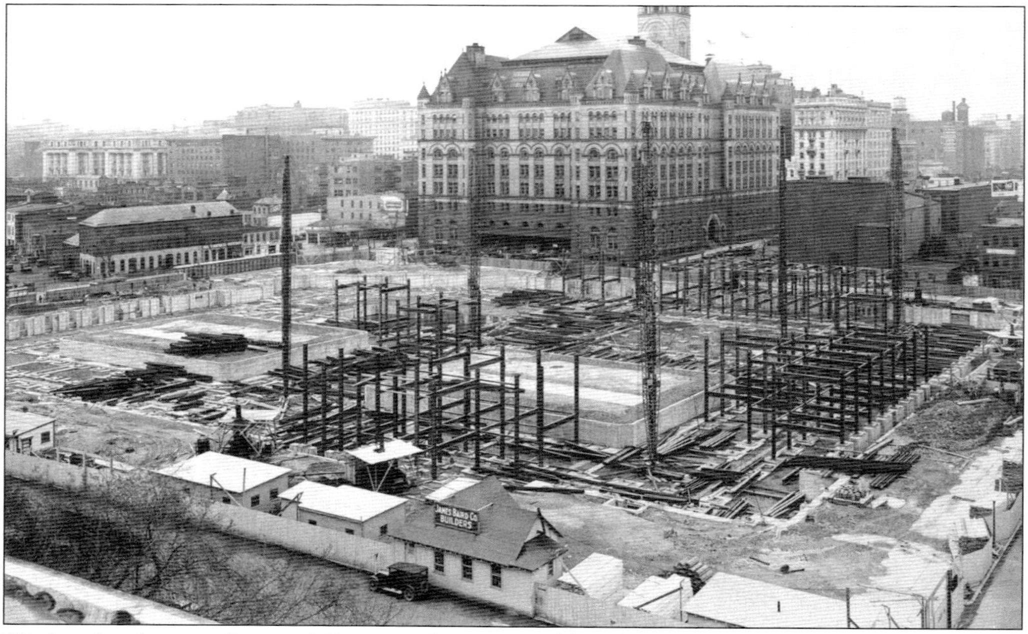

Girders for the new Internal Revenue Service Building begin to rise in this view from April 1929. Construction of the Federal Triangle began with the Commerce Department Building along Fifteenth Street, followed closely by the IRS Building between Tenth and Twelfth Streets next to the Old Post Office Building, which in only a few years would be nearly obscured by the massive structures built around it. At far left center, a slice of Ohio Avenue can still be seen, soon to be obliterated.

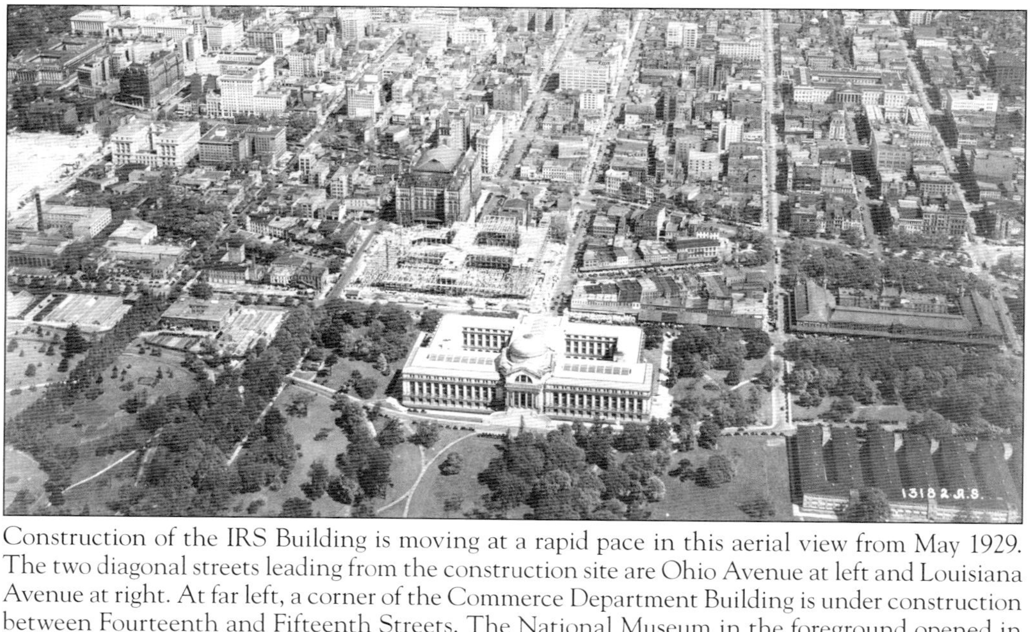

Construction of the IRS Building is moving at a rapid pace in this aerial view from May 1929. The two diagonal streets leading from the construction site are Ohio Avenue at left and Louisiana Avenue at right. At far left, a corner of the Commerce Department Building is under construction between Fourteenth and Fifteenth Streets. The National Museum in the foreground opened in 1910 to house the Smithsonian Institution's art, culture, history, and natural history collections but was dedicated solely to natural history after 1969. (National Archives.)

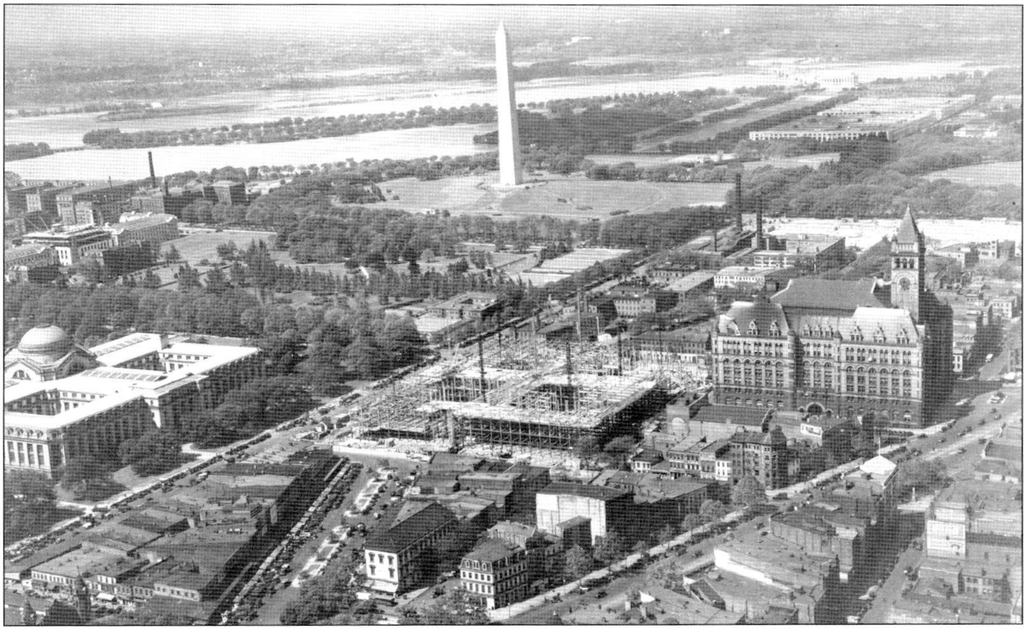

A different perspective from May 1929 shows the proximity of the Federal Triangle to the National Mall and the Washington Monument. Constitution Avenue—then known as B Street and formerly the location of the Washington Canal—is the main road at center between the Mall and the Division, with the new IRS Building. The existence of the canal gave rise to the early neighborhood name of Murder Bay, while the land south of it was once known as "the Island." (National Archives.)

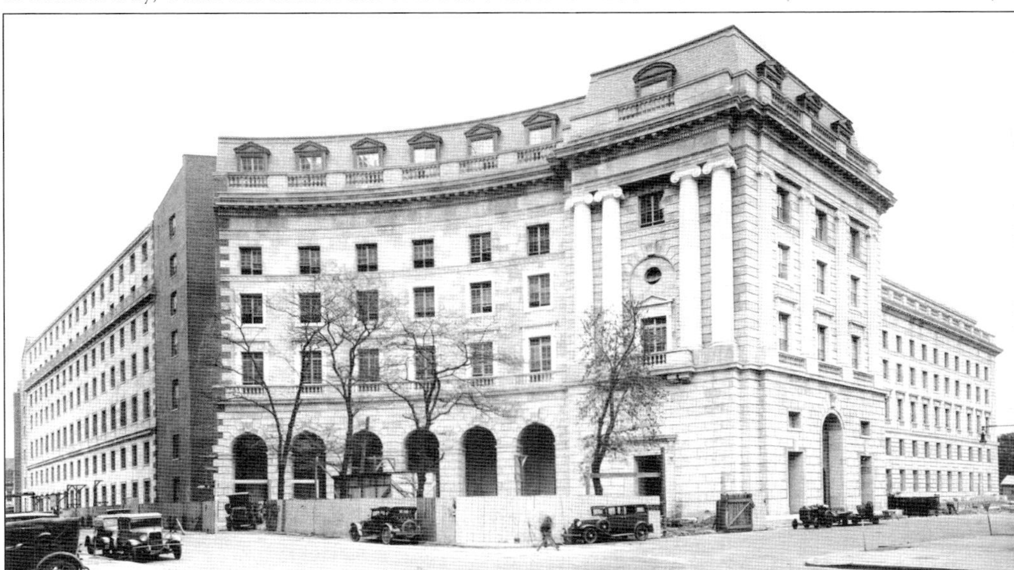

The exterior of the new Internal Revenue Service Building is virtually complete in this May 1930 view of the building's corner at Twelfth and C Streets, although finishing touches on the interior would continue to be made for several more years. The design of the buildings of the Federal Triangle was meant to evoke various classical architecture motifs, including Italian Renaissance, Classical Greek, Beaux-Arts, and even Art Deco.

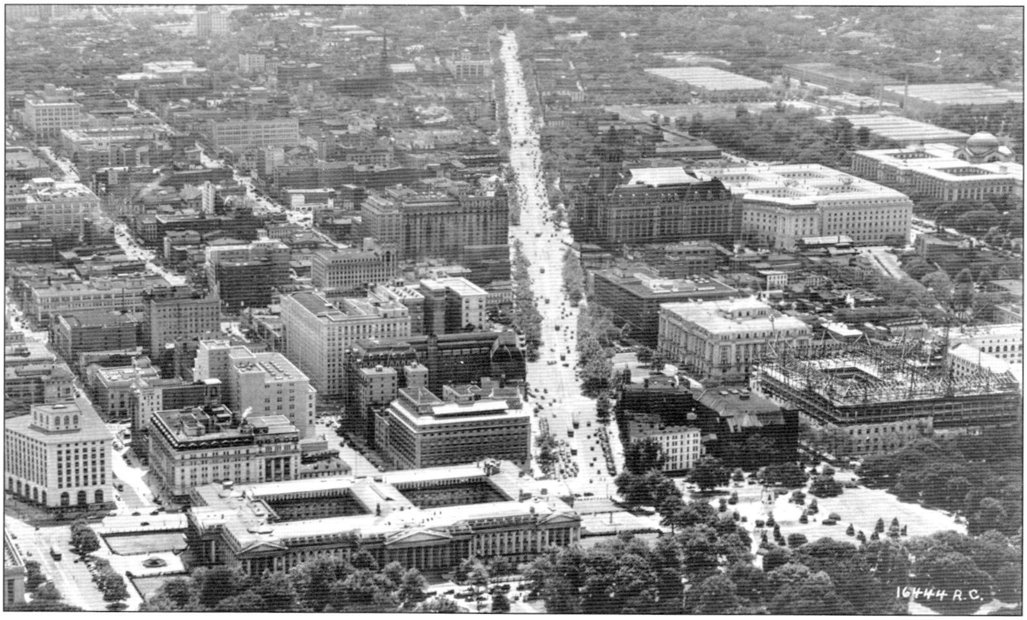

Pennsylvania Avenue stands out in the bright sunshine in this July 1930 view showing how the street makes a right turn onto Fifteenth Street at the Treasury Building in the lower part of the photograph. The avenue picked up onto Executive Drive in the extreme lower left corner to pass in front of the White House, then continued to the northwest about 10 more blocks. At this time, the debate continued over whether to demolish the Old Post Office and District Buildings. (National Archives.)

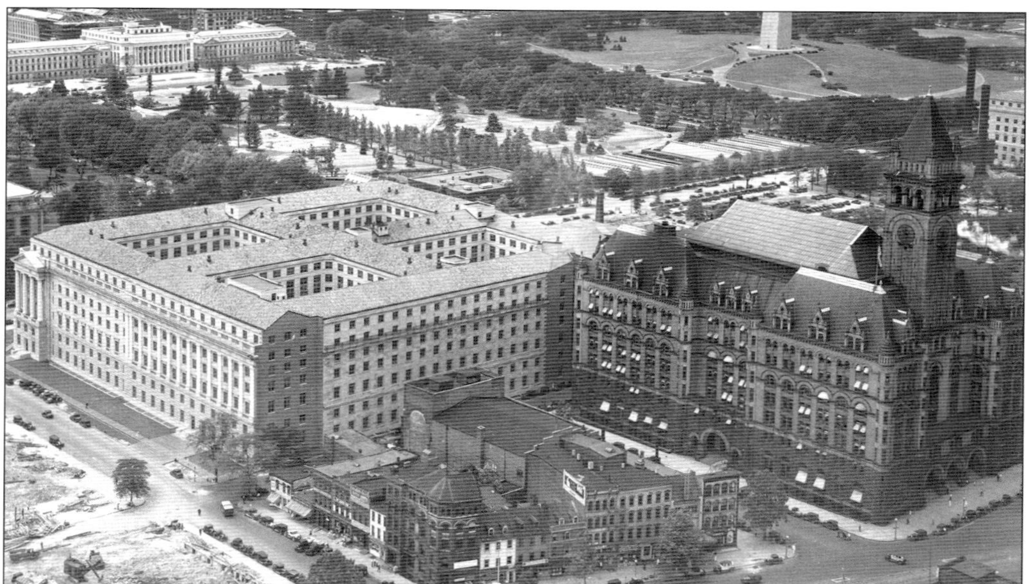

Harvey's Oyster House is on the right corner of the group of small buildings along Pennsylvania Avenue between Tenth and Eleventh Streets, its days numbered in this July 1931 view. All the buildings would be demolished to make way for the northern extension of the IRS Building. At lower left, ground has been cleared for the new Department of Justice Building. (National Archives.)

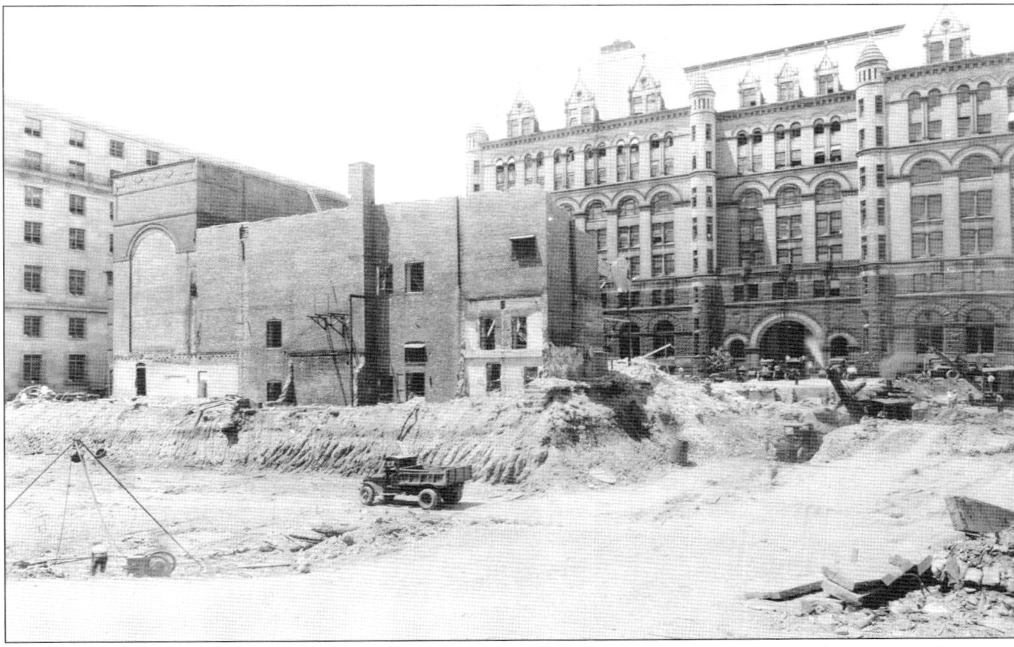

The group of buildings along Tenth Street and Pennsylvania Avenue are nearly gone in this view from June 1934 as ground is cleared for an extension of the IRS Building. The demolition of the old structures in and around the Division was a source of pride for many Washingtonians in the 1930s. The neighborhood had become an eyesore and was turning into a slum, and the emergence of the Federal Triangle was viewed as a major modernization effort.

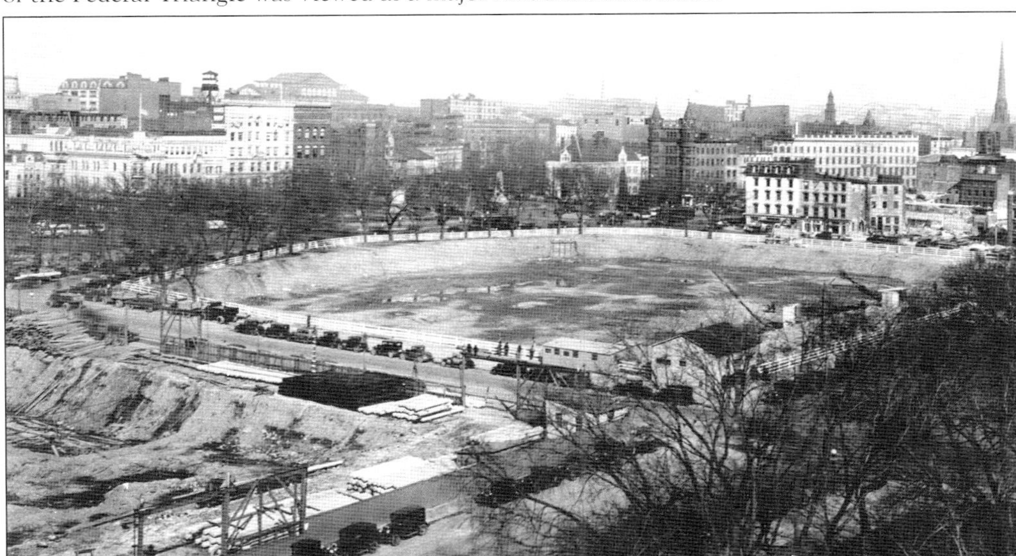

Center Market is a thing of the past in this view from February 1932 as excavation proceeds for the new National Archives. A similar pit along Ninth Street is at lower left for the Justice Department Building. Market Square is at center across Pennsylvania Avenue. The view looks out from the National Museum, with B Street (Constitution Avenue) in the foreground. (National Archives.)

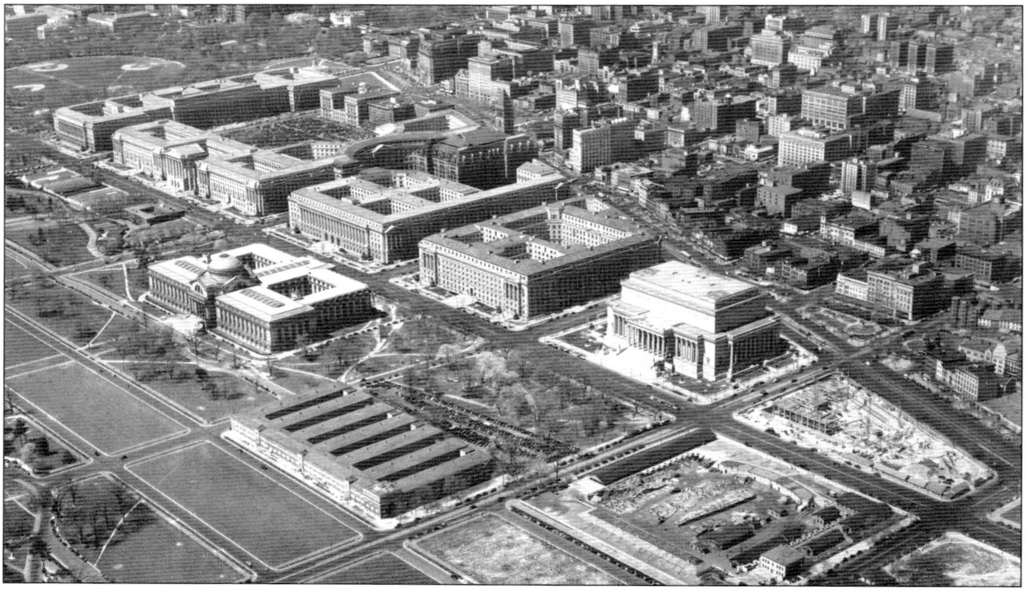

Most of the Federal Triangle is complete in this view from May 1937, with only the last major building, for the Federal Trade Commission (FTC), under construction at lower right. The block with the curved structure next to the FTC Building is the foundation for a structure that was never built, the George Washington Memorial Building. The privately funded project for a huge cultural center stalled soon after its foundation was laid in 1921, and the site lay unfinished for 16 years, finally being cleared in late 1937. (National Archives.)

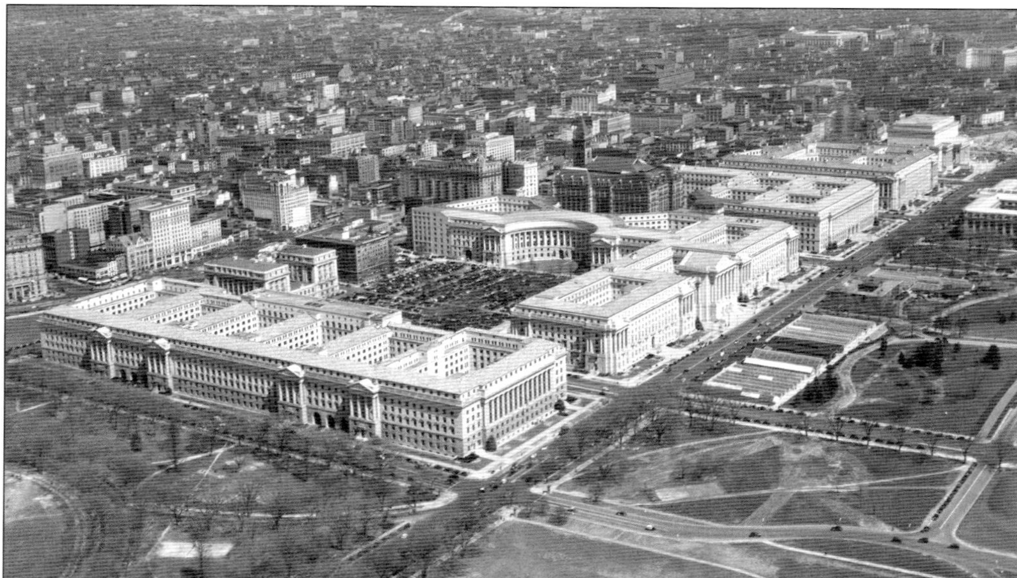

The Federal Triangle stands bright in the sun in this May 1937 view. Depression-era funding shortages left portions of the project unfinished and inadvertently created a large plaza used for decades as a parking lot. As built, the new buildings served the Commerce and Labor Departments, the Interstate Commerce Commission, the US Postal Service, the Internal Revenue Service, the Justice Department, the National Archives, and the Federal Trade Commission. (National Archives.)

Nine

DECADES OF DECAY, THEN REBIRTH

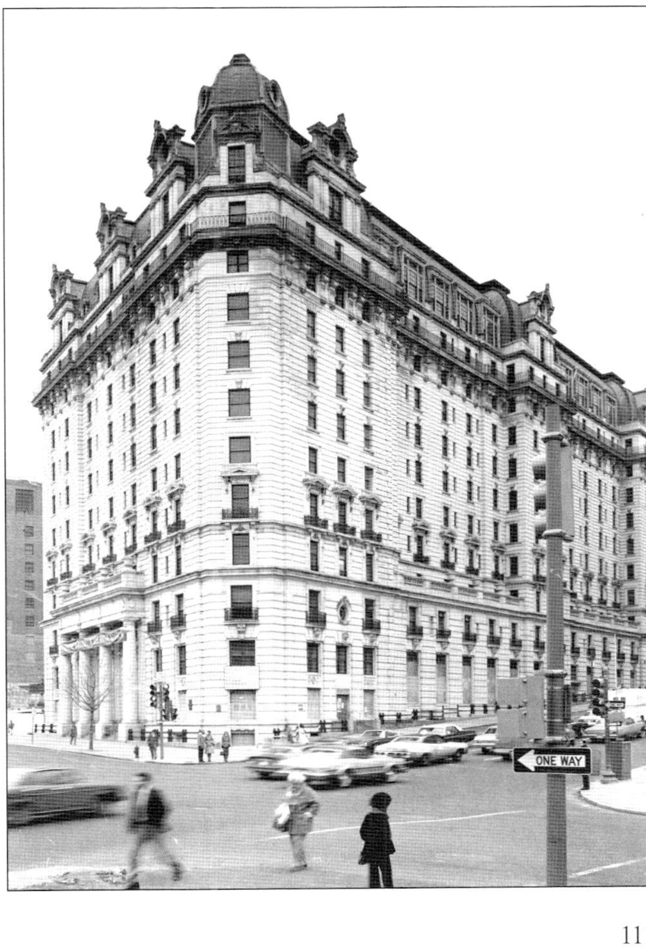

The post–World War II urban blight did not spare Washington. Residents and businesses fled to the suburbs, leaving behind urban decay. The Federal Triangle, while ridding the city of one of its most blighted neighborhoods, also destroyed much of the metropolitan life that had defined the avenue since the 1800s. Cheap businesses proliferated on the avenue's north side, and many buildings, even the magnificent Willard Hotel, pictured, were vacant and abandoned. The President's Council on Pennsylvania Avenue was established in June 1962 to examine the situation and offer proposals, which included urging the demolition of the Old Post Office and the Washington and Willard Hotels. The Pennsylvania Avenue Development Corporation (PADC) was established in October 1972 to oversee the revitalization, but like the council before it, many of its ideas were controversial.

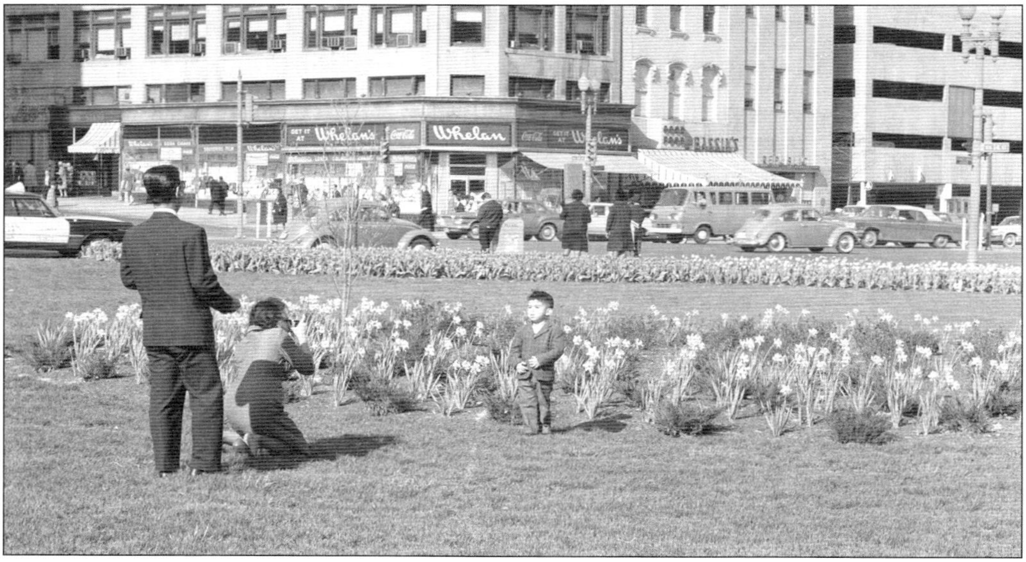

Lady Bird Johnson, wife of Pres. Lyndon Johnson, began a campaign in February 1965 to beautify America, an effort that eventually left a lasting mark in Washington and around the United States. One of her first moves was to direct the planting of flowers in the open space between Fourteenth and Fifteenth Streets just north of the Commerce Department Building. Here, only weeks later in April 1965, a family pauses to photograph their child amidst newly planted flowers.

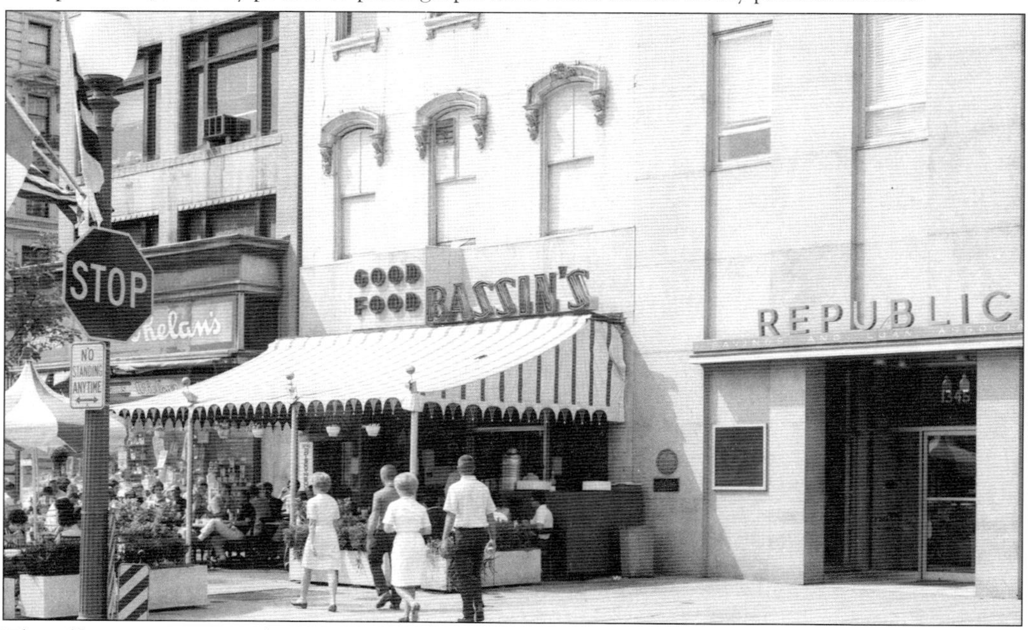

The effort to create Washington's first sidewalk café sparked a running public controversy when first proposed in early 1959 by Harry Zitelman, owner of Bassin's Restaurant, a thriving lunchroom on the corner of what had been Rum Row and Newspaper Row. Zitelman sought to bring some European ambience to Washington, but the DC Board of Commissioners staunchly opposed the idea, citing a litany of concerns over safety, litter, and alcohol consumption. The effort met with success in summer 1961; this scene is from 1967.

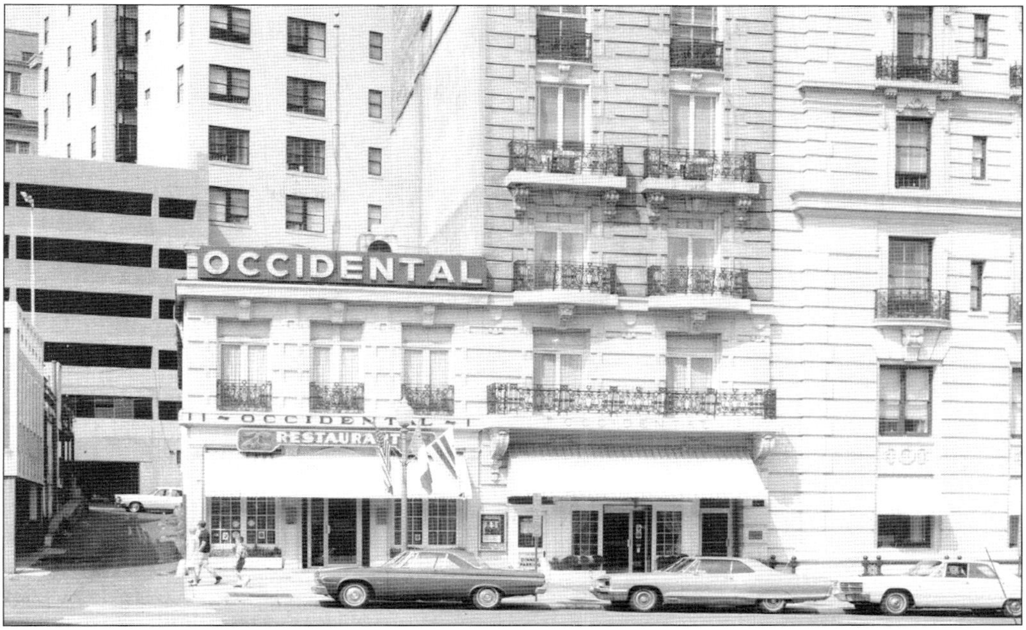

For a time, the Occidental, seen in 1967, continued its reputation as a roost for powerbrokers even as ownership changed and the neighborhood waned. Promoted with the slogan "Where Statesmen Dine," the restaurant even featured the large presidential seal from the Kennedy inauguration stand in 1961 as a ceiling decoration. But business declined as the building deteriorated and debts piled up, and after the restaurant closed in the fall of 1971, its assets were sold at auction.

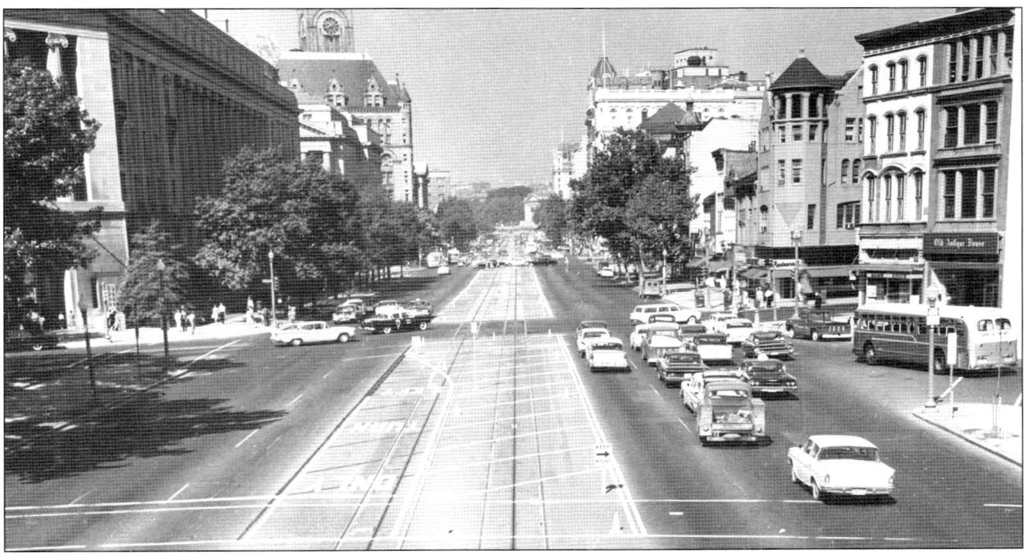

Streetcar tracks still lead down the avenue in this September 1962 view of the intersection with Ninth Street, but the streetcars themselves are gone, replaced in January 1962 by buses. With so many automobiles on the city's streets, the rail system had become an anachronism, and the switch to buses, with their added flexibility, was viewed with approval by most residents. In the middle distance at right is the cupola of the Raleigh Hotel. Fallen on hard times, the Raleigh closed in 1964 and was demolished. (DDOT.)

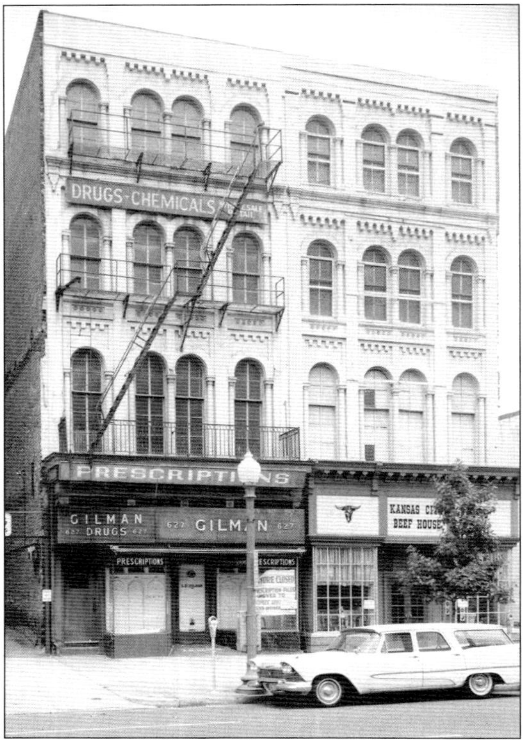

Photographer Mathew Brady's Washington studio occupied the top three floors of the building on the left from 1858 to 1881. Established initially to photograph well-known personalities, Brady's business grew into a major effort to document the American Civil War and develop what became known as photojournalism. But Brady's studio was not the only significant business in this modest building at 627 Pennsylvania Avenue. Zadoch Gilman was operating a store on this site by 1843 and was the building's first commercial occupant when it was built around 1855 as the center of three similar structures, one of which had been demolished by the time of these 1967 photographs. Gilman's remained in operation on this site for over a century, often providing temporary reviewing stands for inaugural parades. When the store finally closed in 1965, it was the oldest drugstore in the country in continuous operation. The interior was considered the most elaborate 19th-century commercial space in the city but nevertheless was destroyed during a remodeling.

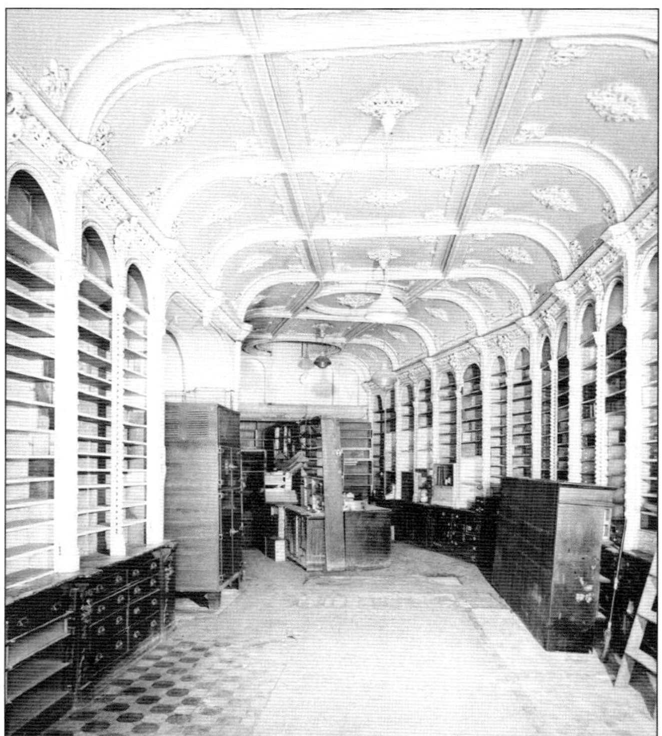

The distinctive twin spires of the Central National Bank building no longer supported huge electric signs, and the building was nearly derelict by the time of this photograph in April 1963. The only business was Apex Liquors, which occupied the ground floor for about 40 years until 1983, when the building was purchased by Sears, Roebuck & Company and thoroughly renovated as the headquarters for Sears World Trade. After less than a decade, the building was acquired by the National Council of Negro Women, which continues to operate there.

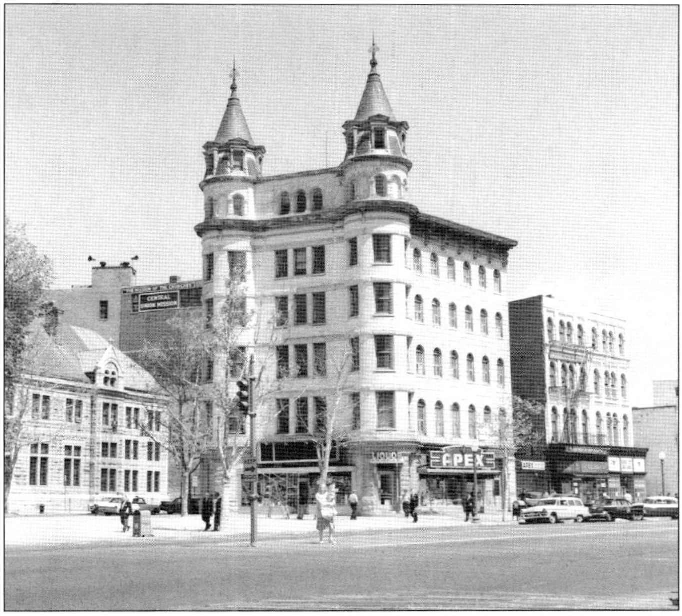

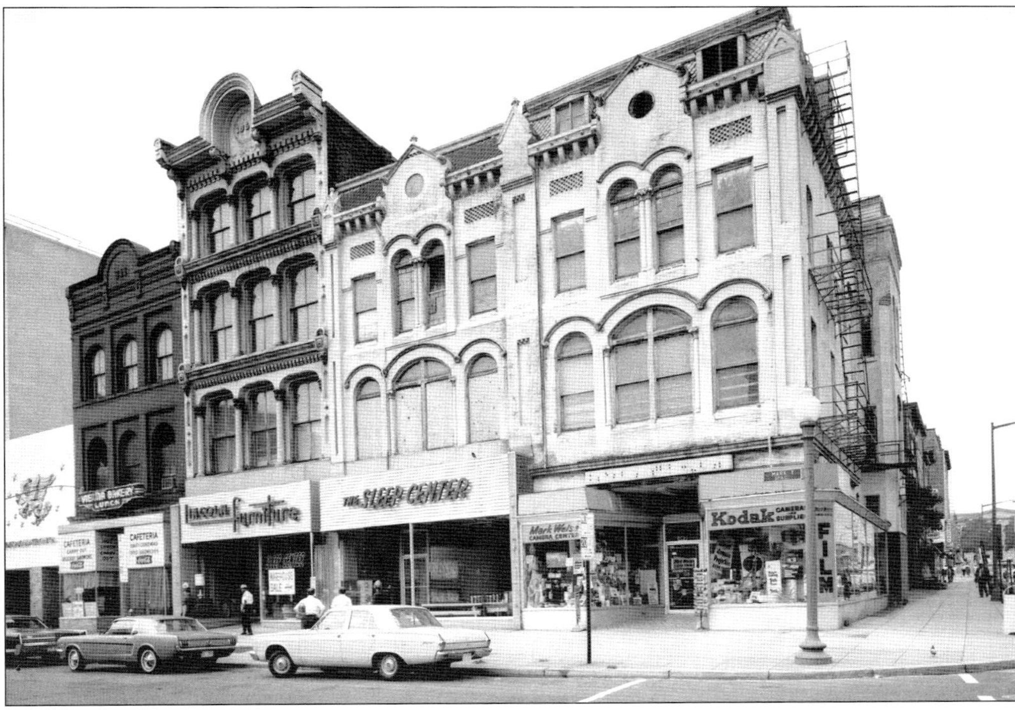

These buildings on Market Square just off Eighth Street and Pennsylvania Avenue were at the heart of Washington's commercial district when they were built in the 1860s and 1870s, but the upper floors are largely unoccupied in this 1969 view. Riots in the aftermath of Martin Luther King Jr.'s assassination in April 1968 destroyed many remaining businesses in the city's already-decaying commercial districts, although the avenue itself saw little trouble. The riots, however, only accelerated the departure of residents and businesses to Washington's suburbs.

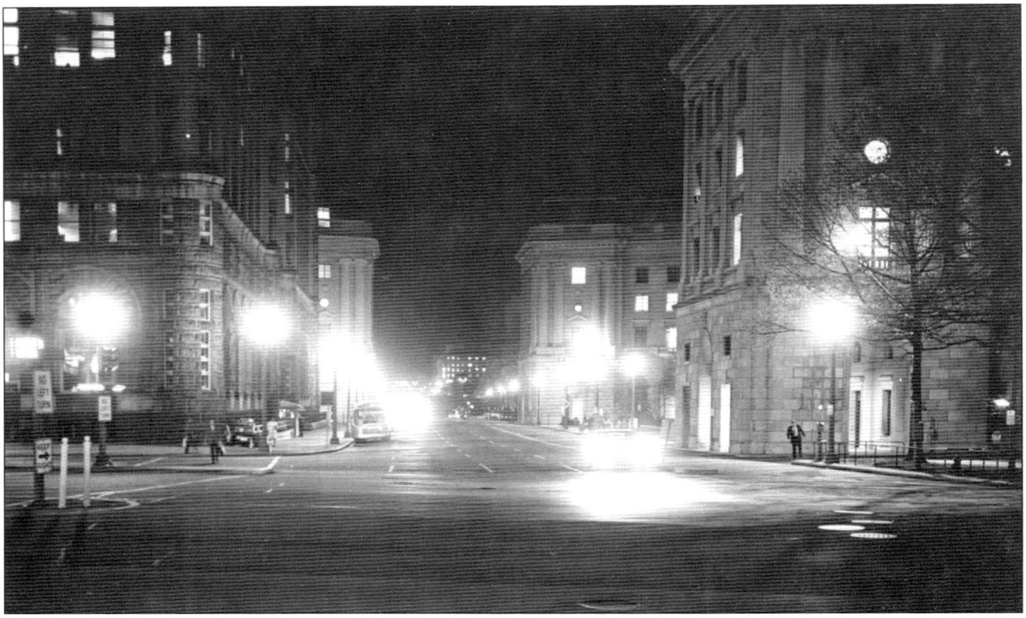

This 1971 night view from Pennsylvania Avenue looks through the Federal Triangle down Twelfth Street, with the Old Post Office Building at left. While thousands of government employees came by day to the offices in the Federal Triangle, the streets were largely deserted by nightfall. The thriving night life that once defined these streets was a forgotten thing of the past. (DDOT.)

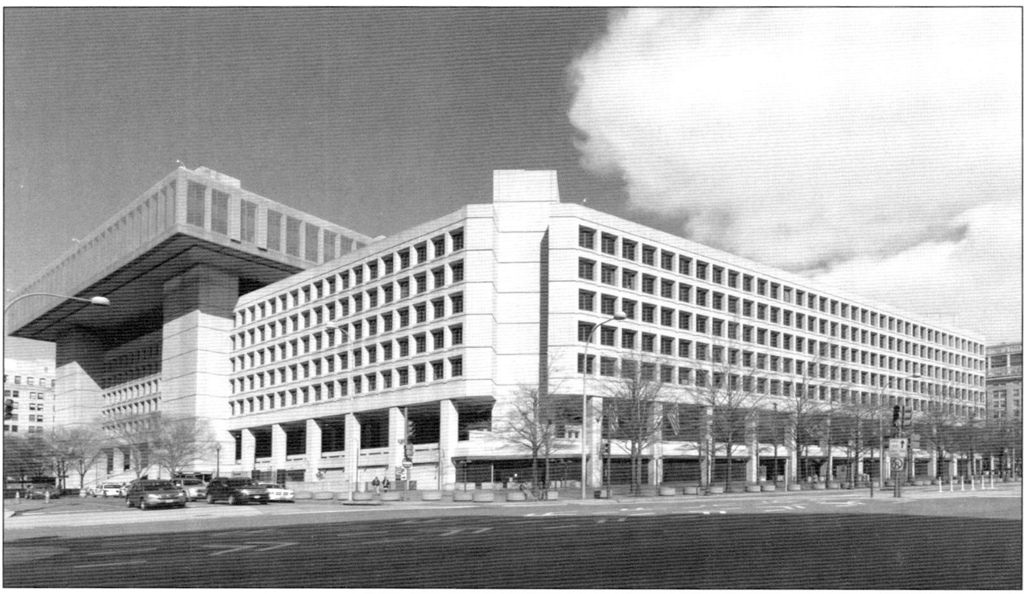

The design of the Federal Bureau of Investigation's headquarters on the avenue's north side between Ninth and Tenth Streets was controversial from the start of the project in 1962 and continues to be so to this day. The fortress-like appearance was no accident: FBI director J. Edgar Hoover was profoundly concerned about security, not even allowing news kiosks to be near the building that eventually would bear his name. Dozens of smaller buildings were demolished to erect the structure, which consumed two city blocks when it was completed in September 1975.

This small two-story building with its modest restaurant was all that was left in 1979 of the once-famous Metropolitan Hotel, known before the Civil War as the Indian Queen Hotel and Brown's Marble Hotel. Most of the five-story structure was razed in 1935, but this small section remained until it was demolished in 1982. Some of the bygone elegance was still visible in the building's neoclassical marble facade and Greek Revival window frames.

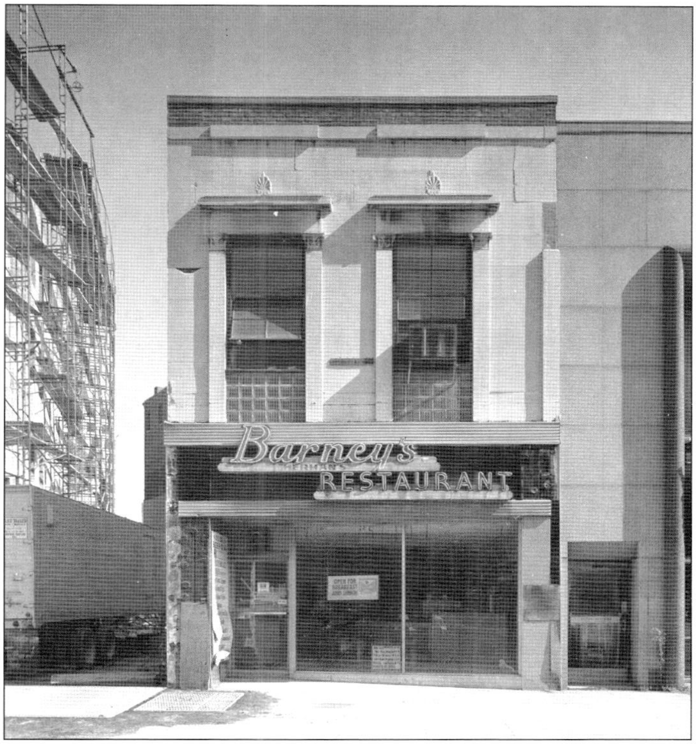

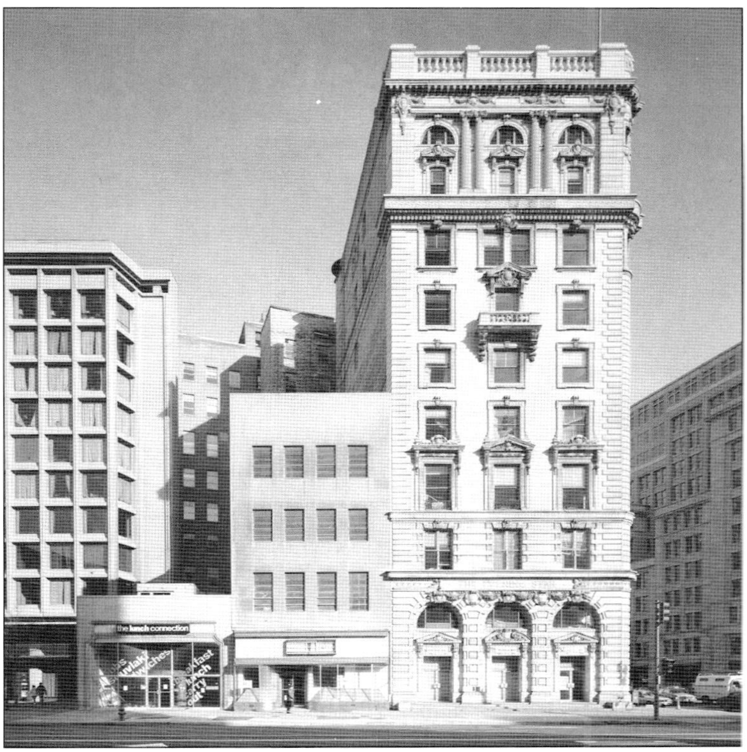

The influence of the *Evening Star*, long Washington's dominant newspaper, waned after the mid-1950s and was not reversed by the company's move to a new headquarters in the city's Southeast quarter. The paper's elegant former home on Pennsylvania Avenue was converted to office space and continued in use, ironically, even after the *Star*'s demise in August 1981. This December 1986 view shows the 1898 structure shortly before a major renovation turned the building into a much sought-after business address.

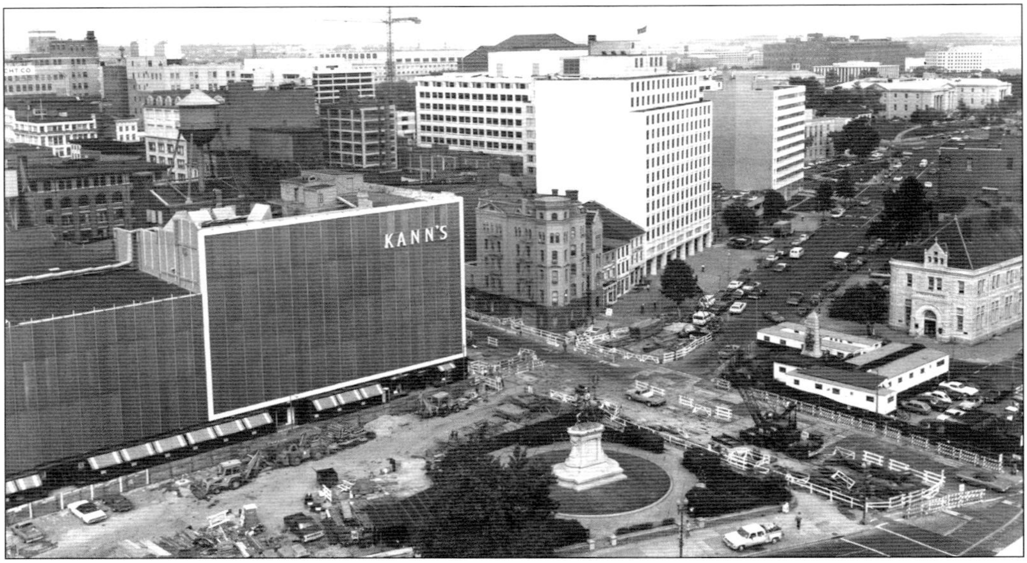

Kann's soldiered on in Market Square despite the urban exodus. In the early 1960s, the company sought to remain competitive with newer department stores by enclosing its aging 19th-century buildings behind giant aluminum siding that dazzled when decorated for Christmas season but failed to draw year-round customers. Business was hurt even more in the mid-1970s when much of downtown Washington was disrupted for Metro subway construction, as seen here in September 1974. (National Archives.)

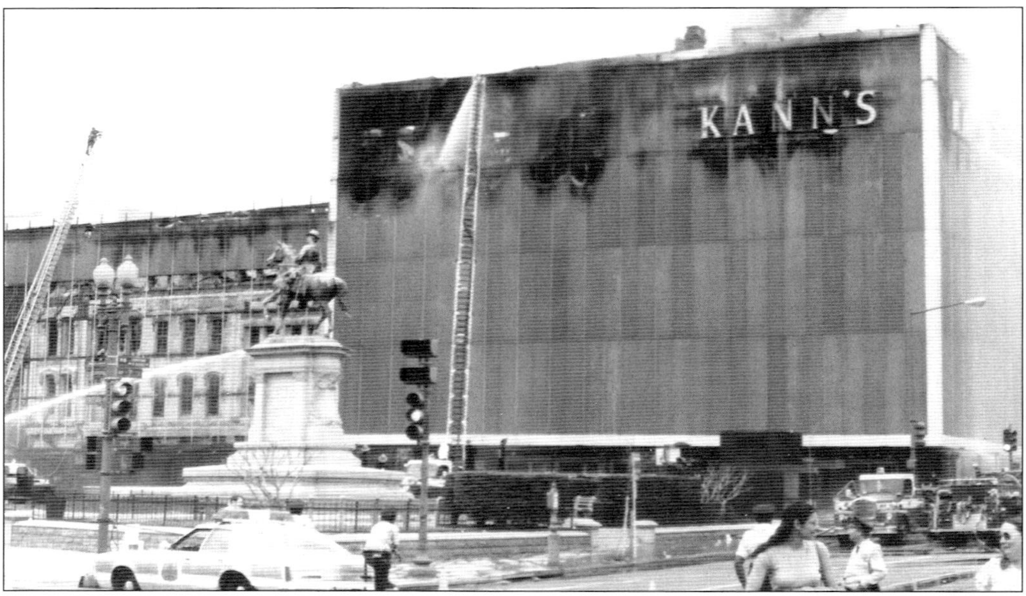

Kann's finally closed in May 1975, but proposals for what to do with the historic site went on for years as preservationists fought the PADC, which acquired the location in 1978 and wanted to demolish the historically significant structures. When some of the siding was removed and the old buildings were revealed to be reasonably intact, the debate only intensified. The question was finally settled when a mysterious fire broke out on March 31, 1979, and most of the structures were destroyed. (Christopher P. Cavas.)

The fire-damaged Kann's structures, seen in April 1979, revealed that much of the store's building facades and original signage had been left intact, enclosed for nearly 20 years by the aluminum siding. But the four main buildings inside the enclosure were essentially destroyed, and all talk of preservation was ended by the fire, which was officially termed suspicious. The cause was never determined, and arson was not ruled out. The Pennsylvania Avenue Development Corporation quickly began demolition of the wreckage, but the site remained vacant for a decade. The debate over what to do with the location included government use and commercial development.

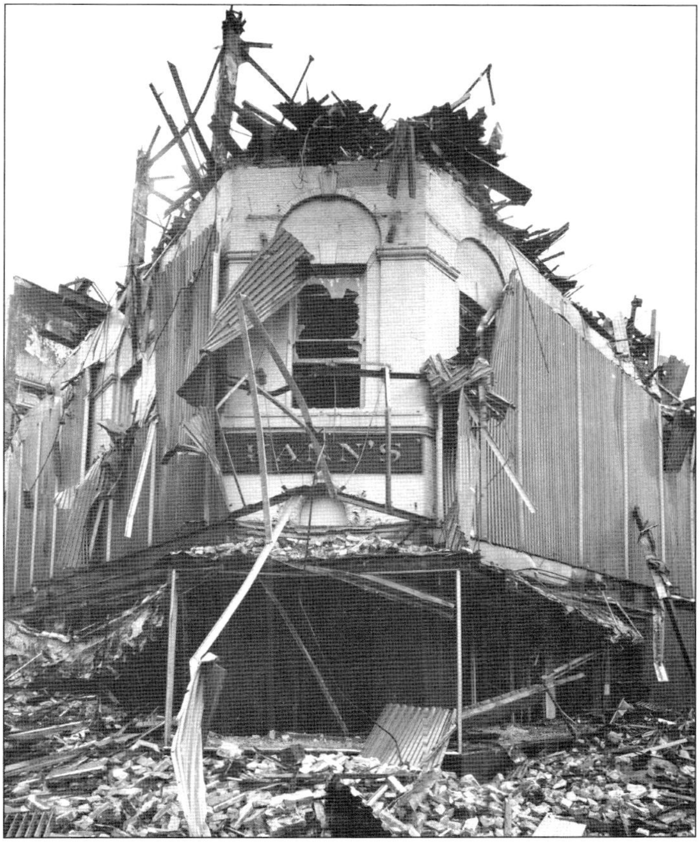

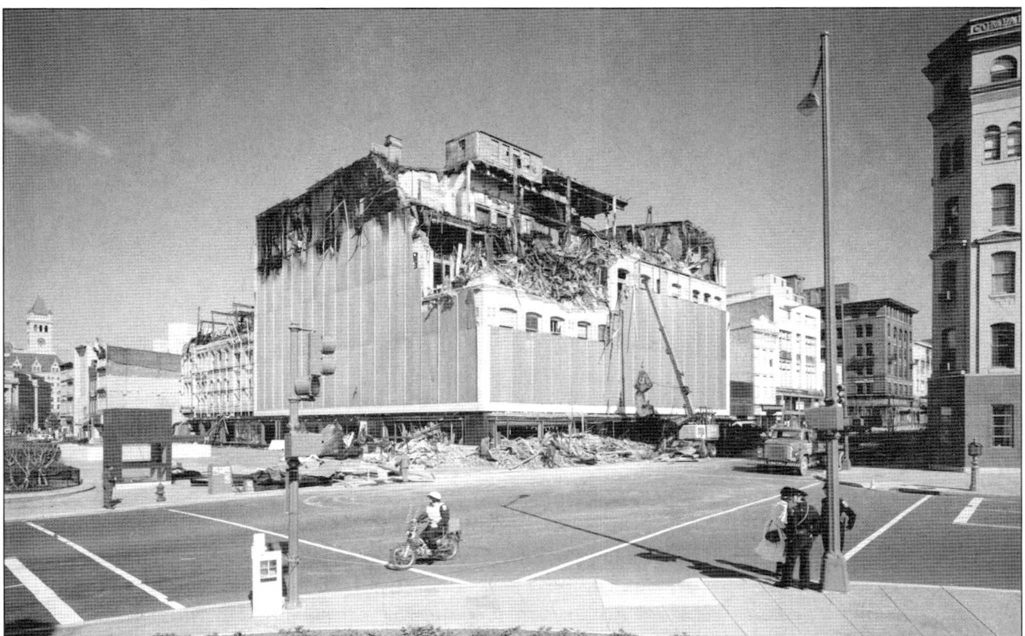

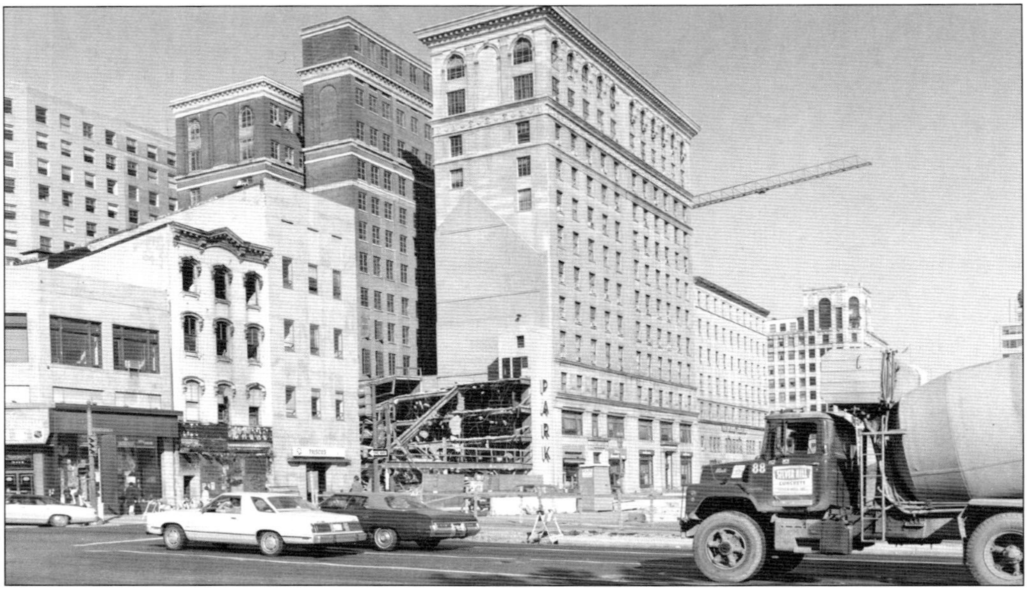

The northwest end of the avenue at E Street also began undergoing major changes in the late 1970s. In this October 1979 view, demolition is about to begin on the Munsey Building, at center, along with all the remaining buildings of what had once been Newspaper Row and Rum Row. After the *Washington Post* moved to a new downtown location, its former headquarters building was razed in 1954 and replaced by a parking garage, but its outline remained on the side of the Munsey Building.

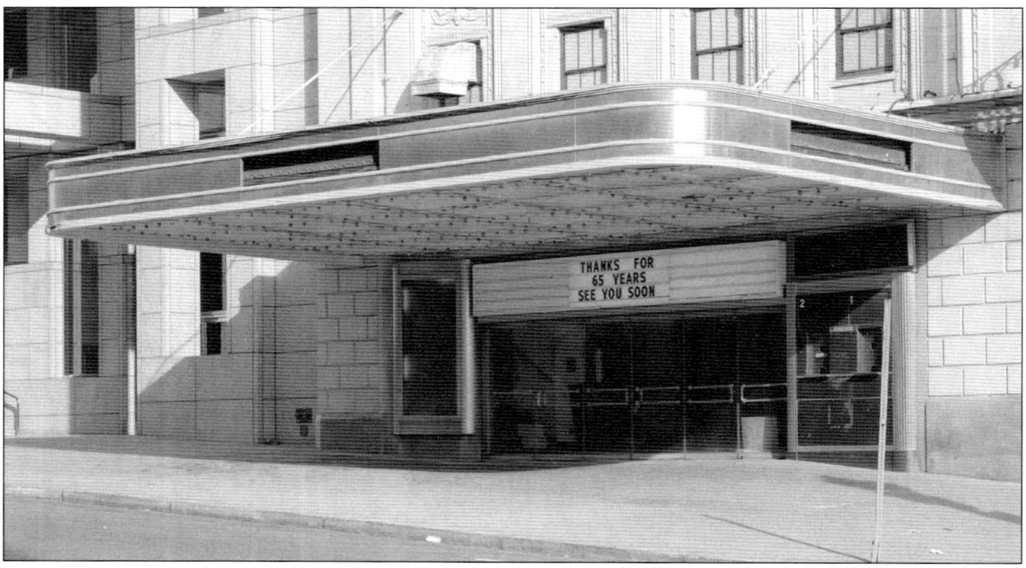

While its stage neighbor the National Theater was demolished and rebuilt, the Warner Theater, which opened in 1924 as the Earle and was renamed in 1947, became the last grand movie palace in downtown Washington. After a series of configuration changes and various reuses in the 1970s and 1980s, the theater closed, as seen here in late 1989, for a major $10-million renovation to return the facility to its former glory. The Warner reopened in October 1992 with a performance by Frank Sinatra, and continues to thrive.

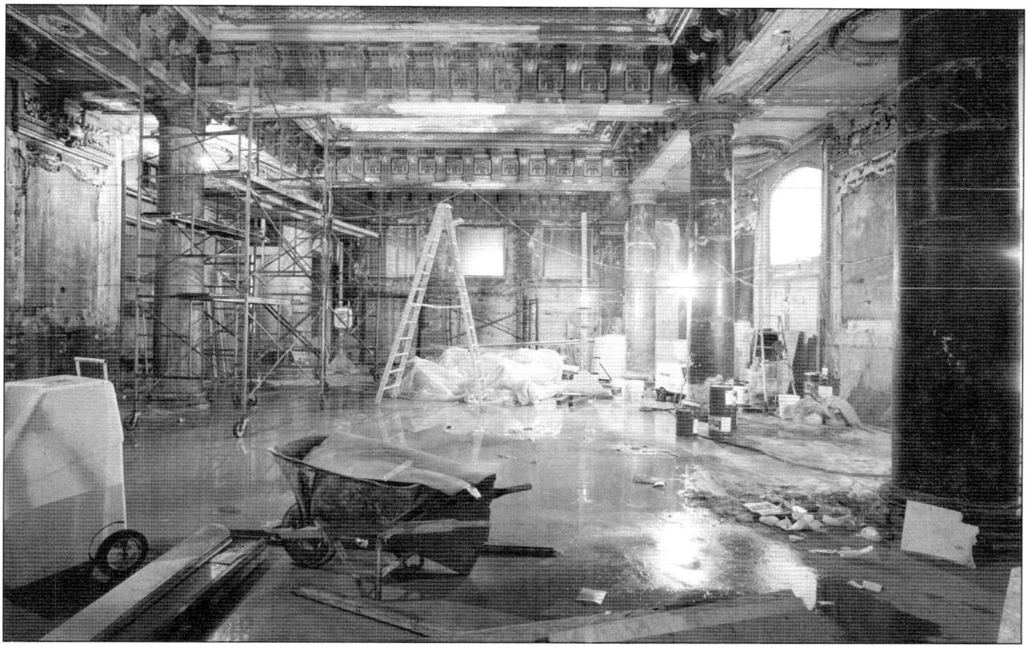

No building epitomized the decay of Pennsylvania Avenue more than the Willard Hotel, which closed in 1968. Vacant and empty, its unlit floors gave shelter to drug users and the homeless, a looming and foreboding hulk only two blocks from the White House. Debate continued whether to raze the hotel to build a new office building or restore it. Eventually all parties agreed to a settlement, and in 1978 the PADC bought the Willard, which became the centerpiece for a public-private partnership to restore the hotel and add office space in the area formerly occupied by the Occidental Hotel and Restaurant. Restoration work on the greatly deteriorated building finally began in 1984, and when the hotel reopened in August 1986 as the Willard InterContinental Washington, the ceremonies were attended by Supreme Court justices, congressmen, and 12 members of the Willard family.

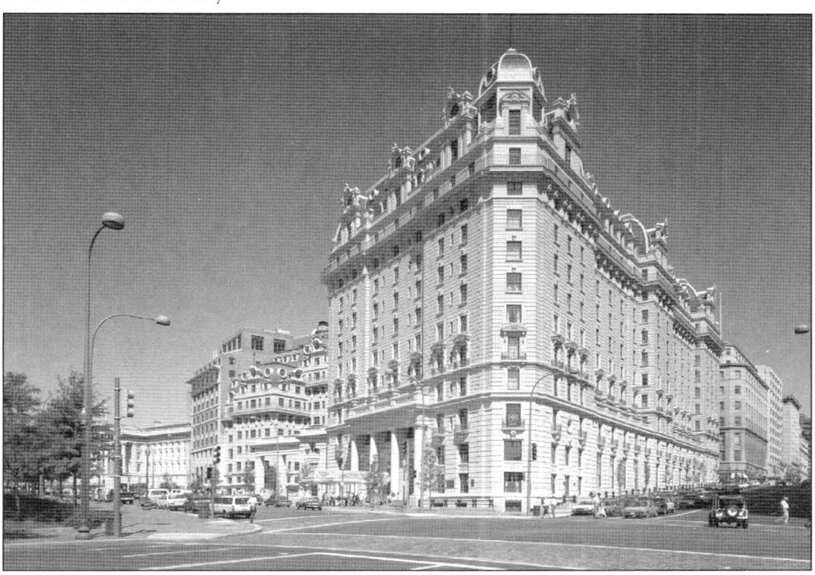

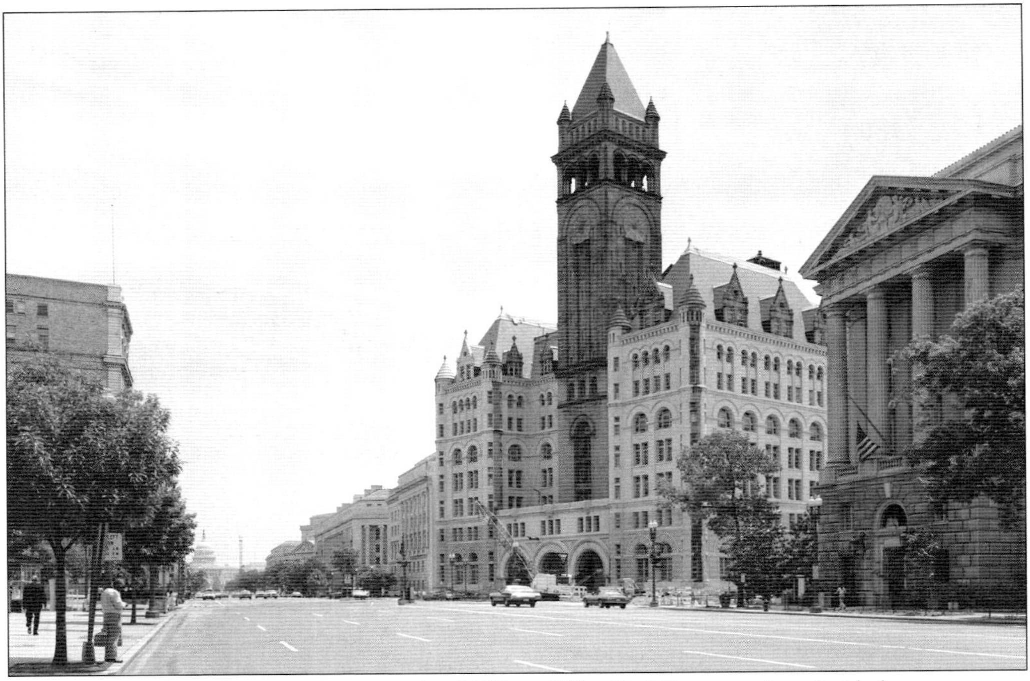

Controversial throughout its existence, the Old Post Office Building was often derided as an eyesore, and its demolition was an early goal for the Pennsylvania Avenue Development Corporation. A preservationist group dubbed Don't Tear It Down fought a long and ultimately victorious battle in the 1970s to save the building, which underwent a major $29-million renovation from 1979 to 1983, during which this photograph was taken. The completed structure became the Old Post Office Pavilion, with three levels of shops and restaurants.

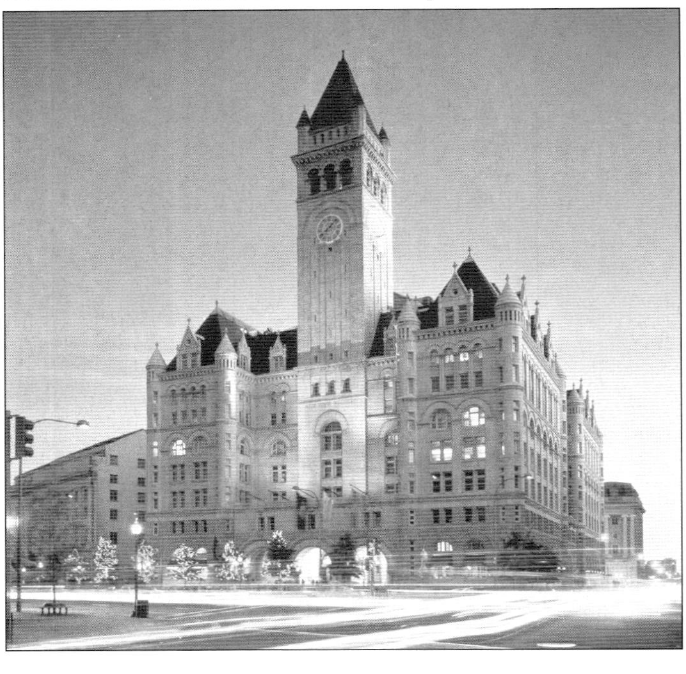

A city-sponsored New Year's Eve celebration started in 1984 at the Old Post Office Pavilion featuring the dropping of a giant love stamp, but costs grew, and the outdoor event ended after 1990. The interior retail scheme also lost money, and the General Services Administration decided to lease the structure as a luxury hotel. The Trump Organization was chosen in February 2012 to redevelop the building under a long-term lease, and the Trump International Hotel opened in September 2016, but the entire structure officially is known as the Old Post Office.

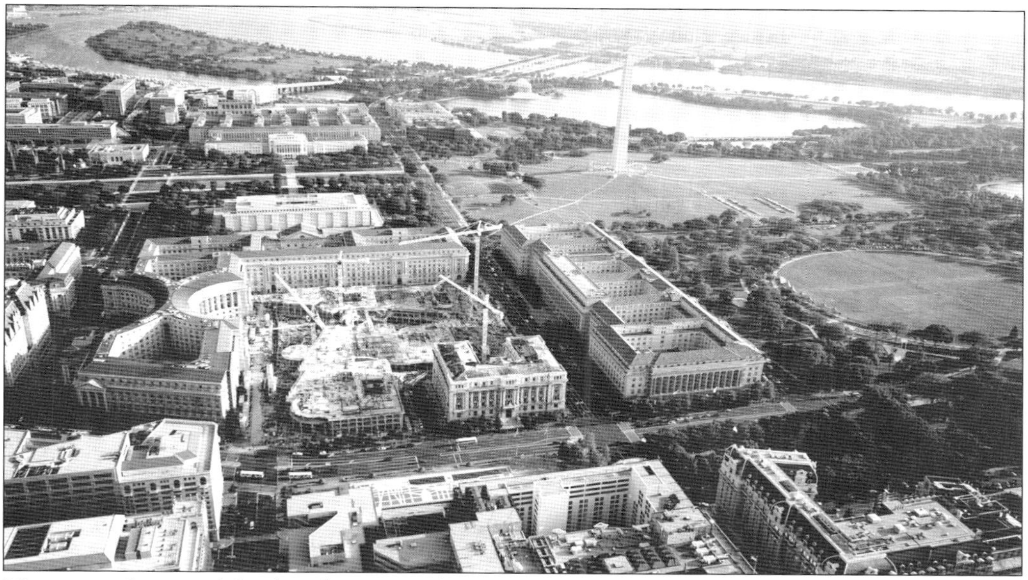

The great plaza used for decades as a parking lot for the Federal Triangle is seen being filled by construction of the Ronald Reagan Building and International Trade Center. Authorized by Congress in 1987, the building was completed in 1998 after eight years of construction fraught with concerns over cost, use, and design. The complex is the second largest government building after the Pentagon and essentially completes the Triangle project begun in the 1920s.

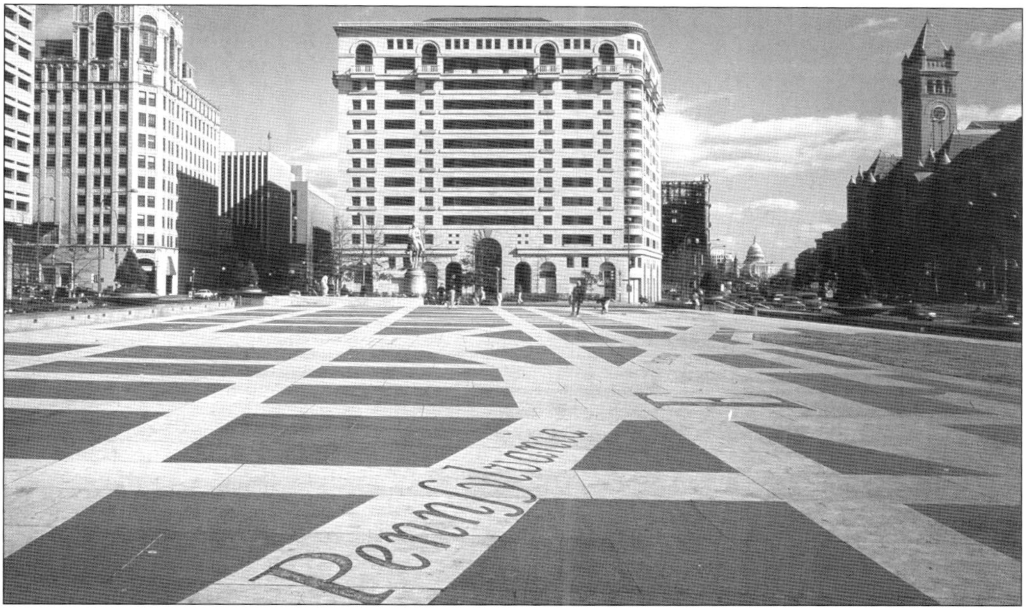

A major PADC project was to redirect the avenue at Thirteenth Street and create a new plaza, called Western Plaza when it was completed in 1980 and renamed Freedom Plaza in 1988 to honor Martin Luther King Jr. Controversies swirled over the design of the plaza until a relatively simple inlaid depiction of the city's street plan was created. The large Pennsylvania Building in the background, built in 1966, was completely remodeled in 1987, when its address was switched from Thirteenth Street to Pennsylvania Avenue.

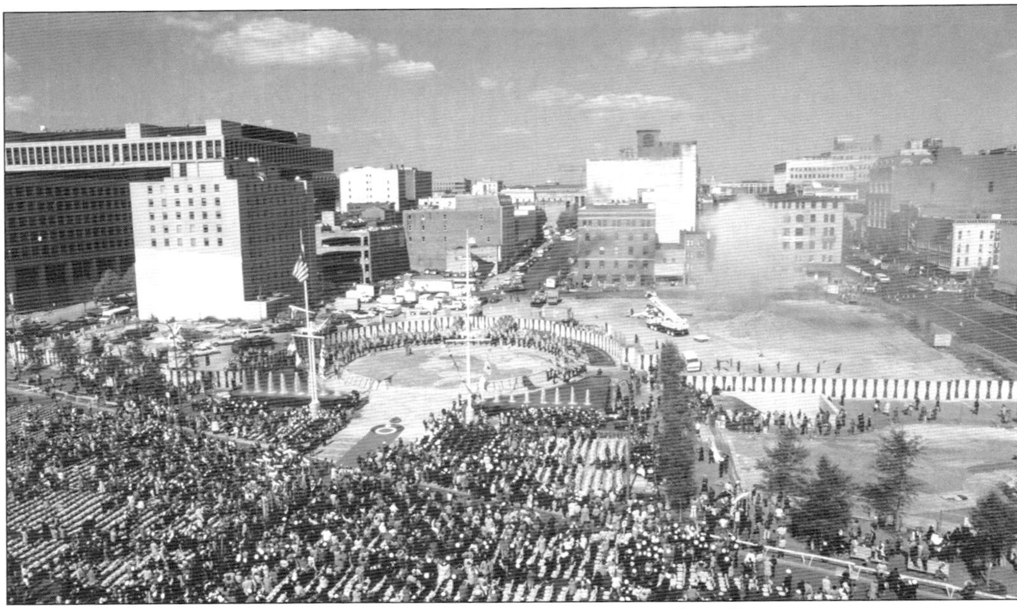

Redevelopment of Market Square took on a new cast in 1980, when Congress supported creation of the US Navy Memorial on the avenue to honor members of the Navy, Marine Corps, Coast Guard, and Merchant Marine. Here, on October 13, 1987, the memorial is dedicated even as construction and demolition continues around it. The memorial is sited on what had been Eighth Street, now cut off at D Street.

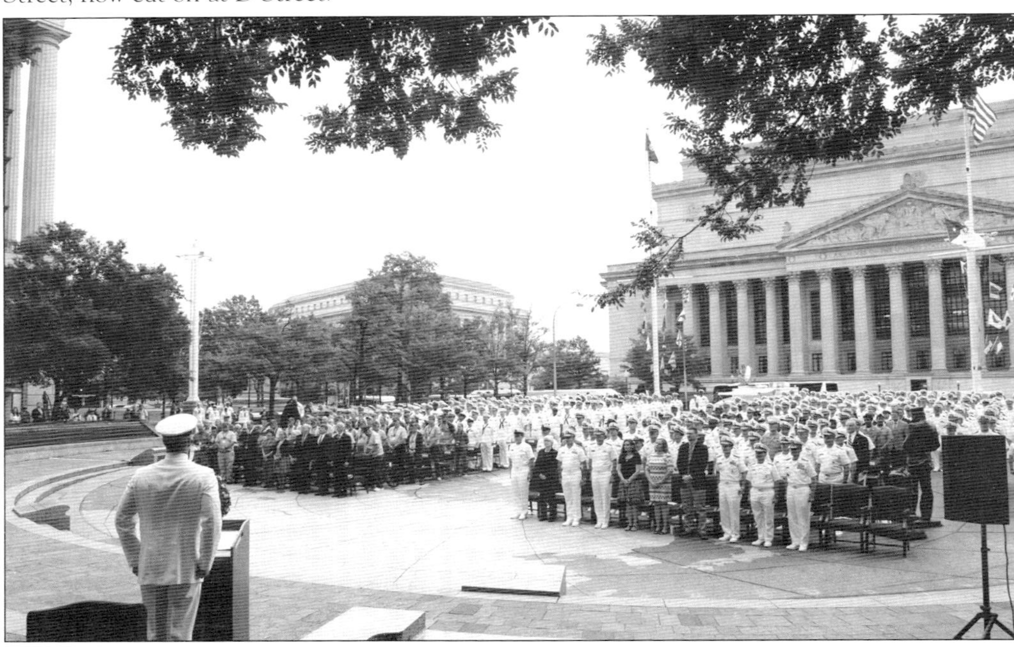

The Navy Memorial has become a regular venue for official ceremonies, gatherings, and concerts, bringing new life to one of the city's oldest public spaces. This ceremony in June 2016 marked the anniversary of 1942's Battle of Midway, a major turning point in the Pacific campaign against Japan during World War II. In the background at right is the National Archives. (US Navy.)

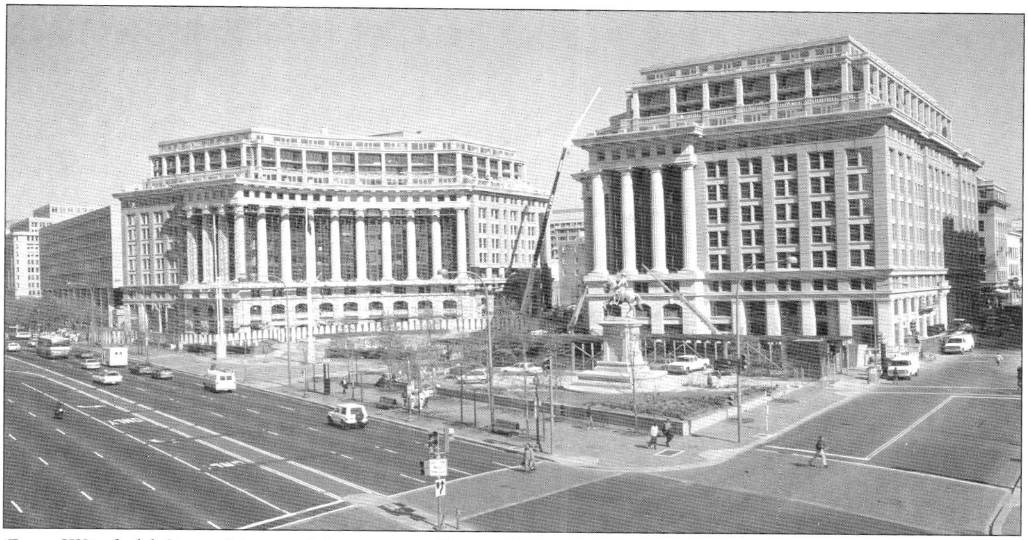

Gen. Winfield Scott Hancock's statue still presides over Market Square, but virtually everything around him in this view from about 1990 has changed. The Market Square East condo and retail development rose first over the former Kann's department store site at right, followed soon by a western twin at left, completed in 1991. A revitalized downtown up Seventh Street at right, along with ceremonies and outdoor concerts at the Navy Memorial, have helped restore some life to the avenue.

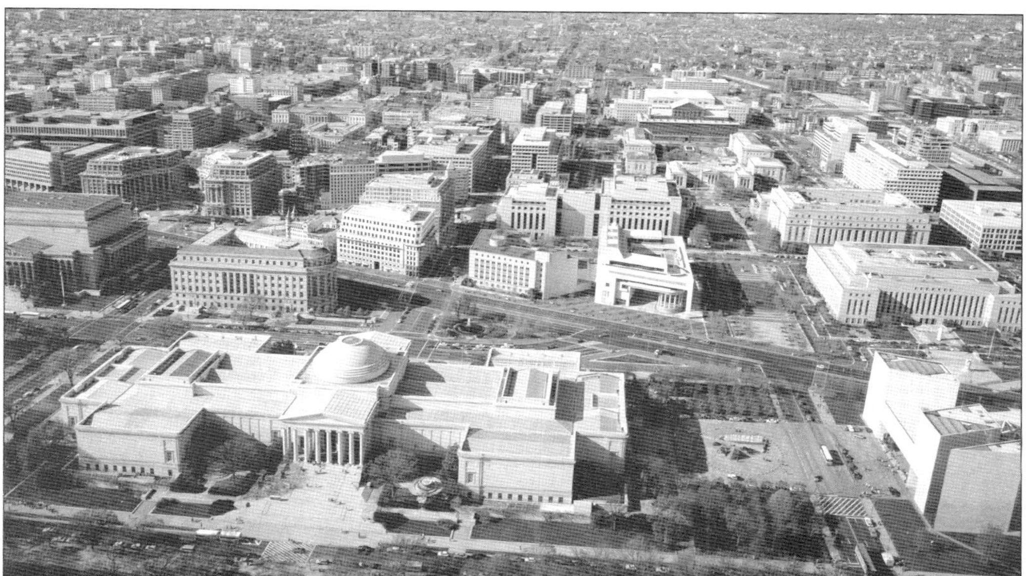

The National Gallery of Art is in the foreground in this view from around 2000, its dome lined up with Sixth Street. The distinctive Canadian Embassy, at lower right, opened in 1989 on the site of the old Ford Service Building, becoming the first foreign embassy situated on the avenue. In 2008, the Newseum opened in a new building next door to the embassy on the site of the old National Hotel.

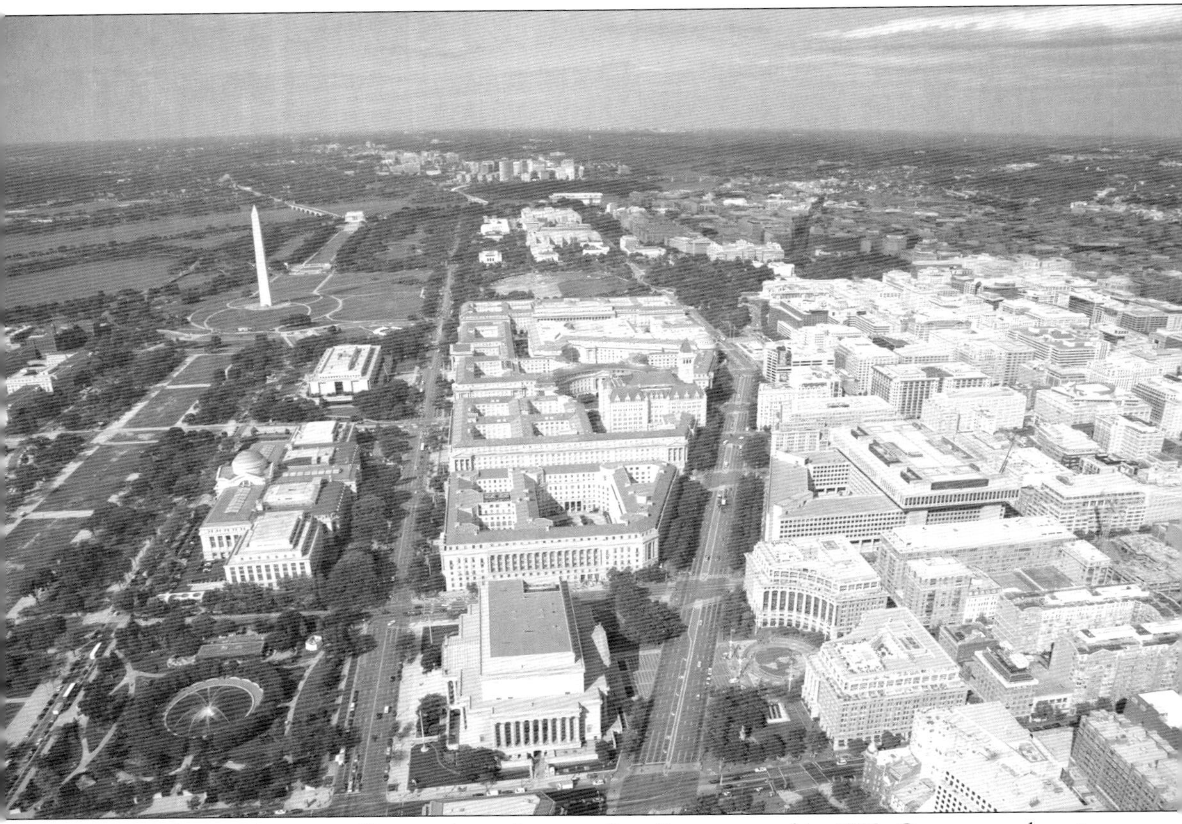

Pennsylvania Avenue still runs along the same line first surveyed in 1792. Over more than two centuries, entire neighborhoods, businesses, technologies, and even cultures rose, thrived, and fell along the 1.2-mile stretch between the Capitol and the White House, but the street's significance as a national symbol carries on. Much of the recent redevelopment had been completed by the time of this September 2006 photograph, but more changes are sure to come.

Bibliography

Brown, George Rothwell. *Washington: A Not Too Serious History*. Baltimore, MD: The Norman Publishing Co., 1930.

DeFerrari, John. *Capital Streetcars: Early Mass Transit in Washington, D.C.* Charleston, SC: The History Press, 2015.

———. *Historic Restaurants of Washington, D.C.* Charleston, SC: The History Press, 2013.

———. *Lost Washington, D.C.* Charleston, SC: The History Press, 2011.

———. "Streets of Washington: Stories and Images of Historic Washington, D.C." www.streetsofwashington.com.

Dickey, J.W. *Empire of Mud: The Secret History of Washington, D.C.* Guilford, CT: Lyons Press, 2014.

Goode, James M. *Capital Losses: A Cultural History of Washington's Destroyed Buildings*. 2nd ed. Washington, DC: Smithsonian Books, 2003.

Green, Constance McLaughlin. *Washington: Capital City, 1879–1950*. Princeton, NJ: Princeton University Press, 1963.

———. *Washington: Village and Capital, 1800–1878*. Princeton, NJ: Princeton University Press, 1962.

Highsmith, Carol M. and Ted Landphair. *Pennsylvania Avenue: America's Main Street*. Washington, DC: American Institute of Architects Press, 1988.

National Capital Planning Commission. *Downtown Urban Renewal Area Landmarks, Washington, D.C.* Washington, DC: US Government Printing Office, 1970.

Richardson, John P. *Alexander Robey Shepherd: The Man Who Built the Nation's Capital*. Athens, OH: Ohio University Press, 2016.